CANINE ENRICHMENT FOR THE REAL WORLD

MAKING IT A PART OF YOUR DOG'S DAILY LIFE

Allie Bender, CDBC, CPDT-KA, SBA
Emily Strong, CDBC, CPBT-KA, SBA

Publishing

Wenatchee, Washington U.S.A.

Canine Enrichment for the Real World
Making It a Part of Your Dog's Daily Life
Allie Bender and Emily Strong

Dogwise Publishing
A Division of Direct Book Service, Inc.
403 South Mission Street, Wenatchee, Washington 98801
1-509-663-9115, 1-800-776-2665
www.dogwisepublishing.com / info@dogwisepublishing.com
© 2019 Allie Bender and Emily Strong

Art director: Jon Luke
Graphic design: Adrienne Hovey
Cover design: Jesus Cordero

Library of Congress Cataloging-in-Publication Data

Names: Bender, Allie, 1980- author.

Title: Canine enrichment for the real world : making it a part of your dog's daily life / Allie Bender, CDBC, CPDT-KA, SBA, Emily Strong, CDBC, CPBT-KA, SBA.

Identifiers: LCCN 2019041789 (print) | LCCN 2019041790 (ebook) | ISBN 9781617812682 (paperback) | ISBN 9781617812699 (ebook) Subjects: LCSH: Dogs. | Animal welfare.

Classification: LCC SF427 .B5174 2019 (print) | LCC SF427 (ebook) | DDC   636.7--dc23

LC record available at https://lccn.loc.gov/2019041789

LC ebook record available at https://lccn.loc.gov/2019041790

ISBN: 978-1-61781-268-2

For Sherry Woodard, without whom this book never would have been written.

And in memory of Dr. Hal Markowitz, without whom the very concept of enrichment wouldn't exist.

TABLE OF CONTENTS

ACKNOWLEDGMENTS

First and foremost, we would like to thank the people who helped us by either peer-reviewing the manuscript, talking us down from the impostor syndrome ledge multiple times, or both. Those people include: Eileen Anderson, Stephanie Edlund, Nancy Tucker, Christie Keith, Lori Stevens, Dr. Erica Feuerbacher, Dr. Lisa Gunter, and Dr. Susan Friedman. Your feedback, words of wisdom, advice, and encouragement were indispensable and kept us going.

A special thanks goes out to the multiple researchers who have worked so tirelessly to help us all better understand many complex and fascinating aspects of mental and physical health, behavior, nutrition, or any other topic related to enrichment. We learned so much from your work and have been able to share what we've learned with other people. The impact you've had and continue to have on our profession is immeasurable. Special thanks to Dr. Sean Delaney, Dr. Kathie Beals, Dr. Anna Johnson, Dr. Roger Abrantes, and Dr. Simon Gadbois for going above and beyond to answer our questions, and doing so with kindness and patience.

We also want to thank Adrienne Hovey, who is the best editor in the entire world. We are so very lucky to have worked with you. You make us want to write another book.

Thanks to our apprentices who read through the manuscript to give us a layperson's perspective. Your feedback was invaluable.

Thanks to our clients, all the shelter and rescue staff and volunteers, and non-human animals we've had the pleasure of working with over the years. Our students have been our best teachers. Thank you thank you thank you for your patience and trust.

Thanks to our families and significant others for being our support system, and for keeping us humble.

And a special thanks to Glenn Pierce for letting us borrow the CPUPS concept. Together we can conquer CPUPS!

Notes From the Authors: Science Matters

Before we launch into the book itself, let's take a brief moment to address the ever-present elephant in the dog training room: science. When we're assessing why and how to meet a dog's needs, science matters. Many people may not want to hear this. Science can feel intimidating or esoteric, or it can seem as if it's belittling emotions and gut feelings. But using intuition and empathy is not at odds with using evidence; the one does not preclude the other, and in fact they work better together. So let's take a little time to acknowledge and discuss the all-too-common aversion to science.

In Chapter 1 we'll discuss how evidence and intuition can be used together. We will also talk about how important it is to be able to objectively assess whether our practices are actually meeting the animal's needs, as opposed to feeling good about what we're doing but failing to be effective. However, some people are also averse to science because they think it's too dry, boring, esoteric, or difficult for them, or perhaps it doesn't have any bearing on real life, or any combination thereof. The authors have heard many people say things like, "That's not how my brain works," or, "I don't have time to sit around with my nose in the books; I'm busy actually training dogs," or, "I may not have spent any time in a lab, but I've spent three decades in the real world, raising and training dogs!" Sound familiar? We have good news for you: it's okay to not have the mind of a scientist. And you don't have to spend your life poring over research or wearing a lab coat. The great thing about a community is that we can each specialize in what interests us, and then we can learn from each other. Just as you don't have to be your own accountant or plumber or doctor or web designer, you also don't have to be your own researcher. And thank goodness for that! Neither of the authors is cut out for academia, either. We find far more joy in reaping the benefits of the labor of hundreds of academics and compiling all of their research into a more palatable and accessible book. That's our niche in our community. You have a valuable niche in our community as well. One of Emily's clients put it best when she said, "Even though I am an artist, I love science. The two aren't opposite; they're sisters. Creativity and intuition need a vehicle in order to become truly great. You have to know the rules thoroughly in order to know when and why and how to break them."

Even more great news: research isn't just something that's done in a lab by a bunch of scientists who have no hands-on training experience. A lot of it happens out in the world. There are so many aspects of animal welfare and behavior that can't be studied in a lab; they can only occur in the real world. And whether it occurred in a lab or out in the world, scientific research nevertheless has real-world applications. Despite being frequently depicted this way in TV and movies, scientists aren't just a bunch of out-of-touch nerds who are too obsessed with their microscopes to be able to function in society, nor are most science-based trainers filled with lots of book-learning but no common sense. In fact, many behaviorists—that is, people who have an advanced degree in one of the behavior sciences—are also highly successful and effective professional animal trainers and behavior consultants, whose research stems from their own real-world experiences training animals and pet owners. So let's once and for all dispel this myth that science has no bearing on real animal training.

Yet another common misconception about science is that it is unreliable because it constantly disproves or contradicts itself. That, too, is a misunderstanding of how science works. Yes, we are constantly learning more and adding to our knowledge, but more often than not we are adding information rather than subtracting it as we learn more. It isn't necessarily that the things we previously learned have no validity anymore; as we continue to hone our understanding of the natural world, we discover more nuances, more subtleties, more complexities, that makes previous understanding less accurate but nevertheless still an important step on our eternal journey.

People also think that science can't be trusted because even within any given scientific field, experts are constantly disagreeing with each other. In fact, it is precisely *because* scientists disagree with each other that a scientific approach is more trustworthy and valid than conventional wisdom. How can that be? Because the peer-review process necessitates transparency and accountability within the field. If a scientist is asked to prove their assertions, they must be able to show their work, so that work can be analyzed and repeated by colleagues who have a comparable education. This is not the case with conventional wisdom. If Expert Dog Trainer is asked to prove their assertions, the response is simply, "Because I'm an expert," or, "Because this is how it's always been done," or, "My results speak for themselves." There is no burden of proof, no accountability, no peer-review process, only anecdotal evidence and a cult of personality.

A trainer once asked Emily a vitally important question: "Aren't we all science-based trainers? Isn't science just collecting evidence? Isn't that what we all do? We try a method, and when it works, we continue doing it, and when it doesn't work, we don't do it anymore? Isn't that what science is?" This is a common misunderstanding of the nature of science and what exactly evidence is. There are actually two types of evidence: anecdotal evidence and empirical evidence. Anecdotal evidence is what this trainer was inadvertently describing: a personal experience in which the observer assigns a causal link between two events that seem to be related to each other. Empirical evidence is collecting measurable data, eliminating variables, and analyzing the data to better understand the nature of whatever is being studied. It is empirical, not anecdotal, evidence that is the heart and soul of the scientific process.

After empirical evidence is collected and analyzed, it then must go through the additional process of peer review and replication to ensure that the study is scientifically sound. Anecdotal evidence is far more prone to human error and logical fallacy. It is the reason for superstitions (a black cat crossed my path and then I broke my leg, ergo black cats are bad luck), misinterpretation (our dogs looks guilty every time there's pee on the floor when we get home, therefore they know what they did is wrong), and persistence of inaccurate ideology (I punished my dogs for barking at the neighbor and they don't bark at the neighbor anymore, so this method works, right?). Anecdotal evidence doesn't tell us whether a method actually works or only appears to work. It doesn't tell us whether it works temporarily and only under certain conditions (for example, only in the continued presence of a threat) or whether it works over the long term. It doesn't tell us why and how a method works (making up reasons why we think it works doesn't count as actually knowing!). It doesn't tell us if it's working in a way that is mentally and physically healthy for the learner. It doesn't tell us what potential collateral damage the method may cause, even if it does work. It doesn't tell us a lot of things. So, the answer to that highly important question is: no, anecdotal evidence is not science, and therefore we are not all using science-based methods.

All of that said, bad science certainly exists. Flawed research certainly exists. Unethical individuals and organizations have certainly abused the scientific method in order to gain power, make money, or in some other way further their own cause. Like any tool, the scientific method can either be used or misused. For this reason, we should not blindly accept something as truth simply because a study says it's so. That isn't science; that's blind faith. In the Resources section of this book, we have included tools for critically assessing research to determine its validity. If you are interested in reading research directly from the source rather than taking our word for it, those skills will come in very handy. The great thing about science is that it self-corrects over time. It may be a slow process in most cases, but the beauty of using empirical evidence rather than relying solely on anecdotal evidence is that, as the scientific community collects data, the inaccuracies, misinterpretations, and missing variables are eventually exposed and eliminated. Think of each research study as a pillar upon which future studies are stacked. The solid science will hold up over time, and further research can build upon it. The flawed science, however, will crumble under the weight of continued study, and those lines of thinking will fall away. Everything that scientists currently understand is built on the pillars that have withstood the test of time.

We do our best in this book to use science responsibly. We only cite sources that have been peer reviewed and published through reputable professional organizations and publications. And even though some of the studies are limited, inconclusive, or performed on a variety of non-dog species, nevertheless we are committed to letting the data drive our beliefs and practices, not the other way around. It's also important to note that just because a study might have been done on a non-dog species doesn't necessarily mean it's irresponsible of us to use it when talking about dogs. Behavior analysis applies to all species. The laws of behavior are as universal as the laws of physics; no living creature is exempt from these fundamental principles. Furthermore, physiological and emotional responses are so similar across species that when scientists have performed similar studies on multiple species, their results across species were the same. So throughout the book, when we reference studies that aren't directly about dogs, we aren't doing so irresponsibly. Until and unless similar studies are performed on dogs, the ones done on humans, rats, and other species can be great analogs in certain contexts.

But this brings up another important point: the scientific study of various aspects of canine enrichment is fairly new and relatively sparse. There's a lot more that we don't yet know than what we do know. So in some cases, the authors by necessity must rely on our personal experiences and anecdotal evidence to fill in the gaps. When we do, though, we'll be honest about it. We all must do the best we can with the information we have.

This is an amazing time to be alive and working with dogs. The things that researchers are learning every year make this profession even more exciting, dynamic, and fulfilling than it already was. We hope our passion and love for behavior science will become contagious.

How this book was written

Finally, a quick note about our process writing this book: we two authors (Emily and Allie) live halfway across the country from each other and collaborate on several big projects together. For logistical reasons, writing the book together wasn't feasible. Instead, we each wrote different chapters of the book and then edited and added to each other's chapters. For this reason, as you read through the book you will probably notice changes in style and tone. When speaking of personal experiences, we refer to ourselves by name so you don't have to guess who the event relates to. We hope you don't find these variations distracting, but instead think of it as a conversation that you are observing and even participating in.

We also want you to think of this book not as an end-all be-all source of information, but as a hub that connects you and points you to even more and better resources. Avail yourself of the Resources section at the back of the book. Explore the books, websites, videos, and continuing education options we provide there. And if you want to dive even deeper, check out the volumes of research in the References section. You can even contact the researchers themselves to ask them more direct questions. The point is, you don't have to take our word for it. This book isn't about our opinions; the goal of this book is to open up for you the whole wide world of information and resources available about who dogs are and how to meet their needs. We hope you'll find it as fascinating as we do.

Introduction: Defining Enrichment for Dogs

You become responsible, forever, for what you have tamed.
Antoine de Saint-Exupéry

Early on in her behavior consulting career, Emily worked with a client whose dog was a nervous wreck. He paced and whined all the time, had difficulty settling down, and didn't want to interact with his owners. His owners had spent thousands of dollars at various veterinary hospitals trying to identify a medical cause, but to no avail. The vets couldn't find anything physically wrong with the dog, so they decided it must be behavioral, and referred the clients to her. Distraught, the clients told her in great detail all the things they were doing to be good dog owners: they made sure he got daily runs, they gave him lots of toys, they fed him in food puzzles instead of in a bowl, they took him to training classes regularly, and the list went on. They weren't good dog owners; they were *fabulous* dog owners.

The most upsetting part for them was that they'd gotten this dog as a puppy and he had never had any problems before, but these behaviors started out of nowhere a few months prior and had continued to get worse. They were convinced it was something wrong with them, because their dog runner reported that the dog was relaxed and happy when away from the house, but always reluctant to come back home.

After a long line of questioning about any potential changes that had happened in their home, the husband finally got this a-ha look on his face and said, "You know, we did buy one of those sonic pest control things. Could that be the problem?" He went to the closet, turned it off, and within seconds the dog started to visibly relax. Over the next several days, the dog returned to his old self and no longer exhibited all the anxious behaviors he had previously demonstrated. All of that stress, anxiety, and expense because of a sound we humans can't even hear.

Situations like this beg the question: How do we define enrichment? The dog had lots of toys, foraging opportunities, and exercise—everything that people typically think of as enrichment—and yet, would anyone who saw him during that sonic-pest-control period of his life characterize him as "enriched"? Probably not. So, if enrichment isn't just the toys and activities that are available to a dog, what is it?

A holistic view
We need to take a more holistic view of what enrichment means. It's not enough to give animals things to do. It's not enough to create an environment that looks good to us. It is our responsibility to make sure that *all* of an animal's needs are being met. Having domesticated dogs, and in doing so created their dependency on us, the onus is on us to make sure they are able to reach their full doggy potential.

For this reason, we need to define enrichment carefully when talking to people who work with and own dogs: *Enrichment is learning what our dogs' needs are and then structuring an environment for them that allows them, as much as is feasible, to meet those needs.* For you as a reader, the easiest way to think about enrichment is meeting your dog's needs. While we will be providing much more breadth and depth to this definition throughout the book, meeting a dog's needs to the fullest extent possible underlies the concept of enrichment.

We also can't stress enough at the beginning that, if we don't understand who dogs are as a species or what their needs actually are, the enrichment process will not get very far. If we rely on myths, misunderstandings, and romanticized notions about dogs, we are bound to miss the mark when trying to enrich them. For this reason, this book covers a much broader range of topics than most people might expect from a book about enrichment. This isn't just about toys and play. It's about who dogs are, the entire spectrum of their physical, behavioral, and instinctual needs, and how we can meet those needs as a part of our daily routine. Dog ownership isn't—and shouldn't be—a job you clock into and clock out of every day; it should be a lifestyle. So we're also going to talk about how to realistically and sustainably make that happen.

How this book is organized

This book is divided into three parts. Chapters 1 through 3 discuss the origins of the concept of enrichment, and provide a clear definition of what enrichment is and is not. The second section, Chapters 4 through 12, delve deeper into the nuts and bolts of enrichment, discussing various types and why they are important. The final section, Chapters 13 through 17, provides practical suggestions for creating and implementing your enrichment plan based on what you learned in the rest of the book.

Chapter 1

ENRICHMENT THEN AND NOW

"Enrichment" has become a buzzword. It gets casually tossed around in conversations about animal welfare and has become paired with the word "training" as if they were two pieces of a whole: enrichment-and-training. Kind of like peanut-butter-and-jelly. A match made in heaven. Everyone knows they're important, and somehow related, right? Easy peasy. But when asked to define enrichment, things get a little less clear for most people. Is it play? Is it toys? Is it preventing boredom? What exactly *is* enrichment? What does it mean? Why does it matter? Isn't it optional? After all, wild animals don't have anyone making toys for them. Maybe it's even spoiling animals? Perhaps we're pampering pets too much with our 21st century notions of enrichment.

When we set out to answer these questions, we realized we needed an entire book to do so. Not only is this topic quite a bit broader than toys or play or pampering pets, it's also much more vital to the physical, behavioral, and emotional health of our pets than most people realize. In order to understand what enrichment is, why it matters, and how to make it a part of our everyday lives, we first need to understand how it evolved.

It started off in zoos
Regardless of your feelings toward zoos, dog owners owe them a huge debt without even realizing it. Our understanding of the concept of enrichment and how it applies to our dogs' lives is a direct result of the actions of zookeepers around the world. For that reason, even though this

book is specifically about dog enrichment, we need to start by talking about zoo animals.

Zoos as we know them are quite different than they were before the mid-to-late 20th century. In the whole history of humans keeping wild animals in captivity, it wasn't until the 1960s that people began to consider the welfare of zoo animals and wonder whether we couldn't do a better job of making them happy and healthy. That journey was a slow and gradual process, but the one man who catapulted the cause of zoo animal welfare forward more than anyone else was Dr. Hal Markowitz.

Dr. Markowitz spent his entire life studying animals in the wild and caring for them in captivity. At the time zoos were, as he called them, "concrete wastelands." Animals spent their whole lives in small, barren enclosures with nothing to do and, more often than not, no other members of their species to interact with. Mealtime was the highlight of their day, but even then it was delivered in a perfunctory, assembly-line manner. During the rest of the day, zoo animals either didn't move at all or they moved in functionless, repetitive motions—a tell-tale sign of deprivation and chronic stress—called **stereotypies**. Even though he had a thorough understanding of many of the behavior sciences and therefore immediately recognized stereotypies for what they were, no expertise would have been required to notice the stark contrast between the active, intelligent, dynamic individuals he observed in the wild and the dull, lifeless beings in zoos and aquariums. This had to change, and Hal Markowitz was determined to change it.

Fortunately for him, the timing was right for him to try to make these changes. By the 1960s, growing concern about the health of ecosystems around the world, and the shrinking populations of animals within them, gave birth to the conservation movement. Zoos were no longer primarily interested in amusing humans but also in helping to save the planet's species. Doing so meant reducing the number of wild-caught animals and implementing breeding programs—not only to populate zoos but also to reintroduce into the wild to help increase and diversify endangered populations. But breeding programs struggled due to the poor mental, emotional, and often even physical health of the captive animals. It was becoming abundantly clear that zoos were not meeting the needs of their animals, to everyone's great detriment.

Dr. Markowitz had a plan, which he shared with the zoological community: "First, learn as much as you can about [each] species both in the wild and in captivity" (2011). From our current perspective it may sound obvious, but we can't meet a species' needs if we don't know what those needs truly are. So, Dr. Markowitz recommended that zoos create an ethogram for each species they had in their collection. An **ethogram** is a list or a table of observable behaviors performed by individuals within a species. Ethograms help scientists to objectively record the natural behaviors performed by a species while reducing the possibility of misinterpretation or varied interpretations among researchers. In this case, Dr. Markowitz used them to help zoos figure out what function those natural behaviors served. He then helped them to create an environment that enabled each species to perform those behaviors. Thus was born the concept of enrichment: learning first what an animal's needs are, and second, how to meet those needs in captivity.

Defining goals and measuring results

Dr. Markowitz understood that it was important, however, to not just *think and feel* that enrichment was helping zoo animals, but to conclusively and unquestioningly *know*. After all, enrichment is about quantifiably improving the quality of life of captive and domesticated animals, which means that it isn't enough for enrichment to look good or feel good to us. Enrichment isn't about us; it's about the animals' well-being. So in addition to the use of ethograms to guide a zoo's enrichment plan, Dr. Markowitz also recommended clearly defined goals and rigorous data-collection to accurately gauge the efficacy of enrichment programs. This means:

- Documenting the clear, observable behaviors of an individual and measuring them against its ethogram.

- Coming up with clear goals for how to change the current behaviors to more closely approximate the species-typical behaviors on the ethogram.

- Documenting how that animal interacts with the enrichment offered, and how successfully those interactions resulted in the desired behavior changes.

- And most importantly of all, whether that animal chooses to continue engaging in those desired behaviors over the long term. In fact, choice is such an important aspect of a successful enrichment plan that we are going to spend a great deal of time discussing it later in this book.

The notion that we must be methodical in our approach to enrichment will undoubtedly displease some of our readers. Many people prefer to take a more intuitive or empathetic approach to interacting with the animals in their lives. To be clear, empathy and intuition are important. People who are already intuitive and empathetic toward non-human species certainly have an advantage, and both intuition and empathy can (and should) be cultivated in people who are not. However, those two skills are not enough to make us as effective as we can be. Basing our efforts on evidence will only enhance, rather than detract from, our intuitive and empathic abilities.

In his book *Enriching Animal Lives*, Dr. Markowitz talks about the first moment when his methodical approach paid off. He had constructed a "forest" in a white-handed gibbon's enclosure and created feeding stations up in the canopy where this species normally eats in the wild. Before building this exhibit, the gibbon who lived in the enclosure had been eating his food on the ground. When he watched the gibbon climb up one of the trees and swing from limb to limb to get to each feeding station to eat his meal, Dr. Markowitz was overwhelmed by a mix of emotions: guilt about how many animals live powerless and unhappy lives, excitement and awe at their intelligence and ingenuity, and hope that humankind could continue to improve the quality of life of all the animals in our care.

Dr. Markowitz's hope has become a reality. Many zoos, aquariums, and aviaries around the world have internalized the importance of enrichment, and their enrichment programs have continued to evolve and progress. Captive and domesticated animals of all species are happier, healthier, and more empowered than they have ever been in the past, and breeding and reintroduction programs are more successful than they have ever been in the past. And we continue to learn and improve every day.

The ingenuity of zookeepers in devising enrichment for the animals in their care is truly inspiring. There are the more recognizable enrichment strategies, such as creating foraging and hunting opportunities for animals to procure their food in a more natural way: papier-mâché prey animals that the predators have to "hunt" and "kill," hanging branches of fruit for birds to fly to and eat from, freezing a hippo's food in a block of ice so they have to swim around and bite at the ice to get the food out, hanging hay from a high branch so elephants have to reach up high and use their trunks to pull it down. Then there are recognizable strategies to encourage play and exercise: bubble baths for primates, hanging animal hides up high to encourage big cats to leap at and tackle their "prey," large, heavy balls for pigs to push around, branches and leaves for parrots to strip, shred, and chew. And then there are less obvious aspects of enrichment that may be easily overlooked or misunderstood by observers. What may appear to be a dirty and stagnant puddle of water is in fact an ideal "swamp" for alligators. If you see a worn-out walking trail along the perimeter of a wolf enclosure, that's intentional: pacing is on the wolf's ethogram, so they need the space to pace. Misters in a tropical bird enclosure aren't just for ambience; they're essential to the health of a bird's skin and feathers, as well as to encourage bathing behaviors in many species. Not only how zoos feed, but what zoos feed the animals in their care has also changed as nutritional research has helped us to gain a better understanding of the dietary needs of captive wild animals. How we treat them medically has evolved as well. Zoos are even using clicker training to teach their animals to actively and willingly participate in medical procedures. This reduces stress and fear, as well as eliminating the need to anesthetize animals for routine veterinary care, which is expensive, time-consuming, and risky. All of that is enrichment, brilliantly and artfully done.

When we combine our empathy, intuition, and a methodical approach to create an enriching environment for the animals in our care, it enriches our lives as well. Both of the authors have been providing enrichment for our own personal pets, our clients' pets, and animals in the shelters, rescue groups, and sanctuaries where we've worked, for many years. Nothing is more thrilling than the moment we see an animal come to life right before our eyes, and it never gets old. It's every bit as thrilling today as it was when we first started. Our lives are better because we have been able to make their lives better.

A growing portion of the zoological community thinks of and speaks about enrichment as Dr. Markowitz developed it. He said, "Enrichment should be a synonym for 'more like nature.'" In other words, enrichment can be defined *as meeting all of an animal's needs as closely as possible to how they would be met in the wild, in order to empower them to engage in species-typical behaviors in healthy and appropriate ways.* Enrichment is not defined solely by what we do, but more significantly by the outcomes of what we do. It can only be enrichment if the result is a physically and behaviorally healthy animal. For that reason, many zoologists and behavior professionals use the terms "enrichment" and "husbandry" interchangeably. However, somewhere along the way, as the concept of enrichment made its way into the pet community, that notion of enrichment as husbandry got lost in translation. When enrichment for dogs is discussed, it usually refers to play, toys, exercise, and marginally some other facets of pet care. As you will see throughout this book, though, it is so much more than that.

Chapter 2

THE ELEMENTS OF ENRICHMENT

As discussed in Chapter 1, Dr. Markowitz defined enrichment as "more like nature." In other words: enrichment is learning what an animal's natural needs are and then structuring an environment for the animal that allows, as much as feasible in captivity, them to meet those needs. That's all fine and good for animals in a zoo, but when using that definition for dogs, we run into some tricky issues.

The largest issue is that, unlike most zoo animals, dogs are not captive wild animals. Instead they are a domesticated species and have been for a minimum of 15,000 years (Larson et al., 2012). Domestication happens when humans exert a significant influence over the development of another species until that species becomes better suited for life with humans than life in the wild. Domestication genetically alters these animals so that they are distinct from their wild counterparts. But unlike some other domesticated species such as goats, horses, and camels, dogs as a species, *Canis lupus familiaris*, have no wild counterparts.

Identifying natural behaviors

How, then, can we determine what a dog's "natural" behaviors are? Natural behaviors are those that evolved in dogs before they became domesticated. Many of those behaviors have been weakened or almost eliminated over the centuries due to selective breeding. However, many are still present today and must be considered in any enrichment program.

Identifying natural behaviors can get tricky given the degree of variation within the species caused by selective breeding. Because humans have been breeding dogs for centuries to perform specific tasks, each breed has its own genetic predispositions toward certain behaviors (Handelman, 2008). For example, sledding breeds are more likely to roam, whereas herding breeds have a tendency to stay near their home. Scent hounds tend to be quite vocal, whereas sighthounds tend to be relatively quiet. Dachshunds tend to dig under things whereas Boxers tend to climb or jump over them. To make it even more complicated, not every dog will exhibit the traits typical for their breed. There are certainly sledding breed dogs who don't roam, and herding breeds who do. There are silent scent hounds and lippy sighthounds. There are Dachshunds who don't dig and Boxers who don't jump. Within every breed there are individuals who never got the memo that they were expected to behave in certain ways! And then of course there are mixed breeds, who have inherited a whole mixed bag of traits. For a behavior to make it onto an ethogram, it must be common and well-documented across the species. With such a wide variety of behaviors offered by the different breeds of dogs, it's not surprising then to see so few of them appear on dog ethograms. In fact, if you look up "dog ethogram" on the internet, most of the ones you'll find are restricted to body language signals and little else.

Research strategies for identifying natural behaviors

Some researchers have chosen to study feral dog populations. "Feral" and "wild" are not the same thing. A feral animal is either a wild animal who has been displaced via human interference and adapted to their non-native environment, or—more salient to our topic—one of a domesticated species who has adapted to life independent of human involvement. They may live in or near an urban area or they may live in the wild, but the defining characteristics are that they do not live where their species evolved and are not dependent on humans to live. For this reason, the scientists who study them feel they can get a good idea of what a dog's natural behaviors are by watching how they live with minimal or no human interference. Other researchers, however, choose to study dogs who are living as the domesticated species they are: either in sanctuary populations or in pet homes, since they feel that human "interference" is one of the defining characteristics of the species. The authors feel that looking at all the combined research of feral, sanctuary, and pet dogs gives us a well-rounded picture of the natural behaviors of the species as a whole, which we discuss in more detail in Chapter 8.

Understanding these limiting complications, we can still accomplish quite a bit in terms of categorizing species-typical behaviors for dogs. And as for the wide variety of individual behaviors, the authors have adopted this mantra from Dr. Susan Friedman: "behavior is a study of one."

We have found that the variations among individuals pose no real obstacle to creating a successful enrichment plan for the dogs we work with. Using the species-typical behaviors as a starting point, from there all we need to do is observe the behaviors being offered by the individual to create their own, unique ethogram. What does *your* dog do, and how can you create an enrichment plan to best meet their needs? Hopefully by the end of this book you'll have a clear answer to that question.

Natural behaviors and instinctual needs

Instinctual needs include: sensory stimulation, safety, security, foraging, and the freedom to perform natural behaviors, which may include breed-typical behaviors. Each of these topics is so important they have their own chapter later in the book. The common thread though is that these needs are often the most frustrating for pet owners, caregivers, and trainers alike, and are often perceived as being "bad" behaviors. However, it is important to recognize them for what they are and find a way to allow dogs to perform these behaviors in safe and acceptable ways. In other words: let dogs be dogs.

For example, counter-surfing or getting into the trash are simply dogs using their powerful sense of smell and their inquisitive nature in order to procure food. This one set of behaviors is meeting three separate but related instinctual needs:

- **Sensory stimulation:** dogs' most powerful sense is their sense of smell, and they are also incredibly sensitive to tactile stimulation

- **Scavenging:** dogs are scavengers, which means they will eat food wherever they find it, hunting only as necessary when easier food isn't obtainable

- **Foraging:** the act of working to find and procure food

What appears to us to be horribly naughty and destructive behavior is actually a dog meeting their needs in the best way they know how given the opportunities they have available to them in their environment. After all, the equivalent of this behavior in the wild is what kept them alive long enough to be domesticated!

So does that mean we should just let them do it? Of course not. We shouldn't have to live in a literal trash pile in order to share our lives with dogs, and digging through the trash is certainly unsafe and unhealthy for them. However, we do need to stop blaming and punishing them for trying to meet their own needs in the ways they currently know how to. Instead, this should be a signal to us that we need to do a better job of creating appropriate ways to meet those needs while also managing their environment so they can't perform the undesirable behaviors.

Another example: you have given up making your bed because your dog habitually unmakes it. If you forget to close your bedroom door and you turn your back for even a few minutes, they have jumped up on the bed and created a nest out of your freshly made linens. They might even have chewed a hole here and there. Why are they such a diva? Why do they *need* to sleep on your bed when they have a perfectly good bed of their own? Why do they insist on messing up your bed to sleep in it? Again, these behaviors are meeting specific needs:

- **Security:** like many other sentient beings, dogs crave a safe space and will gravitate toward the place they feel safest. And just like humans and any other sentient being, comfort is often interpreted as safety, so if a place is comfortable to them, that means it feels safe to them. Furthermore, the act of licking or chewing can be self-soothing to dogs. When dogs are settling into a comfortable space, it isn't uncommon for them to want to lick or chew something to wind down. Sometimes that something just so happens to be your comforter.

- **Sensory stimulation:** no matter how often you wash your sheets, your bed still smells like you to your dog with their super-sniffer. Additionally, dogs have several types of scent glands on their feet, which leaves their own scent on the bedding as well. Home is where your smells are.

Again, though, if this behavior is unpleasant to you, find ways to meet those needs while preventing the undesirable behavior.

Just because dogs have been domesticated doesn't mean they automatically know how to perfectly adapt to our 21st century urban human world. They are still dogs. They still have dog needs. Those needs aren't going anywhere. And they're going to meet those needs in the best way they know how, until and unless we teach them better ways to do so.

Emotional needs

We have reached a point in the advancement of the various behavior sciences where it is utterly impossible to deny that animals experience feelings, pleasure, and pain. Says Patricia Barlow-Irick, PhD, in her book *How 2 Train A __*:

> *Have you ever been chastised for anthropomorphizing? This former breach of propriety has been stepped down quite a bit by new science. Animals do have feelings and even fish feel pain. Scientists can study the physical and chemical changes associated with typical emotional states in humans. Because these same physical changes are found in all mammals in response to situations that would be likely to invoke emotions (such as fear and contentment), we have no basis to say that animals don't feel the same emotions we do. Scientists can produce recognizably similar emotions by stimulation of homologous parts of the brain of species as different as chickens, guinea pigs, and humans. Some researchers suggest that, as in children, emotions might be even stronger in animals than in adult humans.*

We know that animals have their own thoughts, feelings, motivations, and intentions. Recent research indicates that dogs have the cognitive capacity of human toddlers (Stewart et al., 2015; Tomasello and Kaminski, 2009), which means their inner life is far more rich and complex than we previously imagined. Until we invent mind-reading machines, we can't actually know what those inner lives look like. However, we must, if we are going to meet our dogs' needs, acknowledge that those needs exist and take them into consideration when creating an enrichment plan for them.

The implication of a canine emotional life and toddler levels of intelligence is that dogs can also be in a state of mental health or mental illness. This, too, is undeniable. There is an entire field of veterinary medicine devoted to the mental health of animals. Board-certified veterinary behaviorists devote a great deal of their education to understanding the mental illnesses that can affect dogs and the various ways to treat those illnesses. Just as in humans, these illnesses can often be tangibly measured and diagnosed. Again, at this stage in scientific advancement, it is impossible to deny that mental illness can and does exist in non-human animals.

Fulfilling physical needs

Another element to enrichment programs is to recognize a dog's physical needs. Physical needs are those of our physical bodies, and this category is the one people most commonly think of when they think of basic needs.

The physical needs include health, hygiene, nutrition, and physical exercise. We will spend the least amount of time on in-depth discussion of physical needs since veterinary medicine and nutrition lie outside the scope of our expertise. However, there are a few important points to discuss as these needs relate to enrichment.

Hygiene

In the context of our definition of enrichment, bear in mind that hygiene is about what is best for the dog's welfare, not simply what we want or what we think sounds nice. Our number one criterion for how we care for our pets should be, "Is this what they actually need? How is it impacting them?" rather than, "What do I want?" For example, the authors have encountered many dog owners who bathe their dogs religiously multiple times a week because they want to avoid the "doggy" smell, but veterinary dermatologists warn against such practices, as they are not good for a dog's skin. If someone is really concerned about their dog's smell they can use waterless shampoo and thoroughly brush their dog every day but keep the baths down to once or twice a week at most. Unless they have a skin condition for which a vet has prescribed medicated baths, most dogs don't *need* to be bathed on a regular basis. Even dogs with thick, heavy coats generally only need baths every 6 to 8 weeks. By and large, bathing is something we do for our convenience, not their well-being.

Conversely, there are many dogs who need regular brushing, or regular nail trimming, or regular ear cleaning, or regular facial fold cleaning. Humans have bred some dogs in such a way that their bodies require daily maintenance and grooming to stay healthy. To neglect those needs out of some misguided notion that "wild dogs wouldn't get this kind of pampering, so this dog shouldn't need it either" certainly has a detrimental impact on their quality of life, but may also prevent them from performing some of their natural behaviors. For example, dogs whose nails are too long may be less inclined to run or dig or even walk on certain surfaces. Emily had a client who had recently adopted a Pug with a horrible facial fold infection because the previous owner had neglected to clean his face on a regular basis. As a result, the dog avoided using his snuffle mat. At first they thought the dog was afraid of the snuffle mat, but as soon as the facial fold infection was treated the dog immediately started using the snuffle mat with eagerness. It wasn't that the dog wasn't interested in the snuffle mat; he was simply not healthy enough to use it.

Health

The dog mentioned above is only one of many, many anecdotes the authors have encountered that demonstrate what an important role health plays in behavior. Physical health absolutely, unquestionably affects how a dog—or any living being, for that matter—behaves. In fact, it is so important that is the first stop on the Humane Hierarchy.

The Humane Hierarchy is an intervention protocol to help animal trainers and behavior consultants determine which approach to take in training. In-depth discussion of the Humane Hierarchy lies beyond the scope of this book, but the basic gist is this: lots of training strategies will "work" in that they will successfully get a dog to stop performing an undesired behavior or to start performing a desired behavior, but not all strategies are equal in terms of their impact on the learner. We need to do the best we can to ensure our strategies are the most ethical, effective, and empowering options available to us to prevent the risk of collateral damage to the learner's mental, emotional, and physical health.

Hierarchy of Behavior-Change Procedures
Most Positive, Least Intrusive Effective Intervention

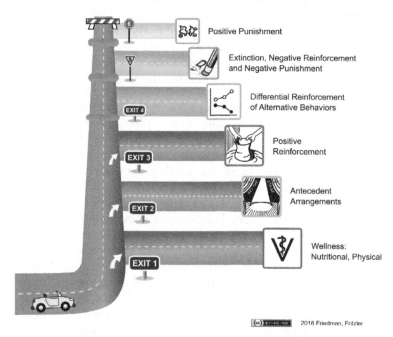

Positive Punishment

Extinction, Negative Reinforcement and Negative Punishment

Differential Reinforcement of Alternative Behaviors

Positive Reinforcement

Antecedent Arrangements

Wellness: Nutritional, Physical

This starts with making sure, first and foremost, that the behavior isn't being caused, exacerbated, or (as in the case of the Pug) suppressed by a medical problem. Emily has another client whose Boxer suddenly started exhibiting aggression toward family members in the household, which he had never done before. These clients went to multiple trainers, all of whom recommended "dominating" and punishing the aggressive behaviors in one way or another: "dominance downs," throwing chains at the dog, hanging the dog by his leash, and shocking the dog with an electronic collar. The dog's aggression only continued to get worse, until they finally ended up hiring Emily. Upon first meeting the clients she noticed that the dog seemed hyperaware of people walking around his sides, and that he walked in a stilted manner and never lifted his head above his shoulders. She recommended taking the dog to a vet before starting any training protocol and, sure enough, the dog had severe neck pain due to arthritis and cervical nerve damage. Every trainer who was just focused on punishing the aggression not only failed to address the underlying cause of the aggression, but they also added more pain and injury to the dog's existing pain and injury. We cannot emphasize enough the importance of making sure an animal is completely healthy and pain-free before trying any other intervention.

We should also specify that starting with a vet visit for behavior issues is not just for issues that you think could have an underlying medical component: it's for every issue. Medical issues play a role in undesirable behaviors in ways that we would never realize without an expert piecing together the puzzle for us. For instance, veterinary behaviorist Dr. John Ciribassi has performed studies suggesting that oral compulsions such as fly biting, flank sucking, and compulsive licking are more often than not accompanied by gastrointestinal issues (Ciribassi and Ballantyne, 2013). Anecdotally, the majority of clients the authors see for anxiety-related issues have some sort of gastrointestinal upset—chronic diarrhea, frequent vomiting—requiring special diets. These clients often report a regression in behavior when the GI upset appears stronger. A reduction in vision can result in not wanting to go outside at night, thyroid imbalances can increase irritability, and joint pain can cause your dog to not sit or lie down when cued. Just because you can't think of how medical issues might be playing a factor in your dog's behavior doesn't mean they aren't!

To successfully address the medical component, we need to have a good relationship with a trustworthy veterinarian. After 23 years of working in a wide variety of veterinary practices, Emily has come up with a list of what she looks for when selecting a vet for her pets:

- **The vet stays up to date on the latest research in their field.** We are making new advancements in medicine every day, and the more we know, the better we can do. It's important that a vet stay abreast of improved technologies and therapies to better serve their clients and patients.

- **The vet is thorough.** You cannot successfully rule out a potential medical issue if your vet does a once-over exam and maybe a small bloodwork panel and calls it a day. Getting a diagnosis means not stopping until you find the answer you're looking for. Don't accept anything less.

- **The vet is flexible and communicative.** Practicing good medicine includes being able to listen to your client and work with them. Having just said "Don't stop until you find your answer," if someone can't afford the gold standard, an all-or-nothing approach is counterproductive. Oftentimes we have to do the best we can with the information, budget, and any other logistical constraints we may have. Look for a vet who is willing to listen to what you have to say and will try to work with you to the best of their ability.

- **The vet recognizes and respects the boundaries of their own expertise.** This means being willing to refer out when a case exceeds their own knowledge. Knowing when to refer to a veterinary nutritionist, a veterinary physical therapist, a veterinary behaviorist, or a certified behavior consultant is every bit as important as referring to a cardiologist or an endocrinologist. Just as it is wildly inappropriate for a dog trainer or behavior consultant who has no formal medical qualifications to make medical diagnoses and drug recommendations, it is equally inappropriate for a veterinarian who has no formal behavioral qualifications to make behavior modification recommendations.

- **You have a good rapport with your vet.** Let's face it: sometimes personalities click and sometimes they don't—and that's okay! Find a vet who meets all the criteria above *and* is someone you like as a person. That's important, too!

When an animal is healthy, they are able to perform their natural behaviors and live an enriched life. So we must address this before anything else.

Nutrition

Nutrition is another aspect of enrichment that may drastically influence behavior. However, it can be a touchy topic since many of us feel passionately about what we feed our dogs, and why. Since Dogwise has many books on the topic, and *Applied Veterinary Clinical Nutrition* by Sean Delaney, DVM, MS, DACVN, provides an even more comprehensive treatment on this topic, we aren't going to spend any time telling you what you should feed your dog. When looking at nutrition through the lens of enrichment, though, there are some important points that need to be made.

Most notably, this is one facet of enrichment where the "more like nature" definition can't come into play. No matter how popular it is to talk about feeding dogs "like they'd eat in the wild," the reality is, there's no such thing as a wild dog diet because, as we've already discussed, wild dogs don't exist, and a lot about nutritional needs and dietary habits can change in 15,000-plus years in ways that we still don't fully understand (Bosch et al., 2015).

So if feeding our dogs "like they'd eat in the wild" isn't an option, what should we do? We should make sure they're eating a nutritionally balanced diet that meets their individual needs. There are standards of nutrient requirements for dogs and cats, aptly entitled "Nutrient Requirements for Dogs and Cats," set by the National Research Council, and for a dog to experience long-term health and well-being, their diet must meet those standards. This is challenging because most of us have a whole lot of feelings and opinions about what type of diet is best for dogs. We watch documentaries, do some internet research, talk to pet store employees, and feel like we have a pretty great grasp on which diet is the best. Here's the problem with that: the reason there are so many widely varying nutritional camps is because each type of diet can legitimately be optimal for certain individuals. Every camp has their success stories because sometimes, in some dogs, that truly is the diet they thrive on most. The implication of that is: nutrition, like behavior, is a study of one. There is no such thing as One True Diet for All Dogs. However, within each type of diet, not all recipes are created equal. In fact, recent research indicates that the majority of homemade diet recipes are not, in fact, nutritionally balanced (Larsen et al., 2013). There are most certainly basic nutritional requirements that all dogs need to thrive, but there's a lot of variation about how those requirements are best met for individual bodies. Says dietician Katherine Beals, PhD, RD, in a 2017 interview with the authors:

> *Just like in human nutrition, there are currently a lot of "fad diets" being marketed to well-intentioned dog owners. While some may adequately meet the needs of your dogs, others could actually result in nutrient inadequacies or toxicities. It doesn't help that pet food labels are not written or displayed the same as human food labels, which only serves to add to the confusion. Luckily most commercial pet foods*

have minimum standards they have to meet that will satisfy the basic needs of most dogs. For those with special needs, there are veterinary nutritionists who can provide more specific dietary recommendations and help with diet formulations.

The authors have worked with many dogs who had chronic health and/ or behavior issues that immediately and permanently improved after being switched to a nutritionally balanced, fresh, whole-food diet. Conversely, we have worked with dogs who could not maintain a healthy weight and generally failed to thrive on a whole-food diet no matter how many kilocalories they were fed each day and were only able to put on weight when switched to a processed kibble diet. We've also worked with dogs who thrived on a vegetarian diet, while others became ill and anemic on the exact same vegetarian diet. Some dogs respond well to prescription diets; others really don't. Some dogs thrive on specific brands of kibble; others do well on a variety of kibble diets. Some dogs do well on a high-protein diet; others experience more fear or agitation on a high-protein diet and are generally more relaxed and calmer on a lower-protein diet (Dodman et al., 1996). Some dogs tolerate a diet high in carbohydrates really well; others behave like children all jacked up on Mountain Dew. Again, there is no such thing as One True Diet. To quote Dr. Delaney from an interview with the authors (2017): "As an omnivore, the domesticated dog has evolved to flourish on calories from many sources. This leads to a wide range of potential approaches to feeding dogs and an ongoing search for what is individually optimal."

What all of those dogs in the anecdotes above had in common was that their owners were willing to set aside their nutritional beliefs in service to their dogs' actual physical and/or behavioral needs. They were willing to change their dietary practices based on the evidence they were presented with, rather than stubbornly feeding what they believed to be "the best diet" despite all evidence to the contrary. If we are going to meet our dogs' needs, we can't let ideology get in the way of observation.

That said, we also can't let anecdotal evidence take precedence over empirical evidence. A huge complicating factor when determining what diet works best for your dog is that, in addition to the immediate, acute changes that are influenced by diet, there are also chronic, cumulative changes that occur internally and may take years to manifest clinical symptoms. On his website, balanceit.com, Dr. Delaney says that a dog's body can:

[conserve] essential nutrients as much as possible over the years, but there may already be problems that have developed. Thinning of the

bones or osteopenia can occur and can be difficult to notice unless you see your veterinarian and they take an x-ray or radiograph or, worse, your pet breaks a bone. Other nutrient deficiencies are much harder to test for and typically won't show up on routine blood work and won't be obvious until a severe problem develops as blood levels are often maintained to the detriment of the rest of the body. ... Surprisingly, many diets that "seem" alright are grossly deficient in numerous essential vitamins and minerals.

This means that just because someone on the internet made up a recipe that sounds great, and your dog seems to be thriving on that diet, doesn't mean all of their nutritional requirements are being met over the long term. Independent, third-party research of many published homemade recipes have shown these recipes to be deficient in one or more essential nutrient (Lauten et al., 2005; Dillitzer et al., 2011; Larsen et al., 2013; and Stockman et al., 2013). So again, it isn't enough to just *feel* like we're doing good things for our dogs; it's important to *know*.

An argument the authors hear a lot is, "Well I don't eat a perfectly balanced, meticulously measured diet and I'm as healthy as can be." That may or may not be true (because, again, oftentimes we pay for our dietary choices decades after we've made them), but here's a critical difference: we can feel what's happening in our bodies and adjust our diets accordingly if a particular food or diet makes us feel bad. Dogs can't tell us what they're feeling. For example, Emily's body does not handle grains well. This doesn't mean she thinks grains are evil or other people shouldn't eat them, but when she eats grains of any kind, for lack of a better term, her insides feel hot and sticky. When she eschews grain in her diet, within just a few days her insides feel cool and clean instead. Externally she may look the same and act the same and no one can tell the difference, but internally she feels worlds different. Many of us in the developed world of the 21st century may (or, again, may not!) be able to play fast and loose with our diets and just modify as we see fit, but since we can't ask a dog how a certain diet makes them feel, we need to take extra measures to make sure we're providing them with a balanced diet.

The good news is, if your dog is one who genuinely does best on a fresh, whole-food diet rather than a kibble diet, balanceit.com has a recipe generator to help people create nutritionally balanced homemade recipes. One could certainly make the argument that a fresh diet, with its variety of colors, textures, and flavors, provides more sensory enrichment than a kibble diet! Just bear in mind that the higher potential reward is also associated with higher potential risk. As with everything in life, there's no such thing as a 100% guarantee of safety or success.

Physical exercise

This topic is so important that we're devoting an entire chapter to it, so we don't need to say too much about it here. However, physical exercise shares this in common with the other physical needs: we don't get to dictate what type of physical exercise is best for our dog. Like everything else mentioned thus far in this chapter, we need to observe what works for each individual dog. What may provide sufficient exercise for one dog, be healthy for their joints, help them to relax, and best meet their needs overall, may not do the same for another dog. Again, we must observe the effect of the practice on the individual dog, rather than deciding how we're going to meet this need regardless of how the dog is being affected. Don't let ideology get in the way of observation.

Chapter 3
AGENCY

Agency can be defined as the ability to have some level of control in our environment and be able to make choices that will result in a desirable outcome. As mentioned in the previous chapter, it is a key component to the mental health of every sentient being, as well as a crucial criterion for meeting their needs. Looking at the lack of agency helps to make sense of why this criterion is so critical. Even though this book is specifically about dog enrichment, let's look at a human example to illustrate its importance.

Patrick Otema was born deaf in a remote part of Uganda. Schools for deaf children had not yet come to this region and, at 15, he had never had a conversation with anyone. Without the ability to communicate, all Patrick could do was watch those around him in confusion. Patrick's father attempted to talk to him through basic gestures, but aside from that rudimentary form of communication, Patrick was isolated and unable to connect with his community. It was impossible for Patrick to decipher the world and people around him. Without that understanding and the ability to voice his thoughts, he could only watch life happen instead of participate in it. He had no way of influencing the events in his life. He was distant and lifeless—his hopelessness painted in his expressions and body language. Patrick was alone, trapped within himself, and afraid (Channel 4, 2014).

We'll find out what happened to Patrick later, but for now let's focus on the aspects of his experience that we can relate to. Most of us have been in a similar situation before: unable to effect change. Whether it's being ignored or chronically silenced by an authority figure, feeling discouraged with a political system and choosing not to vote, or not being able to turn off an incessant car alarm and becoming resigned to listening to it for hours on end, we have all temporarily walked in Patrick's shoes. Often we are left feeling hopeless, frustrated, discouraged, or even frightened, knowing that there is nothing that we can do to change our predicament.

Imagine this from our dogs' perspectives. Like Patrick, our dogs are constantly trying to communicate with someone who speaks another language. They are not able to discuss their thoughts, feelings, motivations, and concerns. And, unfortunately for them, many people in their life are not fluent in dog-ese and consistently misinterpret what they're trying to say. It's no wonder we see many dogs who are like Patrick: despondent and shut down, insecure, and unable to affect many of their desired changes. This hopelessness has been studied in depth; understanding it is vital to realizing enrichment's role in changing it. To illustrate the magnitude of importance of agency, let's first look at the flip side: a lack of agency.

Learned helplessness: what is it?

Patrick was experiencing a state of **learned helplessness**, a condition in which an individual suffers from a sense of powerlessness due to inescapable aversive stimuli—in his case the aversiveness of being unable to communicate with the rest of the world. In essence, the individual learns that nothing they do makes a difference, and therefore they behaviorally—and sometimes even physically—shut down. Scientists have been studying learned helplessness for decades; it's a common topic in psychology and theorized to be a key component of clinical depression in humans. Learned helplessness was discovered by psychologist Martin Seligman in 1967 by studying dog behavior. In this study (Seligman and Maier, 1967), researchers restricted dogs by placing them in harnesses. The dogs were divided into three groups. One group received electric shocks that could be shut off by pressing a lever; one group received the same electric shocks that could be shut off when the first group pressed the lever but could not turn the shocks off themselves, thus making them appear random and inescapable; another group did not receive any shocks. The inescapable nature of the shocks was key to this experiment as learned helpless is dependent on the "uncontrollability of the stressor" (Bland et al., 2003). As Steven Lindsay puts it in his book *Handbook of Applied Dog Behavior and Training Volume 1*, "For learned helplessness to occur, the event must be both traumatic and outside the subject's control" (2000).

The same dogs were then put to the test. Each dog was placed in a box; one side of the box produced electric shocks whereas the other side did not. All the dogs had to do was jump over a low partition to escape the shock. The dogs who did not receive shocks in the first round or who were able to control them with the lever quickly jumped over the partition. The group who previously received the inescapable shocks did not jump over the partition. Instead, they simply lay down and whined when they received each shock. This is learned helplessness; even if you can change your fate, your disbelief causes you not to try and, instead, shut down.

In order to reverse the effects of learned helplessness in this group of dogs, researchers had to physically manipulate the dogs to mimic the motions of jumping over the partition multiple times before the dogs understood that they too could escape the shocks. Watching the other dogs perform the behavior, receiving threats, and being offered rewards were not enough for them to overcome their helplessness. This speaks to how powerful this state of being is.

Learned helplessness in the real world
Learned helplessness can seem esoteric when we talk about these studies performed in a laboratory. It doesn't seem like something we would encounter in daily life. However, learned helplessness is such a common—albeit largely unrecognized—condition in dogs that we frequently see it in shelters, and during grooming, veterinary visits, and obedience training.

You walk into a shelter and head back to the new arrivals. Walking past kennels you see a dog who was surrendered by her family the previous week: Chloe. There's a note from her arrival saying that she will growl when you approach to leash her and will struggle when trying to get her out. You grab your leash and head toward her. To your surprise, Chloe does not growl or struggle being brought out of her kennel. She merely sits still, evading eye contact, as you clip the leash on, and then walks with you to leave. Even though you notice her tail held quite low and ears pinned back, you say to yourself, "She must be improving!" Chloe is not actually improving; she is in a state of learned helplessness.

It's time for your dog Sadie's routine nail trim; you call the vet clinic to schedule the appointment. When you first adopted Sadie, she was terrified of having her nails trimmed, but the clinic has done wonders for her! Each time you go, the techs take her into the back. At first the staff remarked that she was quite difficult, and it required several people to restrain her. Now, when you go to the clinic she gets a blank look on her face, gets very still, and hangs her head and tail low, but she goes into the back with no problem and will remain still even when quicked! The clinic staff, and you, are quite pleased with how much Sadie has improved. Contrary to what you might have been told, she has not "gotten over it" or "submitted to the humans as the alpha." Your dog simply gave up and gave in to learned helplessness.

You visit your neighbor's house to see their "perfectly behaved dog" they've been touting. "Kevin never chews, begs, gets in the way, or barks!" Sounds too good to be true, right? You enter the house to see the dog lying on the rug, out of the way. He opens his eyes to glance at you and then closes them again. He's clearly awake, but uninterested in looking at anything in particular. Time passes and in the hour you've been there you've seen the physical canine shell of a dog, but none of the personality. No happy wiggles, no playing with toys, no active engagement. Kevin just lies there. His owner is ecstatic that he's being so well-behaved around you: "It only took his trainer *four weeks* to get him to be like this!" While learned helplessness can sound equal parts scary and obscure, the more troubling thought is how common it is, and how commonly mistaken for being *submissive* and *well-behaved* it is.

Seligman's research on learned helplessness became a platform for human depression research as he intended. However, the reach goes much further. Learned helplessness has been linked to an array of detrimental outcomes, including:

- Increased pain and fatigue in patients with rheumatoid arthritis (Camacho et al., 2012)

- Decreased performance in school (Diener and Dweck, 1978)

- Increases in fear- and anxiety-like behavior, reduced fight/flight responses, disrupted sleep patterns and food and water intake, and reduction in participants' ability to learn to escape aversive stimuli (Hammack et al., 2012)

- Effects on the neurotransmitters within the individual's brain (Maier and Watkins, 2005)

In short, learned helplessness not only affects psychological well-being on a global scale, but also physical and mental well-being in all species.

While understanding the ramifications of learned helplessness in humans is important, what does this mean for our pets? Let's take a few of the above effects and translate them into what they look like in our dogs. Just like humans, when dogs don't feel well in body or mind they can become more irritable, anxious, or aggressive. And since learned helplessness increases their sensitivity to pain, this means that doing so could also increase aggression as a result (Casey et al., 2013).

Recall that, in Hammack's 2012 paper, learned helplessness caused increases in fear- and anxiety-like behavior, reduced fight/flight response, and affected eating, drinking, and sleep. These can lead to your dog shutting down, being closer to threshold due to lack of sleep and increased sensitivity to stressors, or difficulties maintaining a healthy weight. This phenomenon could also lead to a decrease in ability to learn, making your training more difficult. Oftentimes when people try to train a dog who has been in a state of learned helplessness, they perceive the dog as being stupid or stubborn when in reality we just need to teach them how to learn again. But a failure to recognize the mechanisms at play often means a dog lives a lifetime with unfair labels and a reduced quality of life. The bottom line is: learned helplessness leads to increased stress and decreased mental health.

Why does learned helplessness happen in our dogs?

Often learned helplessness is a product of circumstance: a dog is relinquished to a shelter. No one is actively forcing this animal into a state of learned helplessness. It just happens due to the environment and circumstances. Some people will maliciously induce learned helplessness in others, such as the psychological tactics some abusers use to create dependence within the people they abuse. More often than not, though, we see learned helplessness created by people trying to do the right thing. You need to get your dog's nails trimmed before they crack and cause pain. Your pet has a painful ear infection that requires medication. You're under the impression that forcing your dog who is fearful of other dogs to go to the dog park or dog daycare is truly the best course of action to help them work through their fear.

An earlier example looks at the "obedient" dog. These dogs are created with the best of intentions. Someone obtains a new dog and knows that training is important. They go on the internet or hire a trainer to learn how to do it right: only the best for the new family member! They learn training techniques that focus on punishing undesirable behaviors or maintaining absolute control and mastery over their dog. Or perhaps their dog has a behavior challenge, and the trainer attempts reward-based methods at first. But when they get stuck they resort to more punitive methods like shaker cans and shock collars. Unfortunately, to the untrained eye, learned helplessness in these situations may look like successfully completed training. However, in his book *Handbook of Applied Dog Behavior and Training, Vol. 1* (2000), Steven Lindsay has this to say:

> *Family dogs habitually exposed to unpredictable/uncontrollable punishment are at risk of developing disturbances associated with the learned-helplessness disorder. Traumatic punitive events involving excessive startle reactions or physical pain, which are poorly coordinated with identifiable avoidance cues or response options, meet the operational criteria of inescapable trauma.*

One of the saddest reasons learned helplessness happens is because it's easier for us when our dogs shut down, so we don't necessarily want to fix it. The authors often hear something along the lines of, "They're aggressive when I try to do it at home but will just cower when I take them to the vet for nail trims." The owner often looks reluctant when asked to change their dog's emotional state for nail trims. Why? It's not because the owner is malicious or sadistic. It's typically because they worry that by changing this routine their dog will be aggressive and bite someone or they'll be unable to perform a necessary procedure. It's an "if it's not broken don't fix it" mentality. However, this mentality is only true for one party in this scenario. For the dog, the status quo is definitely broken.

What can we do to help and prevent learned helplessness in our dogs?

Recall the two criteria that needed to be met in order to induce learned helplessness: the event must be traumatic—and only the learner decides what is or is not traumatic—and the event must be uncontrollable. As such, the two overarching things we can do to avoid learned helplessness are: prevent traumatic events from happening to our pets (as much as humanly possible) and give them a sense of control over the events in their life.

Ways we can prevent traumatic events are multitudinous and varied. You can scoop up your small dog on a walk when you see a large, angry-looking off-leash dog running straight for them. You can become more proficient at reading dog body language in order to understand how your dog responds to what you're doing to them and change your approach accordingly. You can choose to skip punitive-based training, and learn how to teach your dog *what you want them to do* instead of punishing unwanted behaviors. There are some traumatic events, however, that are going to be impossible to prevent. For example, moving is often nerve-racking for our pets, but it's better than the alternative of leaving them behind. Another example: there are several legitimate and unavoidable reasons pets are surrendered to shelters. While we can't prevent every traumatic event, nor should we prevent every slightly stressful event (more on that later), we should do our due diligence to help our animals avoid traumatic events as much as possible. Looking out for their safety, discontinuing punitive-training methods, and avoiding flooding techniques (see below) are all ways that we can help in this regard.

Flooding can lead to learned helplessness

Flooding is a method of behavior modification that exposes an individual to whatever stimulus elicits distress of any kind (e.g., fear, anger, frustration, protectiveness, etc.) without any way to escape the stimulus. The idea is to keep exposing them to it until it's no longer stressful and they "get over it." So, for example, holding a dog down on a blanket when they are in the presence of something that scares or upsets them until they "relax" is flooding, because they have no option of escape and they are exposed to the stressor until they learn that they have no control over their situation and they ultimately give up. Another example would be putting a dog who has separation anxiety into a crate and shocking them with a shock collar every time they panic until eventually they stop moving or making any noise.

There are three major flaws with this method:

1. **Ethics/agency/consent:** It was designed by psychologists as a method to help humans overcome their fears. When used for humans, the mental health professional discusses it with their patient, obtains their consent, and the patient willingly subjects themselves to the situation. For example, you have arachnophobia and are choosing to see a professional to help you overcome your fears. The professional explains that they're going to lock you in a room with 100 friendly, non-lethal tarantulas. You will not be allowed to come out of the room until you are comfortable with the spiders, even if it takes several days. You agree to the treatment, sign a consent form, and off you go into Spiderville. Since we cannot tell a dog that we are going to flood them, and they cannot understand what is happening to them, much less give their consent, this presents an ethical problem. For example, shelters may start playgroups as a form of enrichment, especially to help fearful dogs, but forcing a dog to interact with other dogs against their will is removing their agency. Without agency, it isn't enrichment. If, in attempting

to meet their social needs, we violate their need for safety, security, independence, and agency, we defeat our own purpose.

2. **High risk of failure:** If for any reason the procedure must be stopped before the animal "gets over it," and the stressful thing is removed while the animal is still in a state of high stress, that increased stress level becomes the dog's new baseline response to the stressor, making it even more difficult to successfully resolve the emotional state later. This happens all the time with dogs who are forced into group dog settings: they either stay the same or get worse, both in terms of their emotional state and the behaviors that state causes. Then the humans involved erroneously assume that "that's just how they are."

3. **Minimal improvement:** Even if the dog does "get over it," they often feel neutral toward the stimulus, rather than enjoying it or seeking it out. This neutral state runs a higher risk of recidivism than enjoyment or desire does. Think of it like a bank account, where neutral is an empty account and trust or enjoyment is money in the bank. The more a learner likes and trusts something, the more money they have. If you pull them out of the red and bring them to neutral, it doesn't take a large withdrawal to go back into the red. But if they have a healthy bank account, even a large withdrawal won't affect their financial health.

Avoid uncontrollable events

The second criterion to induce learned helplessness is that the event must be uncontrollable. Indeed, the ability to control an aversive stimulus affects our perception of how aversive it is. People willingly pierce their ears and it's rarely a traumatic experience, but if someone held you down and pierced them without your consent, it would likely be traumatic. And if they were to periodically hold you down and give you more piercings, each subsequent experience would be increasingly traumatic. Your trauma may become generalized to the point that you'd be afraid to leave your house because today might be the day that the Piercing People show up. This concept is no less true for dogs (or any species, for that matter) than it is for humans. A dog may shove their head into a cactus while following an interesting scent trail and seem only mildly disturbed by being poked by a cactus needle. But that same dog, when taken to a vet clinic, held down by a stranger, and poked by a needle, would be extremely afraid. Why? Because they had no control over that experience. It's no wonder that at subsequent vet visits this dog gets more afraid, more difficult to handle, perhaps even to the point of needing to be muzzled and sedated any time they go to the place with the Needle People. This infographic by Stephanie Edlund, CPBC, illustrates this phenomenon.

	Intensity of stimulus	Perceived aversiveness	Factors influencing aversiveness
No prediction of stimulus	○	●	Physical sensation. No prediction or escape. Will there be more? When will it happen next?
Stimulus is predictable	○	●	Physical sensation. No escape or prevention. Will there be more?
Stimulus is instigated by animal	○	○	Physical sensation.

Thus, preventing learned helplessness can be accomplished by providing every sentient being with predictability and control—in other words, agency. This principle of being able to make decisions in order to produce desired results is a fundamental need of all sentient beings, just like food, water, and shelter, and it plays a large part in the bigger picture of behavioral health. Agency is incredibly important, powerful, and necessary for our dogs, yet is rarely talked about and often overlooked. But remember that Dr. Markowitz said that choice is one of the defining characteristics of enrichment. As such, we'll spend the rest of this chapter talking about it.

Agency: the power of choice

The thought of dogs as sentient beings is still, surprisingly, debated around the world. But as animal lovers and pet owners have known for a long time, dogs are not robots designed to cater to our every whim. They have personalities, preferences, fears, and desires. And with those come the innate need to have some measure of control over their environment. One of the main guiding principles of enrichment includes "increasing control or contingency between animal action and environmental reaction" (Carlstead and Shepherdson, 2000). This is agency!

For an anecdotal look at the power of choice as it applies to humans, let's go back to Patrick, the deaf Ugandan child described at the beginning of the chapter. A sign language teacher came to Patrick's village to set up a course for deaf children, and the historic event was caught on film.

Throughout the first lesson Patrick walks with the same listless posture. He watches the students around him as they learn to sign animal names. A twinkle comes to his eye. Understanding seeps in. They're communicating—one of the first steps to being able to influence events around you. He could do that too! A smile starts unfolding across his face: the first his father has ever seen. The smile grows wider as he starts signing, communicating, with them. At the end of the class each student stands in front of his peers and receives a new sign name. Finally, Patrick is no longer alone. His new life of interconnectedness and agency has begun.

Ten weeks later, Patrick is completely transformed. He now knows how to interact with those around him and is able to influence the events in his life, and that brings on a new level of confidence. For the first time in his life, Patrick has friends. The teacher has clearly made a lasting impact; Patrick reveals that he wants to follow in his teacher's footsteps and teach other deaf people. He has the ability to bring about the same change for someone else. He can make a difference. Patrick signs that he is now happy. His smile proves it.

We are not alone in this need to be heard and to have control over our environment in order to bring about desired results. This is not solely a human phenomenon. All species, including our beloved pets, need this too. While the authors have experienced many animal cases similar to Patrick's story, a particular cat named Grey stands out for Allie. When Allie met Grey he had been living in an animal sanctuary for several years. He was a shy cat to begin with, uncomfortable with being touched, and suffered from stomatitis, a painful mouth disease that required routine medical care. Because of his fear, Grey required sedation for annual exams. During their first encounter, Grey sat several feet away from Allie—more than an arm's length. He would eat flakes of tuna, but only off the floor, not from her hand. It was clear that he did not trust her.

Allie started working with Grey by teaching him that he had the ability to influence his environment, namely her. Every time he would offer her eye contact she would click and set a flake of tuna in front of him. She wouldn't reach out to pet him, or sit closer than he was comfortable with, and if he moved she wouldn't follow. He dictated how the training sessions went. Grey caught on quickly that he had this power, and by the end of the first session he would eat tuna from her hand. Within a few sessions Allie was able to pet his body, something that took others months to accomplish.

Allie taught his caregivers the "eye contact game"; they taught their interns and volunteers and within a couple months he would play his game with any willing participant, including a caregiver he previously ran from. A few more months and others started to notice. People who rarely saw him would ask about the new friendly cat who calmly gazed into your eyes. All were surprised to hear that it was Grey. Nine months after Allie and Grey's first session, he was due for an annual exam. The vet staff was able to complete his exam without sedation for the first time ever.

Allie chalks Grey's progress up to the power of agency and the amazing caregivers who believed in it. She did work on a few other exercises, including helping him to feel more comfortable with being touched on his head and the sides of his mouth via **counterconditioning**: pairing the experience with things he found enjoyable, like treats or games. However, she did not have to transfer the exercise to other people. He became comfortable with others touching him with very little work, as long as they played his game first. The majority of Grey's work involved the very simple training of clicking for eye contact with a high rate of reinforcement. This simple exercise was enough to boost his confidence and build trust to the point where new people had no idea about the extent of his past fear issues, and he is now able to have low-stress medical exams. Talk about an exercise that gives you more bang for your buck!

Studies in agency

The power of agency is not just anecdotal. In 1984, researcher Joseph Volpicelli set up an experiment similar to Seligman's prior study on learned helplessness, but using rats (Volpicelli et al., 1984). Just as in Seligman's research, Volpicelli had three groups of rats conditioned to electric shocks in different ways: escapable shocks, inescapable shocks, and "naive" rats not previously exposed to electric shocks. However, Volpicelli changed the box set-up so that each side delivered electric shocks; there was no escape. Just as before, the rats previously exposed to inescapable shocks developed learned helplessness. Naive rats tried to escape frequently but their efforts decreased as time went on. Interestingly, though, the rats previously exposed to escapable shocks continued trying to escape over 200 trials. That's some serious persistence. This means that learning history plays a large role in the battle between resilience and giving in. Animals can learn the perseverance necessary to avoid learned helplessness via a learning history that includes high rates of reinforcement. This is called **immunization training**: utilizing high rates of reinforcement contingent on the learner's behavior and limiting the amount of punishment.

We use immunization training to prepare people with high-stress, high-risk jobs. For example, you don't just start being a neurosurgeon. If anyone walked off the street and tried to do that job, they would crumble under the pressure. People become neurosurgeons by first practicing and being reinforced for minimally difficult and low-stress skills, then incrementally more difficult and stressful ones. By the time they become neurosurgeons, they are incredibly resilient to stress, extremely skilled and knowledgeable, and mentally flexible enough to troubleshoot when things don't go as planned. Immunization training will help your dog to become more resilient in the future by teaching them to remain calm under pressure and to be able to work through their choices instead of instantly reacting. Essentially, we're using agency to strengthen a dog's resilience.

This effect was also observed by Dr. Markowitz in his study on the physiological effect of agency on non-human primates (Line et al., 1989). "We have seen that primates given control to deliver food and music to themselves whenever they wished bounced back much more quickly from some of the stresses of captivity (such as being restrained for physical exams) than did matched counterparts with no such opportunity." In fact, this all comes down to a neurobiological level, just as learned helplessness does. Researchers found that in rats, control over stressful stimuli increased ions in a part of the brain contributing to stress resilience (Varela et al., 2011). This means that having control over stress makes your brain better equipped, at the most basic level we currently know of, for handling stress in the future. Immunization training and agency are good for your brain!

Shortly after research on learned helplessness came out, many researchers took to the labs to determine if agency was important from infancy. One of these studies involving early experiences looked at two sets of rats (Joffe et al., 1973). One set was born into a "contingent environment" where they could control the lights, as well as food and water delivery. The other set received the same conditions but were unable to control them. The rats born into the contingent environment were described as "less emotional"—in other words, calmer and more resilient to changes in their environment.

A similar study was performed with 2-month-old infants (Watson and Ramey, 1972). One group of infants was placed in cribs where they could turn the mobiles above their cribs on and off by moving their heads. The other set of infants had no control over the mobiles above their cribs. The infants who could control their mobiles smiled more, cried less, and were generally calmer and happier than the infants who had no control over their environment.

Lack of agency early in life can "produce an animal that later in life is less able to adapt to stressful events and less likely to actively investigate and learn about novel situations" (Carlstead and Shepherdson, 2000). Clearly, the neurobiological effects of agency have a lasting impact. Thus, it's important to start this work with young puppies!

How do we provide our dogs with agency?

Agency in utilization of space

Providing our animals with choice can sound difficult and, as we mentioned, scary to some people. It doesn't have to be either! Something as simple as offering choice through an alternative space can impact stress levels and behavioral well-being. A study in the panda exhibit at the Zoological Society of San Diego looked at the effects of choice on behavioral and hormonal differences (Owen et al., 2005). This study compared the same pandas in two different management conditions: one where pandas were confined to an exhibit area and another where they could move in between the exhibit area and a non-exhibit area. The "pandas displayed fewer signs of behavioral agitation and lower urinary cortisol in the free choice condition."

Providing choice in space in a home environment can be as easy as allowing your dog access to multiple rooms of the house. Pay attention to where your dog chooses to sleep, and put their bed in their favorite spot. Always allow them access to their crate or other safe space. If they move away from you or another person, let them do so. Don't follow. All of these are very easy ways to give your dog more agency.

Allie provides her dog, Oso, agency in utilization of space during thunderstorms. When he was first adopted he would not go outside during a thunderstorm. It was too scary! However, there would be nights when it would be storming for hours and he needed to go outside to potty. It was quite the dilemma. On these nights Allie would leave the door open when they were outside. If Oso got frightened at any point he could easily run back inside without having to wait for her to open the door. Just the knowledge that he could do this made him much more comfortable with going outside when there was a thunderstorm, and it eventually was no longer a problem.

Imagine the impact this understanding of choice in spaces could have on shelter, boarding, and doggy daycare facilities. Installing kennels with two different spaces (often separated by a guillotine or doggy door) is an easy way to decrease stress in shelters and boarding facilities. The animal has a choice as to which part of the kennel to be in. Offering a place to be away from humans or other dogs is another important consideration; kennels with guillotines or dog doors, rooms with places to "hide" like crates, or playground equipment in doggy daycares serve this purpose. Letting your dog hide in the closet isn't such a bad thing after all.

Agency in interactions with humans

Additionally, imagine the implications of simply providing space when working with dogs displaying "behavioral agitation." A common recommendation when working with a dog displaying antagonistic behaviors is to give the dog space—let them approach you. Essentially, you are allowing the dog to make a choice about how the space is used. Take away that choice and the dog will likely aggress or shut down.

Many dogs have learned, for one reason or another, that they do not have this choice. These are the dogs who are uncomfortable with people, but still approach them. When they arrive next to the person, they growl, air snap, or even bite. In these cases, and even in more benign cases as a form of prevention, the authors use what they've termed "flight training." Teach the dog that they have the choice between fight and flight. They have the choice in how they move about their space. There are several ways to do this (detailed procedures are found in the Resources section):

- Retreat & Treat protocol by Dr. Ian Dunbar and/or Treat-Retreat by Suzanne Clothier (in these protocols, a handler tosses high-value treats in front of the dog to lure them closer and tosses lower-value treats behind the dog to allow them to eat and move away).

- Variation of Retreat & Treat protocol: toss treats past the dog so they can move away from you to eat. Remove the part of the protocol where you toss treats in front of them. By removing the part of the protocol where you toss treats in front of them, the reward for approaching becomes letting them retreat and eat.

- Emergency U-turn with cue.

- Luring or cueing your dog to stand behind you so that you are between your dog and an oncoming stranger.

- Recall when your dog approaches a stranger.

Then, when the dog understands that they have a choice in how they can move about in their space, we can give them the choice to approach:

- Retreat & Treat protocol.

- Hand targeting: approach the stranger to target, then go back to the owner for a treat.

- Paw/shake/high five: approach the stranger to perform the behavior, then go back to the owner for a treat.

- "Say hello" behavior chain: Ask your dog to sniff the stranger for a few seconds then come back to you and sit by your side.

All of these approaches allow the dog to make a choice: do I want to approach this person or not? They also ensure that the dog is not lingering near the stranger, in case the dog becomes uncomfortable being around the person too long.

The authors have used flight training on numerous occasions with great success. One particular case that stands out in Emily's mind is a dog named Sammy. Sammy was reactive toward other dogs and strangers, and over time his reactivity had escalated to the point where he was no longer allowed to attend dog daycare. When Sammy's owner hired Emily to consult on his behaviors, one of the protocols she put in place was an Emergency U-Turn with a cue. After four months of training, Sammy had improved to the point that he was allowed to return to dog daycare. To the daycare attendants' delight and astonishment, he came with a new skill. Whenever Sammy gets too stressed in the playgroup, he jumps the 7-foot fence surrounding the play area and puts himself in timeout in one of the air locks! He stays in the air lock until he's calmer, then jumps back into the group to resume playing. Since he learned to choose flight instead of fight, he has had no unhappy incidents with other dogs at daycare.

Agency in daily life
There are a few easy ways that we can create choice in husbandry activities without having to do any additional training first. One of these is simply allowing your dog to choose which direction you take on a walk. Long lines and off-leash walks can take this to the next level if they are appropriate for your dog and situation (the authors believe dogs should not be let off leash in unenclosed locations until they have solid "watch me" and recall cues and have good social skills with dogs and humans). Otherwise, follow your dog as they trail a scent. When you come to a fork, ask, "Which way?" and let them choose which way to go. In this day and age of smartphones and GPS, the risk of getting lost is a sorry excuse for not allowing your dog some fun.

Medical and grooming activities are rarely favorites, and while counter-conditioning is important and necessary to change that, we can build agency into these activities as well. The "Bucket Game" created by Chirag Patel is a way to "ask" your dog if they are okay with continuing a medical or grooming activity. Sometimes these activities become overwhelming, even for a dog who is tolerant of them. This game can provide some mental relief by letting the dog control when to stop and start the session. One addendum we'll add to the Bucket Game, though: if you find that it's difficult to notice when your dog is or is not looking at the bucket while you're concentrating on training, you can modify the game by teaching your dog to place their paw onto a target on the floor, or rest their chin on a chair or on your lap. It's generally easier for people to notice when their dog moves their foot off a target or lifts their chin up than it is for them to notice when their dog stops looking at a bucket.

Does your dog like to play? Let them pick how! Perform a toy preference test, like the one outlined by the Center for Shelter Dogs. This lets your dog tell you what style of toy they prefer playing with. Then, when you're ready to play you can hold two of a similar style up to them and ask which one they want to use today. Do they prefer to destroy toys? Let them! Pick up cheap toys at the dollar store or on clearance and let them go to town. As long as they don't ingest the stuffing, it's really not a big deal how they choose to use them.

What game do they want to play? Some dogs will play any game, whereas others are very particular about the type of game they play. Try playing a variety of games with your dog. If they only like to play one game, that's your answer. If they like to play multiple, attach the name to the action so you can ask them to play it later. Fetch? Tug? Whichever gets the biggest response is your answer!

Problem-solving is a great way to provide agency. When solving a problem, you have to figure out how to behave in order to affect the environment to get what you want. That's the basis of agency, after all. Foraging toys are a great way to employ problem-solving and agency during meal times. We will talk about this more in a later chapter.

As humans, we often don't get something that we wanted simply because we don't ask for it. It always feels better knowing that we can ask, even if we don't get what we want. "Oh well, I tried." We can give our dogs the same agency by teaching them to ask for what they want. Many dogs try to do this in ways we don't appreciate: namely, demand barking or demand pawing. Instead, we can reward our dogs for asking for things they want in other ways. Allie's dog typically sits whenever he wants something, including his habit of requesting that squirrels come down from their trees, which you'll read about in Chapter 11. This is an easy behavior to teach; just ask your dog to sit before meeting their requests! They'll associate the two soon enough and realize that they can ask for other things using the same technique.

Your dog may also be asking for something in a more subtle fashion. Allie has a rule that Oso is allowed on the bed only when invited; he's not allowed when not asked. Oso will rest his head on the bed and look from the bed to her, and back to the bed whenever he wants to be invited up. Sometimes she acquiesces, sometimes she doesn't. Sometimes he doesn't ask at all and goes right to his bed. Pay attention to what your dog is asking of you, and establish a dialogue.

Exercising choice in training

Even dogs who love to be trained get bored of it or sometimes don't want to work. That's okay; so do we! Many people will ask their dogs if they want to work by using a "beginning of session" cue. If the dog responds enthusiastically, the session begins. If they don't, the handler will move on and try again later. Not only can you do this at the beginning of the session, but you can monitor your dog's desire to work throughout the session. Some dogs get bored easily and prefer to not repeat the same task over and over. Others love repetition. Tune in to how your dog is feeling about the session and the work they're doing. Let them dictate the direction and pace.

A great way to assess your dog's desire to work is to notice how quickly and eagerly your pup responds to the training exercise. Trainers accomplish this by monitoring the dog's response latency: how quickly a learner responds to a given cue. If your dog starts out responding to cues within 1 to 3 seconds and performs the behavior with gusto, but then starts performing the cue within 5 to 7 seconds, it might be time to change course. That might include changing your rate of reinforcement, the location, or the exercise you're working on, or it may mean taking a quick play break mid-session, or simply calling it a day before your dog decides they are completely done.

Not all training methods provide agency, so it's important to understand which ones do and how they do so. We will discuss methods such as shaping and free shaping in a later chapter.

Recap: ways to provide your dog with agency

Physical and personal spaces:

- Allow movement throughout multiple rooms

- Provide bedding in your dog's favorite places

- Allow access to their crate and safe spaces

- Allow them to move away

- Flight training

- Allow choice in meeting people

Husbandry, grooming, and medical activities:

- Let them choose the walking path

- The Bucket Game

- Toy preference test

- Allow them to choose the game and toy you play with today

- Foraging toys

- Teach them to ask for the things they want

Training:

- Monitor if they want to keep working

- Shaping and free shaping

- Immunization training

Not all choices are created equal

Providing choice is obviously important, but not all choices are created equal. Every dog owner who has seen their dog spit out a vegetable knows that they have preferences. As usual, though, scientists have put that hypothesis to the test. In one study, researchers measured the value and preference strength of mink for different resources by making them work for what they wanted (Mason et al., 2002). In order to reach the resources, the mink had to push a heavily weighted access door. Sure enough, there were some resources that the mink were willing to "pay" more for. Physiological measures of stress agreed with the behavioral measures seen; mink prefer some resources over others.

From this we know that the value of choices being offered is additionally important. Choice for the sake of choice may not solely be enough. Pay attention to the choices your dog cares about and the ones they don't. For instance, your dog may care particularly about having agency when it comes to meeting new people but care very little about agency on walks. Put more effort into providing agency in the parts of their life that are really important to them. On that note, make sure both choices are actually desirable. Giving your dog a choice between "scary thing A" and "scary thing B" isn't a choice—they'll simply learn that no choice they make is desirable, which can create a state of learned helplessness. Similarly, giving your dog a choice between "scary thing A" and "great thing B" isn't a choice either. No sentient being would choose a punishing operation over a reinforcing operation, so "do what I want or else" isn't actually giving them a choice. When it comes to their learning experiences, choices must be between something good and something *even better*. We need to set up win-win scenarios for our dogs!

Is it possible to provide too much agency?

Everyone is familiar with the expression "too much of a good thing." Agency is no exception. There are times that we cannot, and should not, provide our dogs with complete control over their environment. In these instances it usually comes down to safety. Imagine you're out hiking with your dog. They spot a rabbit and run off after it—right toward the edge of a cliff. Do you allow them the choice to continue chasing the rabbit? No. You do everything within your means to stop their chase in order to protect them. Imagine you have a fearful dog who bites strangers. Do you immediately allow them the choice to go up to every stranger and potentially bite them? No. You manage the environment so that they don't get close enough to bite anyone, thereby avoiding the potential for anyone to get hurt or the law to get involved. Maybe we can give our dogs that choice after extensive training and a risk assessment, but they're certainly not ready without that. There are times—for dogs as well as humans and all other species—that being given a choice just isn't an option.

Are there times other than safety when agency isn't recommended? Occasionally. Imagine you have a dog who counter surfs—a behavior you're trying to squelch. Do you leave a pot roast on the counter and leave them the choice to "do the right thing"? No. You manage the environment and don't give them the chance to lapse into old habits. For instance, Emily had a client with a large juvenile dog, Baloo, who had been described as having no self-control. In actuality, Emily observed that Baloo had not yet learned appropriate greeting skills. Even though he loved every person he met, people were afraid of him because he would jump on them and claw at their clothes and skin, and he was so mouthy that sometimes he would even break skin. His owners loved him, but they were worried that he would seriously injure someone.

Emily gave them a training plan to work on specific behaviors that would help Baloo to learn more appropriate greeting behaviors while having as much agency as possible, but in the meantime also recommended management strategies that prevented Baloo from making undesirable choices. For example, Baloo learned to wear a muzzle, and had to wear it every time he met a new person. He was also only allowed to meet people while on leash or behind a barrier.

By managing Baloo's choices so that he was more likely to make the "right" ones while teaching him new skills in ways that gave him plenty of agency, the family was thrilled when they reported that after only two months, Baloo was able to politely greet people off leash and without his muzzle by sitting in front of them and waiting for them to interact with him.

Know that every time we are managing behavior we are minimizing a dog's choices. Is that inherently bad? Not necessarily. Management is often about safety, preventing the dog from practicing undesirable behaviors (because practicing allows them to become really good at those undesirable behaviors), and is sometimes necessary to provide our dogs with the skills they need so we can provide more agency in the future. Can management be misused or abused? Yes. Micromanaging a dog's behavior by not giving them any or enough choices can be detrimental in all the ways we discussed in the learned helplessness section of this chapter. Well-intentioned management can sometimes be so excessive that the environment creates learned helplessness in the learner or otherwise deprives them of several other aspects of enrichment. Therefore, it's important to keep track of how much you're managing and how much agency your dog is given. You may be able to give them a choice between two acceptable options instead of multiple iffy options. Additionally, keep track of their behavior to make sure that they are alert, lively, and acting like themselves so you know that you're providing the right balance for behavioral health.

By now it should be clear that agency is a fundamental criterion for every aspect of enrichment. It is crucial to the mental, emotional, and behavioral health of learners of all species. For this reason, it will play a large role in every chapter of this book. So let's delve into it.

Chapter 4

PHYSICAL EXERCISE

Now we will move into the part of the book where we discuss the details of how to provide enrichment to dogs. And we start off with what is one of the easiest forms of enrichment for the average pet owner to include in their regular routine.

Physical exercise is widely understood to provide many benefits. We understand how important this topic is for ourselves, and that often makes it easier for us to extrapolate that to our pets as well. It may come as a surprise to hear that there are "right" and "wrong" ways to provide physical exercise, however, and plenty of creativity can go into this category! Additionally, physical exercise can be an important piece of the puzzle when dealing with common behavior issues. Let's start there.

Behavior and physical exercise
Typically we think of physical solutions for physical problems and mental solutions for mental (behavioral) problems. It's not quite so simple, however. The body and mind are inextricably connected; we cannot think of them as discrete, compartmentalized entities. They work together. The more research that's being done in this field, the more we see how interconnected mental and physical well-being are. Thus, it's not that challenging to understand that providing physical exercise to a dog can help with behavior problems.

In humans, exercise has been known for decades to reduce anxiety. However, the type, duration, and longevity of the exercise are important to anxiety reduction. Only aerobic exercise (cardio) leads to the reduction of anxiety, and for certain types of anxiety the exercise program needs to exceed 10 weeks in order to see that reduction. Additionally, the exercise needs to last at least 21 minutes for there to be an effect on all types of anxiety in humans (Petruzzello et al., 1991). Knowing the need for specific types, duration, and timelines for exercise programs is important when creating an enrichment plan in order to maximize our efforts.

In addition to the effects on behavior, exercise affects the brain itself. A study in humans in late adulthood shows that the hippocampus, the part of the brain responsible for memory, increases in size with exercise (Erickson et al., 2011). Exercise has also been linked to increased academic performance in students (Hillman et al., 2008).

Much of the influence of exercise on behavior is neurophysiological. Radosevich et al. (1989) found that exercise affected various hormones, including beta-endorphins and cortisol, and Meeusen and De Meirleir (1995) found that exercise influences neurotransmitter activity. These and other findings explain phenomena like "runner's highs," the elevated mood associated with exercise.

More salient to our discussion, Chaouloff (1997) found that exercise increases serotonin levels. This neurotransmitter has a whole host of functions in the body, including regulation of mood, appetite, and sleep; gastrointestinal motility; and memory and learning. Additionally, serotonin helps to control stress and impulsive behavior and has been found to combat depression.

These effects were greater with daily and long-term exercise, since brain chemistry changes over time and the levels of neurotransmitters stored in the brain improve with chronic exercise. Ultimately, these long-term changes lead to individuals who are more resilient to handling stress in humans (Salmon, 2001). The same phenomenon appears true in rats as well (Dey, 1994). Chaouloff (1997) found that "chronic and free-choice wheel running [helped protect] against [norepinephrine] depletion resulting from uncontrollable and inescapable foot shock." Essentially, Chaouloff found that types of exercise that provide agency help to prevent learned helplessness in rats.

What does this mean for our dogs? These studies on the effects of neurotransmitter production suggest that proper regular exercise can play a role in addressing behavior issues, such as any of the anxiety disorders, and challenges related to impulsivity like mouthing and reactivity. And when the dog is given agency to make choices in their daily physical exercise sessions, it also leads to individuals who are more resilient to stress—and as we've discussed and will continue to discuss, stress is a major contributing factor in many behavior issues. There's no doubt about it: exercise does the body and mind good.

Exercise options with dogs

The majority of pet owners choose to exercise their dogs through walking. For some dogs, especially overweight or geriatric pups, this can be a great form of exercise and can meet their daily needs. However, simply walking for 10 minutes a couple times a day is not enough for other dogs, especially young and/or active dogs and breeds. However, walking can provide a great form of mental exercise by allowing your dog to explore new places and smells along the way. That's often what makes dogs tired after a walk—the mental exercise! Walking is a great base for your dog's physical exercise plan, but know that something more will likely need to be added unless you're walking several miles per day (and even then, walking sometimes is not enough).

Hiking can be a great option for some dogs. These dogs should have a solid recall or be on a long leash if they cannot yet be trusted off leash encountering other people, dogs, and wildlife. This too allows for more mental exercise, as there is typically a problem-solving component associated with more difficult hikes than with regular walks: figuring out how to get over, under, and around obstacles as well as determining where to place feet. Processing all the unfamiliar scents, sights, and sounds is another way that hiking provides mental exercise. If you're an avid hiker, though, know that your new dog may not be able to keep up. You'll likely need to put them through a doggy hiking training plan.

Some people choose to run with their dogs. Some dogs love this activity! Others would prefer to take their time, explore, and sniff. Remember that even if in theory it's great exercise, your dog may prefer not to do something in practice. Respect their wishes and find another way that you two can play and exercise together. Keep in mind, also, that running is a great way to create an athlete. If you religiously run with your dog, that's obviously a desirable trait. If you're just starting out your running program you may want to wait until the program sticks before taking your four-legged buddy along. For seasoned runners, canicross is a cool option. This sport involves cross-country running with dogs.

Swimming is a great option for dogs who need low-impact exercise. In fact, many vets recommend swimming as a form of physical therapy. Swimming is another form of cardiovascular activity and builds muscle tone. Indoor doggy swimming pools are becoming more popular for those who don't have access to other water sources.

Another great resource for people with dogs who need more physical exercise is certified canine fitness trainers. These individuals have specialized knowledge in canine physiology and kinesiology, behavior, and nutrition and can help owners to create a specialized fitness plan.

Canine sports

Many humans prefer to enroll their dog in a sport for their physical exercise. They provide more mental exercise than a "mindless march" (more on this below) and are fun to boot! In similar fashion, many people turn to canine sports to provide exercise for their dogs. Once a niche world primarily filled with functional sports for working dogs, canine sports are growing in popularity and, as they do, more and more options become available to us.

Agility

Agility is a high-intensity sport that provides great physical activity by running the dog through a series of obstacles. People usually think of border collies and other herding breeds when agility comes to mind, but any breed can participate and have fun with it, provided the handler caters to the dog's physical capabilities, safety, and agency. Having your dog go over agility equipment can be a confidence booster even if you don't want to participate in an agility competition. Agility is also a big exercise in impulse control and can help dogs who are lacking in that area.

Parkour

Canine parkour uses elements of agility and elements of human parkour to create a new up-and-coming canine sport. Human parkour, originally derived from military obstacle course training, involves trying to get from one destination to another in the fastest way possible. It's typically seen in an urban setting as people climb over, under, and on top of fences, walls, and buildings. For dogs, it's less intense than that, primarily focusing on balancing and walking on various objects in the environment for core strength and hind-end awareness. While you can earn canine parkour titles, there are currently no competitions. This helps to promote safety.

Herding

Herding, while sometimes thought as archaic, is still alive and well! Many people will travel for several hours to give their dogs the chance to work some real livestock. There are competitions to show off the amazing training that goes into a herding dog.

Treibball

Treibball is a canine sport newer to the United States. This sport, often referred to as "urban herding," is fantastic for herding breeds who don't have access to their own flock of sheep. However, any breed can have fun participating! Treibball involves herding exercise balls into a goal. This sport has lower impact on the joints and teaches dogs helpful behaviors like watching their human, going to a mat, and problem-solving.

Weight pulling and joring

Weight pulling is an old exercise that is becoming popular again in sport form. This can be done in any context from pulling kids in a wagon to competing. Because weight pulling strengthens muscles and helps keep joints in place, this is a good option for dogs who physically cannot do higher-impact sports like agility. In theory, weight pulling seems easy: strap a dog to an object and have them pull. In reality, several factors should be taken into account to make sure that it's done safely, including the type of harness (there are harnesses specifically designed for weight-pulling) and the load size.

Similar to weight pulling, joring involves dogs pulling people on some sort of device: skis, mountain boards, skateboards, bikes. Specific harnesses are made for this sport as well, depending on the type of device you're using. Joring is higher-impact than weight pulling as it typically involves the dog running while pulling.

Dock diving

Dock diving, having dogs retrieve items thrown into water, is another old exercise that is becoming popular in sport form. Dogs are judged on height or distance of the jump. This is a favorite among retrievers but, again, any dog can participate.

Flyball

For dogs who like to retrieve on land, flyball is an option. This team sport involves the dog running over jumps to a special ball-throwing contraption—a flyball box—triggering the mechanism, retrieving the ball, and running back over the jumps. When one dog crosses the finish line, the next dog on their team does the same routine.

Additional sports exist, and more are cropping up all the time! If there's something that interests you, do your research on the sport and the proper ways to train and stay safe. Many amateur sport clubs exist, and you may be surprised by how many are within a couple hours of you. If a sport interests you but you're not the competitive type, know that you can participate without competing. Many owners take that path.

Common exercise mistakes

As with anything, some ways to implement this form of enrichment are better than others. After discussing the importance of exercise in relation to behavior issues, many people, half-jokingly, suggest treadmills. While this does indeed increase the amount of exercise an animal gets, research shows that not all exercise is created equal. "Forced treadmill exercise appears to deplete [norepinephrine] stores in the brain (as observed in learned helplessness) and is physiologically stressful for animals" (Lindsay, 2000). Norepinephrine is a neurotransmitter involved in the "fight or flight" mechanisms of the body and acts on many bodily systems. While consistent exercise generally increases the amount of norepinephrine stored in the brain over the long term, it appears that forced treadmill exercise defeats its own purpose by depleting it. That said, some dogs quite enjoy this form of exercise if they are not being forced into participating against their will but are instead trained to willingly run on the treadmill. Just know that you'll have to provide supplemental mental exercise if you choose treadmill exercising, since it does nothing to provide mental stimulation after initially training the dog how to do it.

Likewise, most of us have been taught since birth that we absolutely must take our dogs on daily walks, and when we do so they must be obedient and walk at a heel to respect our leadership. While there's certainly nothing wrong with teaching a dog a good heel—and in some situations, like service dog training or competition obedience, that skill is necessary—the problem with applying that mentality to regular walks is that most dogs can't get the cardiovascular exercise they need when walking at a human pace, and a strict heel provides very little mental exercise. For these reasons, the authors teach their clients how to teach their dogs to walk on a loose leash, but then to allow their dogs to stop and sniff whatever interests them. This allows the dogs to use their noses to process information in their environment, affording them much more mental exercise. They are therefore more tired at the end of their walk than if we insisted on a "mindless march."

Instead of these mindless march exercises, we should focus on those exercises that are fun for the dog (and human!) and employ mental enrichment as well. Playing games is a great way to maximize exercise. We'll talk more about that in a bit.

Another common exercise mistake is thinking that "more is more." Often the authors meet clients who religiously exercise their dogs, walking or running with them multiple miles per day. Their dedication is commendable. However, eventually what we hear is, "I can't keep up with them anymore. They used to be exhausted after 3 miles and now I'm the only tired one! We come back and they still want to play." Exercise creates athletes. "Exercise training increases the capacity for exercise, thereby permitting more vigorous and/or more prolonged individual exercise sessions..." (Thompson et al., 2001). Marathon runners are happy to train with their canine companions; however, the majority of us simply can't keep up. Don't create an athlete you can't handle.

Along similar lines we often see puppy and adolescent dog owners over-exercising their pups. While the above argument applies in these cases, there is a special point we must address for exercise in juveniles: their bodies are not fully developed yet. There is an increasing amount of literature advising puppy and juvenile dog owners to steer clear of vigorous high-impact exercise, especially on hard surfaces like cement, until their growth plates have fully fused. An increase in musculoskeletal deformities such as hip dysplasia is thought to be caused by inappropriately excessive and/or high-impact exercise during body development (Krontveit, 2012).

While not necessarily a common problem, it is important to note that exercise does increase those fight-or-flight hormones. While the benefits seem to outweigh the drawbacks, there are some animals who seem to make poor decisions when their bodies are pumped full of adrenaline, whether it's fun excitement (**eustress**) or fear, anger, or frustration (**distress**). It's not uncommon for dogs to be playing and for a fight to seemingly randomly break out. The short-term increase in certain neurotransmitters during play and exercise are similar to those found in stressful times. As such, it appears that it's much easier for animals to "flip the switch" during play. This can be mediated through training and behavior modification.

Exercising without a lot of space

Fenced-in yards and big outdoor spaces are wonderful but just aren't the reality for everyone. Many urban pet owners feel frustrated thinking that they need a lot of space to exercise their dog and not having it. Those with leash-reactive dogs can feel even more frustrated when walking (the most common form of canine exercise for urbanites) is a chore. Luckily there are other options for these pets and their parents!

Games are fantastic exercise, and you often don't need much space to make them work. Tug can be enough exercise for some dogs and can be done in quite compact spaces! There is a myth that playing tug will make dogs aggressive. A large basis for this myth is the thinking that tug can lead to dominance-related behaviors and therefore aggression. We'll talk more about social structure and the overwhelming research suggesting that dominance theory is different than we originally thought it to be in Chapter 8. For now know that tug does not impact a dog's social status. Tug can actually be helpful for teaching "wait," "take it," and "drop it."

Fetch takes a bit more space but does not require a massive expanse as many people assume. Fetch can be done down narrow hallways, and for an extra fitness challenge can be done up and down the stairs. Just make sure there's a no-skid rug at the bottom so your pooch doesn't slip. If your dog has trouble dropping their toy, simply use two toys. When they come back with one, act interested in the second toy. Most will drop what they have because yours looks more fun! When that happens throw the second; this method will help you get a solid "drop it." Adding rules, like dropping the toy close enough and sitting and waiting for it to be picked up, can help teach the dog valuable skills that make play more enjoyable for the humans.

Flirt poles are like giant cat lure toys for dogs. Essentially, flirt poles are long PVC pipes with rope on one end and a toy attached to that rope. They are fun for dog and human alike! These require more space but can work nicely in a small yard, park, or a basement. However, they can be modified by making the pole shorter or by eliminating the pole altogether and using just a rope with an attached toy. Like tug and fetch, flirt pole games with rules like "wait" and "drop it" can teach important life skills. Flirt poles can be beneficial for dogs who feel the need to chase things by giving them an appropriate outlet to do so.

Teaching valuable life skills with a flirt pole:

- Ask your dog to sit or lie down before playing.

- Ask your dog to "wait" before they can chase the toy. In the beginning they may only be able to wait for half a second! Give them some cue like "take it" or "get it" to signal that they may chase it.

- Allow them to chase the toy for a few seconds to a few minutes.

- Once they have the toy, play a short game of tug, if desired.

- Ask them to "drop it." In the beginning they'll need to be lured with a treat or another toy if they don't yet know the cue. When they drop the toy, toss a few treats away for them to find. Pick up the toy and hold it against you while they're searching.

- Repeat! Increase their wait time as they're able.

- Additional option: teach them that when you flick the toy to the other side of your body, they must wait. During play flick the toy across the circle. If they go for the toy flick it again until they pause for a moment. Tell them to "take it" or "get it" and allow them to resume chasing.

Safety with flirt pole play:

- Spin the toy in only one direction per round (clockwise or counterclockwise). A round starts when you tell your dog to "get it" and stops when you ask them to "drop it." Rapid changes in direction can cause ACL tears or other soft tissue injuries. Switch direction the next round.

- Depending on what substrate(s) you have available to play on, this can be a high-impact game; exercise extra caution with juveniles and dogs with joint disease. Ask your vet before incorporating this game into these dogs' repertoires.

- Only allow your dog to jump for the toy if they have healthy, fully developed joints. If you're not sure then keep the toy on the ground only.

- If your pole has a bungee rope be very careful about the dog tugging on it—if one of you lets go, you either have a projectile toy or projectile pole! The authors put the top of the pole on the ground and step on the base of the rope to limit risk.

- Be mindful of dogs who show signs of resource guarding around toys.

Some dogs love to jump and need to get in a few jumps before they can settle down. Instead of quashing their delight, let's work with them! We can teach these dogs to jump up to a target: a hand or target stick. This can help with those high-energy dogs who are having trouble learning to plant their feet when people come home. It can also be great exercise. Many dogs are exhausted after a few minutes of jumping up to a target! This, too, is a high-impact activity and should only be performed with dogs whose growth plates have fused and who don't have joint disease.

A warning about laser pointers

Many well-intentioned people think that playing with laser pointers is a good form of exercise. While they do physically exercise a dog, they are considered unsafe from a mental health point of view. Respected veterinary behaviorist Dr. Nicholas Dodman, director of the Animal Behavior Clinic at Cummings School of Veterinary Medicine at Tufts University, notes, "They can get so wound up ... that once they start chasing the light they can't stop. It becomes a behavior problem. I've seen light chasing as a pathology where they will just constantly chase around a light or shadow and pounce upon it. They just spend their whole lives wishing and waiting" (Wolchover, 2012). The issue with laser pointers/light-chasing in particular is that the animal never catches anything; it's incredibly frustrating. That frustration is what develops into maladaptive, compulsive, and sometimes self-injurious behaviors. Redirecting that frustration onto a human in the form of a bite is also common. The authors have worked with several dogs who perform light-chasing behaviors and can attest to how detrimental this practice can be, to the point where some dogs displaying these behaviors in a shelter setting are euthanized because of it. While it is certainly true that not every dog who plays with a laser pointer ends up with a compulsive disorder or some other form of maladaptive behavior, the risks are common enough and detrimental enough that it doesn't make sense to take this risk when there are so many other exercise options available.

Exercise for dogs with limited abilities

Many people treat dogs with limited physical abilities with kid gloves. You don't need to! Your dog knows what they're naturally capable of more than you do, so let them do it unless you notice that it causes soreness afterward or they're on restricted activity per your vet. This is especially true with dogs who don't have all four limbs. The authors have known dogs with two legs who have more spunk and agility than dogs with four! However, while most mentally healthy dogs will naturally self-regulate within their limitations, human encouragement can cause them to stretch those limitations. Keep in mind that humans will often ask for our dogs to do more than they are naturally capable of, and our dogs will happily oblige for food, play, or other motivators. Repetitive stress injuries can happen this way.

If your dog has physical limitations, be sure to speak to your vet or veterinary physical therapist about what is safe and unsafe for them to do. There are some conditions, like partial paralysis, that actually are better served by more exercise than the average person considers. Exercise helps to build those muscles so the dog is more able to get around on their own.

Often we need to redefine what we think of as "exercise." Walking 10 feet may be plenty of exercise for a dog with partial paralysis, or a 5-minute walk may be quite enough for a senior dog with arthritis. Another option for these dogs is physical therapy, like walking over poles or hydrotherapy. The important thing is to be creative and work with your vet or veterinary physical therapist to devise an exercise plan.

Chapter 5

SAFETY AND SECURITY

Two often-overlooked components of successful enrichment programs are the related concepts of safety and security. Like physical exercise, providing safety and security for your dog may seem like a simple thing but in reality can be deceptively complex. Safety and security are topics that we typically do not think about in our daily lives unless they have been compromised. Few people stand in their back yards on level ground and actively think to themselves, "I feel very safe here." On the flip side, scale a cliff face with your hand- and foot-holds crumbling beneath you and safety is the only thing you'll be thinking of! While our dogs aren't mountain climbing, the same feelings of safety and security are true for them.

For the purposes of this book, we'll define **safety** as "the condition of being protected from harm or unlikely to receive harm," and **security** as "the feeling of being protected from harm." It might seem like nitpicking to describe and treat those terms separately. Shouldn't we feel secure if we are safe? In a nutshell, it doesn't necessarily work that way. Time and again the authors hear, "I don't know why they're so anxious or afraid. I've never done anything to them!" Just because you know that your animal is safe does not mean that they feel secure. This can be due to previous history but can also be rooted in mental or physical ailments that we may or may not be aware of. The flip side can also be true: a dog feels secure but is not safe. For instance, the dog who bites at moving tires or runs into traffic during play.

Providing safety and security in the environment

We instinctively set up safe environments when there's a human baby in the house. We cover outlets, put safety locks on the cabinets, block stair access, and make sure there's no access to chemicals. Often it's easier for us to do this for babies because we are the same species; we know what is dangerous to humans. However, many people are not aware of what is safe and unsafe for their pets. Most know that chocolate is off limits to dogs, but what about grapes/raisins, onions, and sago palm? Those too are toxic. Do you know what foods in your kitchen and plants in your house and yard are poisonous for your pup? Chances are you have at least one that your pet shouldn't get into.

It is our duty to know what is dangerous for our pets and to create a safe environment for them. Additionally, that safety should be taken as seriously for a pet as it should for a human baby. Often we assume that putting something slightly out of our dog's reach is sufficient. We would never make that assumption with a baby! We install safeguard after safeguard to ensure a baby is safe; why not do the same for our pets?

While pet safety has become a more familiar topic of discussion over the past few years, pet security is a relatively new concept for most people. Indeed, it can be hard for an owner to realize that their pet does not feel secure in their home, either because they feel bad about it or because it's such a foreign concept. This can also be a hard pill to swallow, as security in an environment is often related to the relationship one has with others in that environment. If you've ever lived with a roommate you don't entirely trust, you understand the feeling. We'll talk more in depth about creating a solid relationship with your pet in Chapter 9; for now we'll simply discuss its importance in relation to security.

One of the reasons a dog's sense of security isn't at the forefront of most people's minds is that scientists have only recently begun to study this topic. The authors could only find studies dating back to the late 1980s at the earliest, with most studies published in the 21st century (which is not a long time in the research world!) This is a growing and fascinating field. Currently, most research in this topic is related to obsessive-compulsive disorder (OCD) in humans. However, there do seem to be components that, intuitively, we would assume transfer to our animal friends in other situations too. This isn't a case of anthropomorphization; dogs and humans share so many similarities in their physiology and neurobiology that it is reasonable in this instance to apply what we've learned about human neurocognition to dogs.

One of the most interesting pieces of research the authors found in relation to this topic is something coined by researchers Woody and Szechtman in their 2011 research paper as the "security motivation system." This research is currently being looked at in relation to humans with OCD. These researchers postulate that there is a mechanism in the brain that is "designed to detect subtle indicators of potential threat, to probe the environment for further information about these possible dangers, and to motivate engagement in precautionary behaviors, which also serves to terminate security motivation." Essentially, they suggest that this mechanism is responsible for responding to potential threats instead of imminent danger. When it detects a potential threat it "activates a persistent, potent motivational state of wariness or anxiety" (Woody and Szechtman, 2013). It's then said that engaging in the precautionary behavior shuts off the system.

To better understand what Woody and Szechtman are hypothesizing, let's look at an everyday human example. You're home alone watching TV in the family room with your pet. You hear a strange noise coming from the kitchen. You detect the noise but don't feel like getting off the couch. As time goes on, worry starts setting in. What if someone is in the house? After several minutes the anxiety gets the better of you and you go to investigate. Once you've determined that it was simply something that fell over on the counter, you go back to the couch. A potential threat—the strange noise—activates a persistent state of wariness or anxiety that motivates you to engage in a precautionary behavior—investigating the kitchen. Once done, the system shuts off.

We see a similar scenario occur with many animals. A dog notices a flag on a fence while on a walk. They initially duck and back away. They continue to look at it for a moment, then tentatively approach. They investigate the item, shake off, and continue merrily on their walk. Could Woody and Szechtman's theory help to explain this behavior?

There seems to be agreement among researchers that "relatively weak [potential threats] readily activate vigilance and wariness" (Brown et al., 1999) and that this activation deteriorates slowly (Wingfield et al., 1998). Even the absence of subsequent potential threats does not deactivate the wariness (Curio, 1993). Think about the implications this could have when considering dogs with compulsive disorders or who often are exposed to potential threats. These dogs must live in a constant state of vigilance and wariness if they're repeatedly exposed to triggers, and that wariness dies off slowly.

Research on the security motivation system is in its infancy, and thus our understanding of it will likely change in the coming years as new research emerges, refining and shaping this theory. However, intuition and observation suggest that these scientists are onto something. For now, though, we'll stick to statements that are more tried and true: "abstract potential threat elicits anxiety and vigilance" (Eilam et al., 2011). Security falls under the umbrella of "abstract potential threats," and anxiety can lead to a host of behavioral problems like guarding, reactivity, and aggression. Clearly it's an important topic, even if it's often not given its due.

Safety and security for a newly adopted dog
One of the only times security is discussed with pet owners is when adopting a new dog. Some trainers, shelters, and rescue groups will recommend setting up a "secure space" for the new dog. This is a great idea and can be a great component to aid in security. This may be a crate, bed, or even closet—anywhere the dog enjoys spending time. You can take this secure space one step further and incorporate calming enrichment activities like those found in Chapter 10.

Many pet owners choose not to follow this advice because of how elementary it seems. They don't understand how impactful this simple action can be. Allie had a client who perfectly illustrated the power of a secure space. This client brought her senior dog in because the dog was growling at her two small boys when she had had enough of them. Amazingly, this dog had developed a response to the boys on her own before choosing to growl. The family had set up their laundry room as a "secure space" for the dog, with a baby gate across the threshold, and had taught the boys to not touch the gate. Often, when the dog was growing weary of the toddlers she would walk over to the closed gate and wait for her mom to open it. If the client didn't notice, the dog would start barking to be let into her room. This dog took it one step further: if, after being let into the room, no one closed the gate behind her, she would bark until someone closed it for her. This dog was making great decisions to remove herself from uncomfortable situations and put herself in her secure space. And because she already had this inclination it was easy for Allie and the client to extrapolate that concept to other situations. Everyone is now living safely and securely together.

This is an extreme example of the power of a secure space, but many people see this in lesser forms as well. Allie saw it with her dog, Oso, when she first brought him home. Unbeknownst to her, Oso was afraid of thunderstorms and fireworks. She adopted him in mid-June during monsoon season in Utah, which yields thunderstorms on an almost daily basis with the 4th of July right around the corner. It was a rough few months. Instead of pacing, panting, and acting frantically, Oso's response was to find what he deemed a "secure space" and ride out the storm. He was very specific in the spaces he chose: they had to be near one of his humans and had to be a confined space. Allie was able to tell when a thunderstorm was about to roll in because Oso would remove himself from his bed and go to his secure space.

The importance of routines

Space itself can make one feel secure, but other forms of security include knowing what to expect. This is why routines are often recommended for dogs who have anxiety. These dogs seem to respond particularly well to structured routines, either throughout the day or surrounding anxiety-inducing events. Essentially we can teach the "investigative behavior" that shuts down the security motivational system and ask the dog to perform it. We can do this by using a consistent word or phrase—such as "Let's check it out!"—and walk with them around the anxiety-producing area, allowing them to thoroughly explore and sniff the space. We don't force them to go where they don't want to go or try to make them interact with anything in the environment, but when they do investigate something, we praise them in a calm, happy tone of voice. If they feel too anxious and want to leave the location, it's important to allow them to do so. Over time, because the dogs know they can leave when they need to and the act of investigating does shut down the security motivational system, dogs become more willing to explore and recover more quickly from stress in those situations. The effects of routine on enrichment provision were studied in 2009 in relation to military working dogs (Lefebvre et al., 2009). Dogs in this study were either provided with routine enrichment or sporadic enrichment; both groups received the same quantity. The dogs receiving routine enrichment produced significantly less cortisol than the dogs receiving sporadic enrichment. Even desirable things are better on a schedule!

Knowing what to expect can also come in the form of household rules. Like children, dogs do well with knowing what they are and are not allowed to do. The authors witness this often in humans in classes where adults are given free rein to select and complete a project. You can see the anxiety set in on their faces as they're confronted with too many options and no clear direction on what they should do. For dogs, these rules can be as simple as sitting for the food bowl and needing to be invited onto the furniture. We don't need to create strict rules that border on being cumbersome for the humans in order to achieve the desired effect. Nor do we need to create rules based on "dominance theory," which, as we will discuss in Chapter 8, is an inaccurate model of canine social behaviors. And contrary to popular belief, aversive corrections are also unnecessary to teach dogs these boundaries. Often pet owners believe that there are strict rules their dog needs to adhere to based on the concept of "good" and "bad" behaviors in the eyes of our society. But this is a moralistic anthropomorphization which has nothing to do with animal behavior. Good and bad behaviors don't exist; there are merely behaviors that are desirable and undesirable to the specific household developing the rules. You have agency to create whatever rules you like! These rules simply serve to make everyone's lives easier and more manageable by giving your dog more predictability in their environment and asking them to exercise some self-control.

Incorporating safety and security in enrichment practices

It's clearly important to include safety and security in our pet's environment, but we also must ensure that we're keeping them in mind throughout every aspect of our dog's enrichment. One aspect of this is the products you might buy to use as part of an enrichment strategy. Alarmingly, many practices and products geared toward animals are not made with safety and/or security in mind. In addition, the safe use of training tools is a key component of an effective enrichment program. Training is critical to enrichment, but not all tools are created equal.

Safe use of enrichment tools

One of the biggest enrichment safety issues arises from not using products properly or not using the right product for your animal. It may be tempting to buy the smaller Kong, antler, or marrow bone for your dog to chew on because it's cheaper, but the vet bills are far more expensive for dislodging these items from jaws and throats when they are inappropriately small for your dog. You should be 100% certain that your dog's jaw can't fit through a bone or that they can't swallow an enrichment item you're providing. If you're not certain, then opt for a bigger size. The authors also see people modifying products in a way that makes them dangerous, like taking out food puzzle components to make them "easier." Products are made the way they are for a reason; leave them and their integrity alone unless otherwise instructed by a professional.

Unfortunately, there are just simply products that are marketed for animals that are unsafe for them. Rawhides are hugely popular but also largely indigestible and are responsible for many intestinal blockages. Cooked bones are often presented as safe alternatives, but cooking bones can cause them to splinter when chewed. Treats and food are recalled on an alarming basis. Being a pet owner and advocate requires keeping up to date on what is and is not safe for our pets. While we'd hope that every company would do their due diligence and test their products for safety before putting them out on the market, it just simply does not always happen.

There are even risks associated with "safer" alternatives that are used and provided properly. That's unfortunately the nature of the beast. For instance, bully sticks are wonderful chewing items. They are fully digestible, unlike rawhides, and are definitely one of the safer options. However, they can pose a choking risk if your dog decides to swallow a big chunk. While it's less common than people think, it is still a reality. With everything, we must weigh the risk versus the reward. If you have watched your dog eat a bully stick and know that they tend to carefully gnaw on it all the way to the end, the risk of them swallowing a large chunk is much lower for your situation. Conversely, if your dog does tend to chew it down to the last couple of inches and then try to swallow the rest, you may want to consider offering a different kind of chew treat. Just make sure you've watched them eat it before and know that they don't swallow large chunks. For example, Oso loves destroying items, so Allie gives him paper products that he's allowed to shred. She's watched him enough with these to know he doesn't eat the paper, and she is comfortable leaving him alone with such items. Knowing your dog is crucial to ensuring their safety.

It's important to note that we're not trying to incite mass panic by talking about safety with our pets. It's absolutely possible to take safety too far and to suck the fun out of your pet's life by trying to create a pristinely risk-free environment and life. Everything we do has some modicum of danger: driving, swimming, eating. Heck, even sitting at a computer is dangerous for your eyes, wrists, and back. With everything we must weigh the risk versus the reward of the activity and that includes with our pets. Don't keep your dog from enjoying life because of the "what-ifs" involved. Simply understand the risks to determine if it's a reasonable option for your situation and if the reward of doing the activity is worth it. Your dog probably thinks it is!

Security in enrichment is related to ensuring your dog is comfortable. A good example to demonstrate the difference between safety and security is nail trimming. We know that the dog is safe for the most part (we should make sure that the groomer or tech is trying to avoid quicking them), but that does not mean dogs feel secure during this routine practice. Providing security often requires thinking outside of the box. If your dog is uncomfortable with nail trimmers, have you tried a dremel? Have you tried modifying their behavior at home to feel more comfortable with either the clippers or a dremel? Have you tried making a scratching board and letting them wear down their own nails? Have you tried going for long walks on the sidewalk to wear down their nails? So often we feel stuck; we feel like we *have* to do something because our animals need it but don't enjoy it. The scenario can absolutely, unfortunately, exist in shelters and vet clinics—although there are many low-stress handling techniques such as the ones in Dr. Sophia Yin's book, *Low Stress Handling, Restraint and Behavior Modification of Dogs & Cats*, which can help to drastically reduce the need for forceful and aversive tactics in these settings as well. When it comes to pet ownership, we have so many more options if we take the time to sit down and learn about how else we can accomplish a task.

Both safety and security in enrichment require understanding your dog's limits. While we've been talking about security more in relation to fear and emotions, it is also tied into physical ability. The majority of us would not feel secure competing in the American Ninja Warrior competition; we doubt our bodies could handle it! Because dogs cannot verbally tell us their limits, it's up to us to listen to their behavior and to give them the benefit of the doubt. Your senior dog has started refusing to go up the stairs? Instead of assuming they've become stubborn in their old age, why not take them to the vet to see what shape their hips are in? Perhaps it hurts for them to use the stairs (safety) or they took a tumble last week while using them and are now fearful (security). Any time a dog has a history of doing something well and then suddenly stops doing it, we have a tendency to blame the dog by calling them "stubborn" or "manipulative," but more often than not there is a medical reason behind any sudden change in behavior.

Safety and security in training and behavior modification

We discussed briefly in Chapter 3 that some training products made for pets are, in fact, harmful from a behavioral perspective. Even more unfortunately from the authors' perspective, many of these products sold in the name of "training" are physically dangerous as well. For instance, choke or chain collars have been shown to cause trachea damage, thyroid damage, vagus nerve damage, brain damage, and to increase intraocular pressure, among other deleterious effects, even when they are being used "correctly" (Mugford 1981; Grohmann et al., 2013). The authors have also seen other aversive training collars such as pinch/prong and electronic/shock collars cause damage (often when used incorrectly), but even a regular flat collar can cause trachea damage. Do not assume that, because a tool seems more humane, it cannot be unsafe. Even the most seemingly benign harnesses can cause chafing and irritation in the armpits and joint damage to the shoulders.

There are starting to be more conversations worldwide about the ethicality and safety of certain training tools and practices. For instance, most people understand the dangers associated with "helicoptering" a dog (lifting the dog off the ground and swinging them around) as there have been many subsequent cases of brain damage, neurological damage, thyroid damage, and/or death associated with the practice. We do not feel like we need to discuss that topic in great detail; we only want to encourage you to use common sense and empathy. If it seems like it could be harmful, don't do it. If you wouldn't let someone do the same thing to you, don't do it to a dog. Instead, we'd like to devote the rest of this chapter to security in training.

Learning is taking place all the time, not just during a training session. Thus, when we're talking about security in training, know that we're really referring to security in learning as a whole, not just in a training session. Many of the more egregious infractions occur outside of training sessions, especially when a dog encounters a fear-inducing trigger in the everyday world. In our culture we're told to simply "get over it." Face your fears! Do things that frighten you! We're all about tackling our fears head on. That's all fine and good when you are making that decision *for yourself*. However, it is not okay to take that stance when you are making that decision *for someone else*. You know what's right for you, not another. You know what you can handle. You do not know what someone else can handle. We discussed in Chapter 3 that this technique is called flooding. Instead of flooding, we should be giving our animals agency to conquer their fears on their own timeline and allow them the opportunity to learn through gradual exposure. Counterconditioning mixed with **systematic desensitization**—the process of introducing a fear-inducing stimulus slowly, increasing intensity only as the animal can tolerate it without displaying stress or fear—is a much more security-friendly approach that a qualified behavior professional can help you achieve.

We already discussed the necessity of predictability in the environment for security. This too applies to learning and training. Some people choose to use a mixture of training methods. An example of this is teaching loose-leash walking with both treats and a corrective collar: rewarding when the dog stays in position but also using the collar when the dog pulls forward. More information is always better, right? We should reward the good behavior but punish the bad behavior, right? Isn't that more balanced? Not necessarily. Confusion is a common occurrence when we choose to mix training ideologies, such as clicker training with a prong collar, especially when we use different methods to try to work on the same thing. As behavior professionals, the authors hear almost daily, "I've tried everything to fix this problem!" How confusing that must be for the dog! Sometimes they get treated, sometimes they get shocked, sometimes ignored, sometimes redirected. The poor dog has no idea what modality is coming next, and some of them are scary. This can add to the anxiety that often is at the root of many behavior problems. Pick a training modality and stick with it. Don't try to do too many things at once.

A secure learning environment involves the dog feeling safe with the training modality and feeling safe to try new things and make mistakes. As humans we so often focus on the "wrong" things our dogs do, even when they're first learning. We're quick to tell them that they've tried something that isn't what we were looking for. What can happen in those cases, though, is that they give up trying. Allowing dogs to make mistakes without the fear of being punished encourages them to try new behaviors, which ultimately works in our favor.

Many people balk at hearing that we should allow our dogs to make mistakes. It's scary to give up that control! We've been conditioned, incorrectly, into thinking that punishing mistakes leads to faster training. On the contrary, mistakes help dogs learn, and making mistakes without harsh consequences helps keep them feeling safe in the process. However, there are times where the mistake a dog might make would be unsafe to either the dog or another being. We're not saying to allow your dog to make egregious mistakes. Beyond preventing danger, we should set up the environment to enable our dogs to choose the "right" path. Make it so easy for your dog to do what you're asking that they won't even consider another option. Good environmental management typically mitigates the risks associated with making mistakes.

Finally, a secure learning environment takes frustration into account. A key to helping your animal choose the preferred behavior involves rewarding approximations toward that behavior. Don't ask for collegiate-level behaviors when your dog is still in kindergarten. Understand what your animal is capable of mentally and behaviorally, and expect only behaviors they're capable of performing.

Chapter 6

INSTINCTUAL BEHAVIORS

Remember that earlier in the book we noted that allowing a dog to engage in instinctual behaviors is an important part of the enrichment process. Unfortunately, the notion of "instinct" is a tricky one. The role genetics plays in behavior is highly complex, and as such is often misunderstood and misused. Furthermore, individual dogs may display a wide range of what are believed to be instinctual behaviors based on the environment they have lived in and what they have learned. Discussing the sophisticated interplay between genetics, instinct, and behavior lies beyond the scope of this book, but in order to explain how enrichment factors into a dog's instinctual behaviors, we do need to spend a little time discussing what instincts are and are not in dog behavior.

Oftentimes, when people encounter a behavior they can neither explain nor change, they tend to dismiss it as "genetic." We, as a species, have a bad habit of talking about certain sets of behaviors as "drives," and then talking about drives as if they are permanent, immutable behaviors, or as if the only way to "reduce a drive" is to crush it with dominance and punishment and keep those beastly tendencies—our dog's "inner alpha wolf"—under control forever. However, it may surprise people to learn that there aren't actually any genes for specific behaviors. That's right: there are no "prey drive" genes or "aggression" genes or "tracking" genes. There is a combination of genetic traits that sets the stage for a behavior or set of behaviors—called **modal action patterns**—to be more or less likely to occur. Explains Stephen Lindsay in the *Handbook of Applied Dog Behavior and Training, Volume 1:*

> *Although behavior itself is not directly encoded into an animal's ge-*
> *nome, various genetic instructions are orchestrated by the genome that*
> *provide the biological substrate for the expression of a species-typical*
> *behavior.*

He goes on to explain that patterns of behavior will vary greatly among individuals, and an individual's likelihood to perform any given instinctual behavior also varies greatly. Some individuals within a species will need almost no stimulation to perform an instinctual behavior, whereas others might need an extreme amount of stimulation to perform the same behavior.

So, for example, all dogs bark. They don't need to learn how to bark; it is a species-typical behavior that all dogs know how to do from birth. However, what a bark sounds like differs among dogs, and when, why, how often, and how readily a dog may bark also differ among dogs. The same is true for digging, chewing, trailing scents, and the list goes on. Like all living beings, dogs have inherited the sensory and mechanical traits that enable them to perform behaviors that ensure their survival.

In other words, modal action patterns are unlearned, innate, species-typical behaviors that serve a functional purpose. But! That doesn't mean that learning can't occur surrounding these behaviors! In his series of studies on instinctual behaviors, William Thorpe found that even though instincts start off as a spontaneous response, individuals can learn to perform instinctual behaviors intentionally (1956, 1966). This is great news, because it means that we can influence when, how often, and why an animal may perform an instinctual behavior. Instead of trying to punish or suppress an instinctual behavior for the rest of the animal's life—which is both exhausting and unpleasant, since it creates a relationship dynamic founded on conflict and opposing wills—we can instead provide an acceptable outlet for those instinctual behaviors and teach our dogs when it is and is not appropriate to perform them.

Meeting your dog's sensory needs

As we have already discussed many times throughout this book, enrichment means meeting all of your dog's needs. This includes sensory needs, which are plentiful in dogs, especially given their incredible sense of smell. "Environmental enrichment" is often what we think of when we refer to enrichment catering to sensory stimulation. Environmental enrichment "can be defined as improvement to the biological functioning of captive animals resulting from modifications to their environment" (Bender et al., 2013). Essentially, if we add the right things to our animals' environments, the environment itself will enrich them. This passivity in enrichment is a godsend for those of us with busy lives! But what are "the right things"? The authors believe this involves something for every sense.

Smell

Scent plays a huge role in our dogs' lives. Olfaction is a dog's primary sense, and thus a large portion of their brain is devoted to this sense. Dogs have more than a hundred times more of the nerves located between the nose and the brain than humans, and the olfactory epithelium devoted to trapping and analyzing odors is 30 times larger than a human's (Bradshaw, 2012). As important as smell is to dogs, it's often underutilized in enrichment programs, since most programs primarily focus on play and exercise. This is a huge disservice to both the dogs and the humans involved: to the dogs, because scent is such a huge part of their lives; to the humans, because we limit our own efficacy when we omit this crucial component, and therefore have to work harder to provide enough mental engagement for the dogs we work with.

The great thing about enriching our dog's sense of smell is that it can be done passively. Throw a few drops of essential oils in a spray bottle full of water and you have a source of enrichment. Some pet owners, boarding facilities, vet clinics and shelters have a "scent of the day": Monday vanilla, Tuesday lavender, Wednesday peppermint, and so on. While this won't provide hours of entertainment to your wards, we have noticed several instances in which dogs take a moment to sniff the introduced scent. At a bare minimum this can provide some variety for dogs who enjoy it. We have also personally seen some dogs respond physiologically, especially with Blackwing Farms Calm Balm: taking a deep breath, dilated pupils constricting, and a decrease in activity and barking. Before making up your own essential oil bottles, please do your research on essential oil toxicity in animals and remember that their noses are far better than ours; a very little goes a very long way for them.

If your dog is one of many who prefer animal odors to plant odors, one option is to find synthetic animal scents and put a drop or two on a toy for them to explore. Some companies will also sell real animal urine diluted down to the point that humans can't detect it but dogs can—a popular product for many dogs! Either way, you can also use an animal-scented toy to play tug or flirt pole, or even bury it somewhere and let them dig it up to combine multiple forms of enrichment in one. At shelters the authors often take bedding from one species and put it with another instead of finding synthetic scents (as long as it's not a predator scent into a prey species' cage). Many dogs spend several minutes investigating this new scent. You can get as elaborate as you want with this!

While working at a sanctuary the authors received moose poop from a remote employee living in Colorado. Allie put some in an enclosed PVC pipe with holes and gave it to a young dog, Stymie, who promptly proceeded to bury it. He had a blast!

With such a large focus on "the perfect heel" in the dog training community, we are missing out on the opportunity to provide our dogs with one of the best scent enrichments we can offer: sniffing on walks! As noted in Chapter 4, the authors' approach to leash walking is that as long as the dog is not pulling they can go wherever they want and do whatever they want (within reason). Walks are less physically taxing for athletic dogs than we care to admit, so let's focus on the mental aspects. Mental exercise is more exhausting than the same duration of physical exercise, often considerably so, and processing information via scent is one of the most exhausting forms of mental exercise for dogs. So by simply letting them stop to smell the smells on a walk we are getting more bang for our buck than if we rigidly require a mindless march at our heel.

Scent work games are becoming more popular as the sport K9 Nose Work is gaining traction. Classes focusing on the competitive route of Nose Work are cropping up everywhere, and dog owners are falling in love with this sport even if they have no intention of competing. One of the great things about this sport is how cheap it is: all you need are some treats and cardboard boxes! Many games have branched off from the technical sport: hiding treats around the house like a treasure hunt, hiding treats under a blanket or in a snuffle mat where the dog has to sniff them out, and playing a shell game with a treat under cups. A quick Google search will come up with as many variations as there are people to think of them.

Scent work offers a number of benefits including confidence-building, relationship-building with you and your dog, and giving your dog a job. All of these can indirectly improve a variety of behavior problems. The authors often recommend and use scent work for shy, insecure, and fearful dogs as a confidence booster. Allie worked with a shelter dog, Jodee, and her caregiver on formal nose work. Jodee was a Nervous Nellie, especially going to new places. They first started in an area where Jodee was comfortable so she could learn the game. Then they tried taking it to a new location. The first time, Jodee walked tentatively into the new building, clearly uncomfortable and nervous. She saw the boxes but it took her a minute to start searching. Her caregiver took her back outside while Allie hid more treats for the next round. This time Jodee walked in a bit more confidently and started searching immediately. The next time

Jodee strutted in, went to work, then proceed to explore the rest of the area once the game was over. Her caregiver was amazed! A process that would have normally taken several visits over multiple days was accomplished in a matter of 15 minutes.

Scent work can also do wonders for dogs with compulsions (functional repetitive behaviors) and stereotypies (the functionless repetitive behaviors described in Chapter 1) as well. Emily worked with a shelter dog, Kyla, who constantly licked the walls, chased lights, and herded rocks. If she was awake and not eating or being taken on a walk, she was performing one of those three behaviors. Obviously these are not behaviors that would endear her to potential adopters. They are also a sign of extreme stress and poor behavioral health. Kyla was already on an anxiolytic medication and had a training plan in place, but her progress was slow and her behaviors hadn't abated significantly. In an attempt to improve her quality of life they started doing nose work three times per week. In her first session, Kyla could only handle one round before she started chasing lights. But in her second session she was able to do two rounds, and in her third session she was able to complete three. By the end of the second week, Kyla was an eager and enthusiastic participant in nose work— and better yet, all of her compulsive and stereotypic behaviors had significantly decreased to the point that she was able to rest, play with her runmates, and engage with her caregivers and potential adopters. Kyla was adopted shortly thereafter and continues to thrive in her home.

The authors also like to use scent work to help dogs who are struggling to learn important life skills such as polite greeting manners. Emily worked with an 18-month-old, 80-pound American bulldog mix named Ziggy, who had not had a great start in life and had always been characterized as extremely hyper, distracted, and easily overstimulated. His previous owners had tried every training methodology imaginable, but he only seemed to get worse. When he arrived at the sanctuary, he was so over-the-top excitable that the caregivers struggled to interact with him in any way without getting clobbered. Even more troubling was that he would make rapid progress in each daily training session, but the caregivers reported that by the next day he would have completely forgotten everything he learned the day before, so every day they had to start from scratch. He had a veterinary appointment scheduled to rule out physical or mental health issues, but in the meantime Emily suggested that the caregivers do nose work with him. What they discovered was that, as long as Ziggy got one 15-minute nose work session a day, he could relax, focus, and remember. He was able to progress through training plans and develop better skills.

Scent work can even be used to help dogs meet new people. Allie worked with a sanctuary dog, Dusty, who was very uncomfortable meeting new people and had a bite history. He had historically only been able to make friends with a couple of people: his main, full-time caregivers. He was having a lot of trouble trusting his part-time caregivers. He would react at the fence at them and made it clear they should keep their distance. Allie started doing a modified form of nose work where his caregiver would block him on one side of the gate while Allie hid treats, then she would leave the enclosure while he searched (so Allie was never in the enclosure with him) just as a form of mental enrichment. After a couple times he would no longer react at Allie on the other side of the fence; he'd look, wag his tail a bit, and go back to searching. His caregiver was amazed! She explained that it was taking months for him to trust new people, but here he was just a couple weeks in and already friendly with Allie. Could it work with other people? Sure enough, Allie and Dusty's caregiver started having other people play this game with him and he quickly became their friends too.

While the authors are clearly advocates for scent work and have several success stories that include its use, it's important to note that scent work is not a panacea, and not every dog will improve as dramatically as the above examples. However, we have had enough experiences like this that we feel it's a significant pattern and worth including as a component of a behavior modification plan.

Sound

When providing sound enrichment, remember that your dog's hearing is different than your own. Dogs are able to hear sounds at higher frequencies (while we can hear sounds at lower frequencies and are better at locating sound). We can hear sounds at about the same volume, so no need to have music either blaring or barely audible for your dog; if it's a comfortable volume for us, it's generally a comfortable volume for them. But again, as always: observe your dog's response!

Sound enrichment can be as easy as turning on the CD player or radio before you leave for work in the morning. There are some forms of music that are more calming than others (Wells et al., 2002; Kogan et al., 2012) (see Chapter 10), and one study indicated that many dogs found the sound of a male voice speaking in even tones more soothing than any type of music (Brayley, 2016). The key here, as always, is to observe your dog's response to any type of soothing sounds you play for them and observe which one(s) relax them best. An important note is not to play music/radio all the time. Your dog needs some silence too! Don't underestimate the importance of silence, especially in a shelter or boarding environment.

For puppies, sound enrichment can be fundamental to preventing sound sensitivities later in life. Exposing puppies in a fun, happy way to city sounds, animal sounds, human sounds, household sounds, and more will be helpful later in life. One of the easiest ways to do this is YouTube videos. You can find pretty much any sound effect you want there, and while there is a frequency difference between a recording and real life, it will still help lay some ground work. For those dogs who already have sound sensitivity you can use these videos to countercondition while playing at a volume that allows your dog to stay under threshold.

Sight
In some regards, dogs have a worse sense of vision than we do. For example, they have trouble seeing stationary objects at a distance, but are better at seeing moving objects at a distance. That's why you can see a rabbit that is sitting still from afar before your dog does, and they only see it once it starts running. It's also speculated that this is why dogs are sensitive to changes in human silhouettes brought on by wearing different clothing and accessories. They truly don't recognize you.

Sight enrichment can vary greatly. It can include presenting dogs with people wearing different clothing and everyday household objects. We can use different items like bubbles and pinwheels. Some dogs even enjoy watching TV now that there are HD TVs (they are not really able to see the images on tube TVs). We can get creative with this category. One of the easiest ways to provide sight enrichment is to take our dogs on a walk or car ride. New sights galore!

Touch
Tactile enrichment can involve either the dog touching something or being touched. We often forget about the first. Dogs have an impressive number of touch receptors in their paw pads and can feel what they're touching quite well. It's important to expose them as puppies to a variety of surfaces: carpet, tile, linoleum, concrete, gravel, grass, sand. If they don't experience different surfaces as puppies they often have a hard time walking on various surfaces as adults. Additionally, each dog has a different texture preference for mouth touch. This is why some dogs love chewing on wood, others on plastic, and others on fabric. You'll also find that dogs have different preferences regarding comfort. Some love mounds of blankets and orthopedic beds while others would prefer a cold tile floor—especially in the summer!

We can provide tactile enrichment in the form of regular petting, TTouch, massage, or Jin Shin Jyutsu, which is a type of acupressure massage that allows the dog to have more control over their experience. Many dogs love these! However, dogs do not come out of the womb innately loving human touch. Human touch is a learned reward, not an instinctual one. For most pet dogs, the love of being petted may seem innate because human touch (the learned reward) has been paired with tactile stimulation (the innate reward) since birth. However, anyone who has worked with a feral dog can testify that human touch is by no means universally desirable to all dogs. Some dogs do not enjoy being touched at all, or in certain ways, or certain places, and may even bite someone who tries to pet them in a way they don't enjoy. The first step is changing our mindset that all dogs love to be touched. Once we realize that this is a teachable behavior, like learning to enjoy nail trims, many people have an easier time understanding the behavior modification necessary to change the way dogs feel about being touched.

Similarly, dogs do not come out of the womb loving to be hugged. In the primate world chest-to-chest contact is a sign of affection. In the canine world, chest-to-chest contact means something along the lines of "I'm going to kill you now." How sad for us primates living with canines! Some dogs learn to like hugging, and some will learn to even hug you back (Allie's dog Oso gives the best hugs, except for Emily's dog Brie, who actually gives the best-best hugs). However, the key word in the previous sentence is *learn*. This is a learned behavior, not an innate one.

Taste

Dogs have fewer taste buds than humans, so their palate is less refined than ours. That doesn't mean that they don't enjoy different tastes though. Try different meats, cheeses, veggies, and fruits with your dog. You might be surprised by how many different things your dog enjoys. Minimize processed foods and stay away from toxic ones (a list of these can be found in the Resources). This enrichment can be as easy as just giving your dog a few different foods to try or mixing up what kinds of treats you use in training, but you can get more elaborate too. You can freeze broth ice cubes or buckets with different foods or treats (and toys) for fun summer treats. You can also freeze canned dog food, pureed pumpkin or sweet potato, unsweetened yogurt, peanut butter, or any combination thereof into muffin tins or baking sheets for your dog to lick. And, of course, there's the ever-useful Kong, which can be stuffed with anything your dog likes. The Kong website has some great recipes if your pup is getting bored. In a pinch you can put some peanut butter on a tile floor or cookie sheet for them to lick. Being a scavenger species, most dogs aren't picky—and that's a good thing!

Meeting your dog's need to engage in instinctual behaviors

Not long ago people were more okay with dogs being dogs. Dogs roamed the neighborhood, dug up the flowerbed, and if they bit you, you probably did something to deserve it. In recent years that has changed: now we expect perfectly programmed dogs who act more like four-legged adult humans than dogs. Conventional wisdom discourages many of our dogs' natural, instinctual behaviors such as barking, chewing, and digging. There are likely a variety of reasons behind this, but we most often hear that it is because it's inconvenient for the human, or the owner is afraid of "rewarding and encouraging bad behavior."

While humans typically don't appreciate many of our dogs' instinctual behaviors, that doesn't mean that we can just suppress or discourage them. That would be akin to us never being allowed to hug or be hugged, which is an instinctual comforting behavior in primates (but only primates). We need to embrace *all* of our dogs' needs and find a way to work with, rather than against, our dogs. Both our lives and our dogs' lives will be better for it.

In reality, no behavior is good or bad. Behavior merely serves a function. Humans are the ones who attribute morality to it, not our dogs. And sadly, many behaviors that humans deem "bad" are merely normal dog behaviors.

Regardless of how we feel about a behavior, a dog's need to perform certain behaviors isn't going to go away. This disparity doesn't have to become a behavioral showdown though. If we provide appropriate outlets for these instinctual behaviors, we can meet the need while reducing the undesirable means by which dogs attempt to fill those needs. It's a win-win.

Dogs are a crepuscular species

Crepuscular means being most active at dawn and dusk, and sleeping throughout the day and night. This is why your dog gets crazy zoomies shortly after you come home from work or in the morning when you're trying to get ready. Knowing that your dog is crepuscular is half the battle. Many clients, especially those with puppies or adolescents, come to the authors with problem behaviors that only appear around dinnertime. "My dog is mouthing, running around like crazy, and being destructive! Help!" After learning that dogs are most active at dawn and dusk, and therefore get bursts of energy during those times, most people have the same reaction: a look of relief and a big "ohhhhhhh." Understanding that those behaviors are natural for the species helps most clients to feel less offended by them, and we haven't even done any behavior modification with the dog yet. Truly, half the battle with many instinctual behaviors is human understanding.

For those dogs who are overly rambunctious at dawn and dusk, ramp up your mental and physical enrichment right before these times when possible. If your dog usually gets hyped at 7 a.m. and starts getting mouthy, start providing physical and mental exercise at 6:30 a.m. Even if you're not able to time it perfectly, providing extra mental and physical exercise at any point throughout the day will help. The unwanted behavior is much less likely to happen in the vast majority of cases. Many clients who see the authors for these behaviors never even need a training plan; increasing the right forms of enrichment solves the problem almost immediately.

The great thing about dogs being crepuscular is that it fits best into the typical human's life. Humans are diurnal (awake throughout the day), but most of us work or go to school throughout the day. It's perfect. Our dogs are active when we're home in the morning and evenings and asleep while we're gone and while we're asleep. That midday nap is so important for most dogs, to the point where some behavioral problems can develop when they don't get enough sleep (like human toddlers): more on that in Chapter 10.

Digging

Many dogs need to dig. While that's unfortunate for your yard and floors, for those dogs it's a necessity. Instead of fighting your dog on this, work with them by giving them a specific place where they're allowed to dig: a digging pit. This can be a specific place in your yard, or you can fill a plastic kiddie pool with sand or dirt as the designated space. Bury treats, bones, and toys (bonus points for toys that have other animal scents on them) in the digging pit so the dog is rewarded even more so for digging there. Whenever you see them digging elsewhere, calmly lead them to the digging pit and encourage them to dig there. Then, put a piece of poop in the unwanted hole or block it off with garden borders to discourage digging where you don't want it. While this strategy will work for some dogs, know that it won't work for all; for many, inappropriate digging is more about management and consistency than anything.

Barking

Barking is a way for dogs to communicate with others. They bark to warn others; tell off intruders; out of fear, anxiety, frustration, or pent up energy; to tell you they want something; to greet friends; and because they're bored. Some dogs also seem to bark because they like to bark (though this is less common than people think). The way to decrease your dog's barking depends on why they're barking in the first place. If they're demand barking at you while you cook dinner, keeping them out of the kitchen will likely do the trick. However, if they're alarm barking at a stranger coming in the room, we'll have to focus on the underlying fear. Whatever the reason, figure out why your dog is barking, and work with the underlying reason. Just as with the majority of behavior problems, excessive barking is a symptom of another problem.

That said, expecting a dog to *never* bark and making it *always* off limits is neither fair nor realistic. That would be like expecting a human to *never* talk. Barking is instinctual. It is a huge part of how dogs communicate. For this reason, it's important to give them times and places when they are allowed to bark. This might look like letting them yell to their friends during a playdate, teaching them a "speak" and "quiet" cue, allowing them to bark only one time to alert you to visitors approaching your house, or turning it into a game. Emily's dog Brie, who was a feral dog before she was adopted, used her voice excessively when they first met. She would bark at anything new. She barked at things that scared her. She barked when people came to the house. She barked when she wanted to go outside. She barked when she wanted Emily to give her something. Emily had to work on reducing all the excessive barking. However, Emily rewarded the cute "woo woo" barks that Brie would do when she wanted attention and turned it into a game. Brie and Emily "woo woo" at each other a few times a day, especially during times when Brie wants attention while Emily is working and the "woo woo" game is the most interaction Emily can afford to give her. Brie is also, along with Emily's other dog, Copper, allowed to alert bark when a stranger approaches the house, but they have learned to stop barking when Emily cues them to stop. Think of it like we're acknowledging that they did their job of protecting the house and then allowing them to go off duty. After their job is completed and their work has been acknowledged, they don't need to keep doing it.

Chewing, shredding, and destroying

Some dogs chew vigorously and others do so only occasionally. However, chewing (and the similar behaviors of shredding and destroying) is a natural and instinctual behavior for dogs as a species. Be sure to provide them with appropriate things to chew on if you want to spare your furniture! This can include raw bones (do not give cooked bones; they splinter), antlers, bully sticks, and Nylabones. Different dogs have different preferences for what they chew, so experiment! Dogs can have texture preferences for what they chew as well. If your dog has a knack for chewing up your utility bills, then offer newspapers, egg cartons, or take-out beverage trays to chew instead. If they have a thing for remote controls, try a Nylabone. If they go for shoes, give them scraps of leather (bonus points for adding a scent enrichment to the leather, since part of the appeal of shoes is that they're smelly). Find an appropriate object that has a similar texture to the inappropriate objects your dog has chewed up, to meet their needs and preferences. By encouraging your dog to chew on and destroy those appropriate items, you're making them less likely to chew on things you don't want them to have.

Chapter 7

FORAGING

Foraging is the act of searching for and working to obtain food. Dogs' undomesticated ancestors foraged for their food, consuming just about anything that was edible. Feral dogs today are also expert foragers. Most pet dogs will forage if given the opportunity; almost every dog owner has experienced dogs who counter-surf, pre-wash dirty plates in an open dishwasher, and vacuum up the floor of any food items that fall. It turns out that the act of working for and seeking out food is not only satisfying to dogs, it is a fundamental need. As such, it should be used to help enrich their lives and to teach them useful behaviors.

The concept of contrafreeloading

It is a universal law of nature that all living beings have an inborn need to work for their food. When most people think of primal needs, they usually think of things like food, water, shelter, safety, and sleep but, interestingly enough, gainful employment is also on that list. This principle was first discovered by a scientist named Glen Jensen, who published a study showing that rats would choose to press a bar for food rather than eat the same food available in a dish nearby (1963). Since his groundbreaking study was published, several other studies went on to test that hypothesis with a variety of species and examine a variety of aspects of the phenomenon (Neuringer, 1969; Osborne, 1977; Inglis et al., 1997; among others), and each study found the same thing: the desire to work for food is innate, even though the skill to do so is learned. When an animal is taught how to work for their food, they will choose to work for a meal even when the exact same meal is available for free. Thus, the term

contrafreeloading was born: "contra" means opposed to or against and "freeloading" means getting things without giving anything in return.

Since the discovery of the contrafreeloading phenomenon, many scientists have offered a variety of possible explanations as to why it exists, any or many of which could be true. However, one thing we do know is that the act of seeking is its own reward. It's why people will go on treasure hunts, even if there's nothing particularly exciting at the end (to the point where the entire hobby of geocaching was created). It's why we love a good mystery novel, or a bend in the road. The excitement of discovery is as fun as the thing discovered.

Contrafreeloading is one of many reasons it's actually a good thing to use food in training. We *want* animals to work for their food. They *need* to work for their food. Using food in training is like giving them a paycheck for a job well done. It isn't bribery; it's payment for services rendered, just like you receive at your job. It doesn't create a dependence on food. What actually creates a dependency on food is—wait for it—being alive. Yes, that's right: being alive is what creates a dependency on food. Using food in training is simply meeting some primal needs: you learn a skill, you perform the job, you bring home the bacon. That's it.

That said, there isn't a whole lot of seeking that occurs in most training sessions, and there are many, many other ways we can encourage dogs to forage for their food. Having a variety of options available is important for many reasons, one of which is purely practical: we need to be able to provide for our dogs' needs without turning it into a full-time job that runs our whole life.

The Goldilocks Zone: not too hard, but not too easy
Think of foraging like grade school. We know that sounds weird, but bear with us. Different dogs have different levels of skill, experience, and motivation, which means they have different capabilities. They might need kindergarten-level foraging opportunities or they might be in the foraging equivalent of 12th grade, or anywhere in between. It's important to figure out exactly where your dog's skill level is and provide them with the right kind of foraging opportunities.

If foraging is too easy, they will get bored and lose interest pretty quickly. In fact, this is such a consistent behavioral pattern that researchers were able to observe this while studying contrafreeloading. If the food always occurred in the same place and was obtained in the same way every time without variation, the animals being studied would stop foraging and start eating the freely available food instead (Wallace et al., 1973). It may seem counterintuitive, but the thing that can make a behavior persistent is that *it sometimes isn't rewarded*. This is called intermittent reinforcement—or the "slot machine effect"—and it is why gambling is such an addictive behavior: you never know when you're going to hit the jackpot, so you just keep on playing! For more in-depth information about this phenomenon you can check out the Resources section at the back of the book. For now the important thing to consider when it comes to foraging is that, by definition, it involves a mixture of success and failure for the participant. That seeking component is a powerful motivator, as is the opportunity to overcome a challenge. This act of facing a challenge and using both mind and body to triumph is called "constructive discontent." It's that feeling you get when you solve a particularly difficult math problem or beat a level in a video game. It's another key component of behavioral health and an overall feeling of satisfaction and confidence. So, foraging needs to be challenging and varied enough to maintain a dog's interest.

Conversely, however, it needs to not be so challenging that they give up, or don't even try. Imagine putting a typical first-grade student in a high school calculus class. Do you think they would pass the test? Do you think they would even try? Of course not. Why is that? Is it because they don't like calculus, or perhaps because it's so far beyond their current skill level that they wouldn't even know where to begin? That's what it's like for dogs when we present them with foraging opportunities that are beyond their current abilities. They don't lack interest; they lack skill.

So, when determining what type of foraging our dogs need, we need to find the Goldilocks Zone: not so easy that it's boring, but not so hard that they get discouraged and give up or, worse, don't even try. We need to put them in the right "grade," and then determine when they're ready to graduate to the next one.

Troubleshooting motivation

But what about dogs who legitimately lack interest? Those dogs certainly exist. As we discussed in Chapter 3, when a learner has been chronically deprived of choice and lives in a state of learned helplessness, it doesn't just change their behavior. It also affects their cognitive abilities, their problem-solving abilities, their resilience against frustration and discouragement, and their interest in the world around them. What appears to be a well-behaved dog may actually be a dog who has no idea how to use their big brains and super-powered senses, because someone else has made every decision about every little detail of their life for as long as they can remember. Or what about dogs who are so filled with anxiety and fear that every decision they make is in service of those emotional states? Or what about dogs who compulsively perform one specific set of behaviors over and over with little to no interest in anything else? The authors have met and worked with numerous dogs who fit into one or more of those categories, and the common thread is that their owners and caregivers described them as being "uninterested" in foraging.

In a sense, they are right: seeking behaviors require a certain amount of motivation, and if the motivation isn't there, no food on earth, no matter how appetizing, will be compelling enough to get a dog to put forth an effort to forage.

But as mentioned earlier, while the need to work for food is innate to all sentient beings, the ability to do so via foraging is a learned skill set, which means it must be taught. And the learner needs to be behaviorally healthy enough not only to learn, but also to want to learn. If there is a severe mental disorder at play, it might require medication—preferably under the guidance and direction of a veterinary behaviorist. Regardless, we have a tool available to us to create motivation and confidence in a dog who currently lacks either one, and that tool is called "errorless learning."

Errorless learning is when we create an environment where the learner can't make mistakes. It simply isn't possible. No matter what they do, it's the right choice. Every choice is rewarded. And since making the right choice is easy and rewarding, they want to make another choice. And then another. And then another. Over time, they develop enough interest, motivation, and confidence that you can present them with small challenges that are relatively easy for them to overcome. When they succeed at that, you can gradually increase the difficulty of their challenges just like any typical learner of their species. By that point you're no longer relying on errorless learning; they can and will thrive on constructive discontent like the mentally healthy learners they have become.

Troubleshooting preference
But wait! There's more! Just as grade school has different subjects, and a student may have more interest and aptitude in one subject than another, foraging can be done using a variety of materials catering to different play styles and skill sets, and a dog may have more interest or aptitude in one than another. A child may have a second-grade grasp of math but be reading at a ninth-grade level. Similarly, a dog may be quite skilled at food puzzles that require holding and tearing but may not be as successful at ones that require pushing. So in addition to difficulty level, we also

have to look at the dog's behavioral tendencies and textural preferences, and create foraging opportunities accordingly. Some dogs really like to use their mouths; others like to use their paws. Some dogs like to beat the heck out of something until it gives up the goods like Conan the Barbarian; others like to meticulously solve puzzles with an almost surgical precision like Bobby Fischer. Some dogs really love to shred and tear up paper or fabric; others like to gnaw on hard objects or push things with their noses. By starting with foraging options that play to their strengths, we can generate more interest and then perhaps later generalize their skills to other styles and textures.

By now you may have noticed a recurring theme in this book: the key is to observe the behaviors of the individual dog and modify your approach to meet their needs, rather than just buying a foraging toy based on what appeals to you and expecting them to figure it out.

Troubleshooting food motivation

All of that is fine and good, but what about dogs who aren't food-motivated? The authors hear so many variations on that theme they could write an entire book just about the concept of food motivation alone. The complaints vary: "I tried using food in training, but my dog isn't food-motivated." "I tried switching my dog to a different diet, but they won't eat that." "I tried food puzzles, but my dog just doesn't like food very much." "You're lucky your dog likes food; otherwise that would never work."

Here's the thing: as we mentioned earlier, every living being on earth is dependent on food for survival. There are no exceptions. There are no breatharians among us. Okay, there are *some* exceptions, because some extremophile bacteria can live off of crazy stuff like sulfur vents in the deep ocean and some microscopic critters like tardigrades can live for a decade without food or water. But all the creatures that we typically see and interact with need food to live. So when we encounter an animal who isn't showing an interest in their food, we need to ask ourselves *why* instead of just slapping a "not food-motivated" label on them and then moving on. You may be surprised at how many possible reasons there are! We discuss some of the most common ones later in this chapter, but for now just know that if a dog doesn't appear to be food-motivated, we need to spend some time sleuthing the underlying cause of this apparent disinterest in food. Again, it's important to observe each individual dog's behaviors to be able to meet their needs. We don't do anyone any favors when we slap a label on them and call it a day.

One note of caution before we move on: one of the researchers we cited earlier, Allen Neuringer, discovered that animals' desire to work for food wasn't contingent on deprivation. It's important to note that not only is contrafreeloading not contingent on deprivation, deprivation actually makes animals *less* willing to work for their food (Osborne, 1977). Regardless of species, when we are in a state of survival, we will do whatever it takes to obtain food in the easiest way possible. Likewise, if an individual already experiences constructive discontent in other aspects of their life, and is already working hard in other ways, needing to then work for their food can create choice fatigue, and their motivation to forage will severely drop off. Imagine working a 10-hour day at your job and *then* having to come home, hunt and forage for your food before you even get to do your dinner prep. Doesn't sound appealing, does it? There's a reason most of us don't forage for our dinners; our lives are already full of constructive discontent! We already aren't freeloading! This is why the science of contrafreeloading doesn't support a pure NILIF (Nothing in Life Is Free) protocol: when life is already challenging for our dogs, sometimes a free meal is exactly what they need. In other words, weight management isn't necessary to teach dogs how to forage, and if your dog already has a job and is too tired to forage, don't make them forage.

A word on safety

Before we look at tools you can use to meet your dog's need to forage, we should address the safety of those tools. Pick a product, any product, that is made for dogs, and you will find someone on the internet devolving into Chicken Little histrionics about how unsafe that product is. They will have personal anecdotes. Other people will join in with their own personal anecdotes. It will look like that product is more dangerous than Ebola-soaked asbestos covered in fire ants. To be fair, most people don't make those claims unless they legitimately did have a traumatic experience with that product, and their grief over the death or injury of their beloved pet is real. But this is the reality: there is no such thing as a 100% guarantee of safety of anything, anywhere, ever, on this planet. Everything has some potential for accident or injury. Everything. But when determining the safety of a product, statistics matter. People die every year from falling out of their own beds, but no one is screaming for increased bed safety measures or banishing beds. Why? Because those deaths are rare and, in general, a bed is not a dangerous object.

Some products are legitimately quite dangerous, even when being used according to manufacturer recommendations, and really have no business being sold in pet stores. Other products have only proven dangerous in bizarre, freak accidents. And everything in between. The recommendations of toys and products in this book come with this disclaimer: closely monitor your dog the first few times you let them play with a product, and if they show signs of interacting with it in a potentially unsafe way, discontinue its use. There are so many options out there you don't need to use one that might hurt your dog. Also use common sense: if your dog has a health issue that might make a generally safe product riskier for him, don't use it.

When recommending products, we are doing so under the assumption that your dog does not have pica (a compulsive disorder wherein they eat inedible objects) or any medical issues that would render the products riskier than usual.

Foraging toys

Foraging toys can be separated into two basic categories: the ones you make and the ones you buy. We generally recommend to our clients that they start with making toys until they figure out their dog's skill level, play style, and texture preferences so they aren't wasting money on a bunch of toys that may not be appropriate for their dog. That said, there's no reason you can't continue to use do it yourself (DIY) toys forever! They aren't just for starting out!

DIY toys

Easiest food puzzle ever. One of the easiest ways to get a dog to forage for their food is to literally throw it outside. Put their meal in a cup or a bowl and scatter it out as if you were spreading seeds or chicken feed.

If a dog doesn't know how to use their smelling super-power yet, you may have to help them. For the first few times, go out to the yard with them and search with them. If they find a kibble, give them lots of praise. If you find a kibble, point it out to them and praise them when they find it. Before long, most dogs start to use their noses. It's fairly obvious when they do: nose goes to ground and they start making deep snuffling noises as they breathe through their nose more than their mouth. When that happens, you shouldn't need to help them anymore; you have successfully taught your dog to use their nose to seek out food. This activity is surprisingly exhausting for dogs. Most of our clients who do this with their dogs report that it can easily take their dog an hour to finish breakfast, and when they're done they take a long nap. Using their nose and their brain to seek out and find their breakfast is hard work!

Don't have a yard, or your yard is made of concrete? Or perhaps your yard is buried in 12 feet of snow? No problem. You can create the same effect indoors with snuffle mats. Snuffle mats are easy to make (the internet is full of instructional videos) or buy, and once they're made they last forever.

When your dog is first learning how to use a snuffle mat, it's best to use just one. But as they learn how to use it, you can create the same effect as tossing food in the grass by putting several snuffle mats around the house, but only putting food in some of the mats. They'll have to use their nose to figure out which mats have food and which ones don't. But remember: switch it up! Maintain the challenge by changing how many mats have food and where the mats are located in the house.

Destructibles. If your dog is a rough-'em-up kind of pup, they may do best with foraging toys that they can utterly obliterate in the process of eating their food. There's nothing quite as fun as watching a dog tear a toy to shreds and then gloat over the carnage.

These are easily modified to make them easier or harder. For example:

Paper towel roll

- Fill with food. Pinch ends. Boom. Doggy kindergarten.

- Fill with food. Pinch and fold ends.

- Fill with food. Twist and tie off ends with twine. Punch a few holes in the tube.

- Fill with food. Twist and tie. Punch two holes.

- Fill with food. Twist and tie. No holes.

- Fill with food and stuff with newspaper. Twist and tie. No holes.

- Fill with food and newspaper. Twist and tie. No holes. Hidden around the house.

Cereal box

- Cut off one surface of the box. For a very easy toy, choose the front or back of the box. For a harder one, opt for one side or the other. For the biggest challenge, cut the top or bottom. Put food in cardboard awkwardly-shaped "bowl."

- Cut half of one surface. "Bowl" is half covered!

- Food in intact cardboard box with lid open.

- Food in intact cardboard box. Close lid.

- Cardboard box in cardboard box. Close lids. Food in both boxes.

- Increasing layers of Russian nesting doll of cardboard boxes. Food in each layer.

- Russian nesting doll layers of cardboard boxes. Food only in some layers.

Plastic bottles

- Cleaned and dried. Lid off. Punch or burn several holes in it.

- Cleaned and dried. Lid off. Fewer holes.

- Cleaned and dried. Lid off. Two holes.

- Cleaned and dried. Lid off. No holes.

- Cleaned and dried. Lid on. Must be destroyed to yield its riches.

- Cleaned and dried. Attached to wooden dowel set on frame. Must be flipped or destroyed. This will tell you a lot about your dog's play style! Are they a Bobby Fischer or a Conan the Barbarian?

The common theme among these toys is that they are single-use, will be destroyed in the process, and then their remains can be swept up and chucked in the recycling bin. But because they are literally made of trash and are therefore a low-investment enterprise, you can really play around with difficulty level until you find out what grade your dog is in. When you figure out where the Goldilocks Zone is, it will help to inform your decision about other foraging options you provide for them.

Non-destructibles. More permanent homemade options can also be created with varying difficulty levels. For example:

Cupcake pan

- Food in cupcake pan. Essentially 12 miniature bowls instead of one big one.

- Kibble mixed with smeary food (e.g., canned food, canned pumpkin, yogurt, etc.).

- Kibble and wet food frozen.

- Kibble and wet food frozen. Balls or other objects placed in each hole.

- Kibble and wet food. Balls or other objects frozen into place.

- Kibble and wet food. Frozen balls. Wrapped in paper or placed in box.

Cookie sheets

- Kibble on cookie sheet. A really shallow, flat bowl!

- Kibble mixed with smeary food on sheet.

- Kibble and wet food frozen.

- Kibble and wet food frozen on a few sheets, then stacked.

- Kibble and wet food stacks frozen together.

- Kibble and wet food frozen stacks wrapped in paper or placed in box.

Empty peanut butter jar

- PB jar with no lid.

- PB jar with lid and several punched or burned holes.

- PB jar with lid and a few holes.

- PB jar with lid and only two holes (never do just one hole, to prevent creating a suction that could pull your dog's tongue into the hole and cause permanent damage!).

- PB jar with two holes and filled with toilet paper rolls.

- PB jar with two holes and filled with toilet paper rolls and wadded up paper towels.

PVC pipe food bomb

- PVC with a bunch of holes drilled in it and only one end capped.

- PVC with a bunch of holes drilled in it and both ends capped.

- PVC with two holes and both ends capped.

- PVC with two holes, both ends capped, and stuffed with other inedible objects that are too large to fit through the holes.

- PVC stuffed with objects, two large holes, ends capped, suspended by a rope a foot or so above the floor.

- Suspended just above the height of the dog's head.

Easter egg hunt

- Plastic Easter eggs stuffed with food. You may first have to start with them open.

- Then only partially closed.

- Then fully closed.

- Then fully closed and scattered around one room.

- Then scattered around multiple rooms.

- Then hidden around multiple rooms.

These are just a few popular examples of DIY food puzzles, but the sky's the limit when it comes to creative foraging opportunities at home. Emily has one client who was given a bunch of miniature gift boxes she had no real need for, so she turned them into Russian nesting doll food puzzles for her dogs and hid them in different places around the house every day. Another client's dog enjoyed licking plastic, so she started using her Tupperware containers as frozen food puzzles and hiding them around the house. As long as your individual dog is not demonstrating any potentially dangerous behaviors, such as ingesting inedible objects or breaking things into sharp points and cutting themselves, feel free to flex your creativity muscles and play around with foraging ideas!

Purchased toys

There are plenty of advantages to buying toys instead of making them: they're made of sturdier materials and come in a wide variety of play styles, sizes, colors, and difficulty levels. Once you have an idea of your dog's grade level and play style, you can decide which types of food puzzles to try and go from there. Each style contains many toys with varying shapes, textures, and difficulty levels, so bear that in mind when purchasing one for your dog.

- For dogs who like to use their feet to hit and slap at objects: weebles are a type of foraging toy with a weighted or heavier based and a lighter top. They wobble but they don't fall down, so your dog has to bat them around to get the kibble to fall out a hole higher up.

- For dogs who like to push things with their noses: treat balls aren't always actually ball-shaped, but come in a variety of different materials, shapes, and difficulty levels. The general premise is that your dog rolls them across the floor so food falls out of one or more holes.

- For dogs who like to solve puzzles: stationary toys are meant to be stationary while your dog lifts up, slides, spins, and pulls out different components to get to the food. The easiest versions of these are slow-feed bowls, which simply require the dog to eat around obstacles in the bowl, and Kongs, which require the dog to lick food out of the hole at the end.

Pretty much every purchasable food puzzle falls into one of these three categories, but you'd be surprised at how many variations there are on these themes. The internet is full of options; all you've got to do is search!

Troubleshooting foraging activities

As already mentioned, a common thing we hear from clients or caregivers is, "I tried that; it didn't work." As this mindset relates to foraging, it usually looks something like this:

"I have tried so many different foraging toys for my dog, but they're just really not into foraging toys. They're way too lazy and stubborn! Haha! No, but seriously, believe me: they just don't like to forage."

To this we respond: challenge accepted.

There are so many reasons that something might appear not to work that we could write a whole other book on that topic, but for now let's focus on troubleshooting foraging and why it sometimes may appear to "not work."

Not the right grade

As we've already discussed, finding your dog's skill level and play style is a crucial first step in teaching your dog how to forage. But sometimes, this may be trickier than it seems.

For example, what do you do when even kindergarten seems too hard? Something we think of as being extraordinarily, obviously, stupidly easy may not necessarily be so for a particular dog. Emily once worked with a dog named Lazarus who had been hit by a car and had a permanent brain injury as a result. He was a sweet, smart dog who thrived with regular training sessions and could learn quickly, but he struggled with problem-solving and wouldn't generally try anything new unprompted. His caregivers told Emily that he just couldn't forage, no matter what they tried. Even the easiest possible food puzzle was too hard for him. When he came to Emily's office for his next office day, she tried the easiest food puzzle she could think of: scattering his food on the floor. He just stared at her. The floor isn't a bowl! That's not where food goes! Does not compute! Interestingly, Emily knew that if anyone dropped a treat on the ground during a training session, Lazarus would find it and eat it without any problems. So she scattered the food in a small area only slightly bigger than a bowl, and sprinkled treats in among the kibble. Then she sat down with him and pointed out the treats. When he'd find one and eat one, she'd give him lavish verbal praise. Then she started pointing out kibble sometimes, too. When he'd eat it, she'd give him lots of praise. After he ate that small pile, she scattered a mixture of kibble and treats over a slightly larger area, and repeated the exercise. This time, Lazarus got it and didn't need her to point out the food. The third time, she scattered the food over half the office floor, and he eagerly went around hoovering up all the food he could find. By gradually increasing the difficulty level like that, Emily and the caregivers were able to teach Lazarus how to forage like any other dog, and it didn't take long for him to become an enthusiastic forager. But it all started with an exercise that seemed so painfully simple that the average observer would never characterize it as a challenge.

Conversely, some dogs are already so advanced at foraging that their disinterest comes from foraging being too easy rather than too hard. Emily's own dog Brie is a good example of this. Brie was feral for the first year of her life, living in the desert and having to use all of her wits to survive. As a result, when Emily first adopted her, the entire house was a food puzzle to Brie. She had no idea how to be a civilized dog. She jumped on counters, opened pantry doors, pried off the trash can lid, and even learned how to get food off the top of the fridge. How she managed that Emily can only guess! But Brie's super survival skills, which served her quite well in the wild, meant that for the first year of their life together, Emily and her partner had to keep all their food in those thick plastic containers with locking lids, had to keep the counters and fridge top meticulously clear of any food, and they still to this day have to keep the trash can locked away in the laundry room. Any food puzzle that Emily could find, Brie could solve in a matter of minutes and then go right back to being a little hellion. Since Brie's skills already exceeded the difficulty level of any toy Emily could find, she takes a different approach to providing foraging for Brie. Emily scatters and hides frozen stuffed Kongs and marrow bones throughout the house, which Brie (as well as their other dog, Copper) has to find with her nose and those gigantic survival-skill brains. Additionally, since they are stuffed and frozen, it still takes a lot of time and effort to get all the food out. In this way Brie is still presented with challenges, she still has to seek out and work for her food, and she no longer thinks of the counters and pantry as her foraging zones.

Not the right style

Just like finding the right grade, finding the right style for a particular dog may be more challenging than it seems. Most of the time troubleshooting this is as easy as presenting them with a variety of styles and textures and observing what they most eagerly interact with. However, what do you do when a dog won't play or interact with any kind of toy or object when people are around? The authors have worked with many shy dogs who know how to play, and enjoy playing with toys, but get "stage fright" and won't do so in the presence of humans. Teaching these dogs how to forage can be especially challenging because it's difficult to gauge what their play style is when you never actually get to watch them play.

Emily had a client with just such a dog named Flower. Flower came from a hoarding situation and had only been in the client's home for a couple of months when Emily started working with them. Flower was so shy that the only reason the clients knew she was playing with toys was that they would come home or wake up in the morning to discover the toys in different places than they had been. The clients purchased a nanny cam so they could see what was going on when they weren't home, and discovered that Flower loved playing with her toys when she was alone! By watching how she played and what she played with, they were able to figure out what type of foraging toys to start her off with, and then started using the foraging toys as a kind of collaborative game to form a bond with Flower.

No interest in food/play/toys

As noted earlier, if we had a dollar for every time someone told us their pet "isn't food-motivated," we'd be millionaires. Here's the thing, though: all living beings are food-motivated, because we all need food to live. While it is true that some animals would eat themselves to death while others stop eating as soon as they are no longer hungry, here are some of the most common explanations for times when people think their pet isn't food or toy motivated:

Needs to be shown how. We've already touched on the fact that foraging and play are learned skills, so if your dog hasn't learned those skills as a puppy, they'll need to be taught as an adult. We've also discussed that a dog may lack interest in a foraging opportunity because it's either too easy or too hard. In addition to those issues, some dogs do better at trying new things when they are shown how to do it. Some dogs can really benefit from watching someone else perform a behavior before they are ready to try it for themselves. As in the Lazarus example, sometimes you have to show them what to do by doing it yourself, pointing it out to them, and then praising them when they give it a shot. This may even be true if your dog has graduated from a few "grades" of foraging. Sometimes the next difficulty level can be a bit overwhelming for them, so playing with them or just playing with it while they watch can create enough motivation to encourage them to try it.

Not hungry enough. Some dogs are really good at regulating their intake, and will only eat when they are actually hungry. For these dogs, trying to teach them how to forage after they've eaten a large meal is not going to be successful. It's best to introduce a new foraging opportunity to them first thing in the morning, when they are at their most hungry. They might be more likely to give it a try when their motivation is high! (Please note: this is not the same thing as depriving them of food to force them to be more "food-motivated." We never recommend such a strategy. Simply harnessing their regular hunger cycles throughout the day is more than sufficient.)

Overfeeding. Sometimes, we humans overestimate how much our pets really need to be eating. Many clients have come to us with concern that their dog isn't food-motivated and isn't eating enough, and leaves a large amount of food in their bowl every day. And yet! The dog is a healthy weight, has a glossy coat, and is bright, alert, and responsive. All of these signs indicate that the dog is getting plenty of food. So the problem isn't one of insufficient caloric intake or motivation, but of misperception. Some dogs, like some people, can have astonishingly efficient metabolisms and don't require much food to maintain a healthy weight. So for them, it's simply a matter of figuring out exactly how much they need to maintain their current weight, then only feeding that amount and using their daily portions primarily for foraging and training. Familiarize yourself with the canine Body Condition Score chart provided in the Resources section of this book. If your dog falls anywhere between 3/9 and 5/9, they are eating plenty. If they score 6/9 or above, they are eating too much or they have a medical condition that causes weight gain. Either way, they are plenty food-motivated; they just don't need as much food as you think they do.

Not valuable enough. The pay isn't worth the job. If a task is hard for a dog, or if the environment is distracting to them, we need to use higher-value food in training or foraging to make the effort worth their while. Over time, the job itself becomes so pleasurable to them that they will happily work for lower-value food again. The authors often start training shy, fearful, or hyperactive/easily distracted dogs with high-value treats and then over time can switch to just using their regular food in training sessions and foraging toys.

Not safe and secure enough. Most dogs won't eat at all, or will barely eat enough to survive, if they feel unsafe in their environment. If you have a dog who is so shy that they seem to be cowering and flinching all the time, or are otherwise experiencing extreme stress, where even getting them to eat their regular food is an adventure, focus on creating a secure space for the dog, as discussed in Chapter 5, and make sure they feel safe enough to comfortably eat in your presence before teaching them to work for their food. Many people fail to recognize that a dog is in survival mode because they aren't in a state of fight or flight, but freeze, or are chronically close to threshold but not quite over it yet. If this is the case, we need to focus on helping the dog to feel more secure and calm before trying to work with them.

Not up to snuff. Some dogs, like some people, have very specific likes and dislikes, and may not be thrilled about the food you're offering them. Alternately, they may like a wide variety of foods for short periods of time but get sick of them quickly and crave variety. Either way, it may be that the food you're using is not their cup of tea, so finding something they really love or providing them with a wide variety may be the key. We'll discuss this in greater detail in Chapter 9 but for now remember: only the learner decides what's reinforcing!

Aversive association with food in training. If a dog's learning history includes any training method in which both food and aversive punishment are applied (e.g. "reward the good and punish the bad"), the dog may have made an association between the food and the punishment, and as a result has learned to avoid food in the presence of humans. It makes sense, after all! If someone regularly told me, "If you do what I want I'll give you a $100 dollar bill, but if you don't do what I want I'll punch you in the face," I wouldn't want to risk taking money from them, either. Furthermore, if the dog is in a state of learned helplessness and isn't able to problem-solve, they may have no idea how to get the food. In either case, we need to use errorless learning to teach them that not only is getting the food possible, but doing so is safe and fun.

Underlying medical issue. If your dog legitimately isn't eating enough to maintain their weight, and you are struggling just to get them to eat anything at all, you need to take them to a vet ASAP and find out what is causing their inappetance. *It is not normal for animals to not eat enough to maintain their weight.* Anorexia in animals only occurs as a result of a physical illness or, much less commonly, severe depression or stress. Some illnesses that cause anorexia may not be immediately apparent with a standard exam and bloodwork. Your dog may need additional bloodwork, a urinalysis, radiographs, an ultrasound, a CT scan, a food trial, an endoscopy, or any number of other diagnostics before your vet finds the ultimate cause. Whatever the case, it's important to take that seriously, and get to the bottom of their physical illness before focusing on any kind of training.

Aggression around food and/or toys

If you are afraid to allow your dog to forage for food because they become aggressive toward you or another pet in the house in the presence of food or food puzzles, it is important to take this seriously and be proactive in addressing this maladaptive behavior. This is called **resource guarding**, and there are many things we can do to help a dog learn that they don't need to guard their things from their friends and family. First of all, it is crucial to hire a professional who has in-depth knowledge of behavior science as well as ample experience working on cases like this. What types of professionals can help and where you can find them will be listed in the Resources section at the back of this book. We also highly recommend reading the book *Mine!* by Jean Donaldson.

In the meantime, if your dog is guarding from other pets in the house but not from the people, you can still provide them with foraging opportunities through careful management:

- Separate the dogs before bringing out the food puzzles. Ideally have two closed doors between them to prevent accidental escape/contact. This can include a kennel door and a bedroom door.

- Provide them with the food puzzles and other toys in these separate spaces consistently, so they know what to expect.

- Pick up all puzzles and toys and put them out of the dogs' reach *before* letting the dogs come back into contact with each other.

Don't have time

We understand! Life gets crazy busy! Fortunately, the last section of this book is entirely devoted to how you can implement enrichment in sustainable, efficient ways.

Chapter 8

SOCIAL INTERACTIONS

It's safe to say that the overwhelming majority of dog trainers, behavior consultants, and behaviorists would agree that it's critical to recognize that dogs are dogs. Dogs aren't humans. Dogs aren't cats. Dogs are dogs, and we need to treat them as such, which means that we also need to let them have social interactions that are natural to dogs. That said, in order to do so we need to know who dogs actually are as a species, and what their social structures actually look like. And in order to do that, we need to look at the entire body of data that has been collected on dog social structure over the past century or so, rather than relying on outdated belief systems that are based in old, bad science that has been debunked time and again over the past several decades.

Canine social structure

So let's talk about who dogs are in the context of their social structure. We can most easily start by discussing what they are most certainly *not*: a species with a rigid hierarchical social structure in which individuals in the pack fight to achieve and maintain alpha status. That's right: there's no such thing as an "alpha dog."

The belief in the alpha dog started back in the 1940s when a man named Rudolph Schenkel published a study he had done on wolves in which he concluded that wolves fought for status and formed an established ranking system (1947). The alpha got priority access to resources, then the beta got next priority, then the gamma, and so forth and so on. This study became the foundation upon which future studies of wolf and dog behavior were founded. The scientific community took this hierarchical social structure for granted, and then went on to apply that same logic to dogs as well. If wolves have a ranking system led by an alpha, dogs must too, right?

More like a family than a pack

This general belief system went on for a few decades until a man named David Mech, a wildlife biologist who specializes in wolf behavior, noticed some serious methodological flaws in Schenkel's work. First and foremost, Schenkel didn't actually study wild wolves, but observed captive wolves in a zoo. Remember, this was in the 1940s, two full decades before the conservation movement began, and three full decades before Hal Markowitz defined and implemented enrichment programs. This means that zoo animals at the time were rarely born in captivity, and were often wild-caught. And the only wolves that are practical or easy to catch are the "lone wolves": juvenile males who have left their pack and have not yet formed their own. Which brings us to the second problem: not only were these wolves living in an unnatural environment, but due to the utter lack of enrichment they had no way to perform their natural behaviors. So Schenkel was observing a bunch of displaced and stressed out juvenile males who were unnaturally crammed together into a concrete wasteland. Sounds a little bit like prison, doesn't it? Imagine that aliens come to Earth and decide to study humans, but instead of observing us all living out our lives they decide to study prison environments. Then they go back to their home planet and publish a study that says, "Humans are a completely crazy species! They wear bright orange jumpsuits! They file the end of their tooth-cleaning devices down to sharp points and stab each other with them! Their primary form of currency is these little sticks that give them cancer!" Does that accurately describe your behavior? Or your family's? Or your friends'? Would you call that a good, accurate study of human behavior? I certainly wouldn't. And yet, this was Schenkel's methodology.

When Dr. Mech recognized these flaws, he realized how important it was to study wolves in the wild who were subjected to as little human interference as possible. As a result, he and many other venerable scientists have followed suit. What they have collectively found is that wolf packs comprise the alpha male and female, their offspring from multiple litters, and sometimes their own siblings who have yet to go off and start their own families. Wolf packs are families, and the alpha male and female aren't the pack leaders because they fought their way to the top; they're the pack leaders because they're the parents (Mech, 2000). No sane human parent would go into their 6-year-old's room punching their fist into their palm and say, "Alright, kiddo, let's take this outside. You or me: who's gonna be the dad? Throw down, bro!" Likewise, the wolf parents don't need to throw their muscle around to gain superior status. They're just Mom and Dad.

Comparing apples to oranges

So that's wolves, but here's another major flaw in the dominance theory logic: dogs aren't wolves! Up until now, all of our discussion about social structure and defining dominance has been a bit of a moot point, because we're not even talking about the right species! While wolves and dogs belong to the same genus, *Canis*, they are two distinct species. Let's go back to that hypothetical alien study. As inaccurate as it was, how much more inaccurate would it be if they went on to say, "And since this is how humans behave, we can assume that this is also how gorillas, chimpanzees, and all other primates behave!" I don't know about you, but my behavior differs quite a bit from gorillas and chimpanzees. We are related, and we share many similarities, but we are not the same.

Fortunately, the scientific community realized this several decades ago as well, and scientists began to study dog behavior to learn about dog behavior. What a novel concept!

As we discussed in Chapter 2, scientists faced a significant challenge when deciding how to study dogs: since they are a domesticated species, there are no wild dog populations to study! How then might we understand what dogs' "natural" social behaviors are? Different scientists went about this in different ways. For example, some scientists like Ray Coppinger studied many different populations of feral village dogs. Other scientists, such as John Bradshaw, studied groups of altered dogs living in sanctuary environments. Still other scientists like Marc Bekoff studied feral dogs in wild environments. A group of scientists studied street dogs in Rome, but in order to do so they needed to create a centralized food source to artificially bring the dogs together (Cafazzo et al., 2010). And although we have never done any kind of formal research on the topic, the authors worked together at a sanctuary that took in many feral dogs from nearby reservations as well as dogs from puppy mills, hoarding situations, dog fight busts, and pet homes, and as a result we, too, have had the opportunity to observe and work directly with hundreds of feral and otherwise non-pet dogs, and observe the differences and similarities in their social behaviors and those of pet dogs.

Fluid rather than strict hierarchies

The truly fascinating thing about all of this research and anecdotal evidence is that, among the various populations, the only consistent pattern in group behavior is how inconsistent it is. The consensus among the scientific community—which we agree with wholeheartedly—is that dog social structure is highly fluid and adaptive to their environment. So while temporary, highly contextualized hierarchies do exist, no rigid hierarchy exists in dog social structures. And perhaps even more importantly, those hierarchies are not established via acts of aggression.

Moreover, we cannot with any accuracy or certainty claim that dogs are even pack animals. Dogs are unquestionably social animals, and they can and will demonstrably live in packs—either temporarily or long term—when it benefits them to do so or when environmental pressures render it impossible or unsafe not to. Dogs will also "pack up" momentarily to achieve a common goal. However, they are equally likely to live alone or in pairs when the occasion merits it. Interestingly, a large body of research from the past three decades has shown that, even when groups of dogs do live in a pack, the pack structure remains fluid and will undergo seasonal or other types of changes (Bekoff et al., 1984). So even at their most packiest, dogs still nevertheless have a fluid social structure.

The difference between species that have a well-defined group social structure and those with a more fluid social structure is beautifully illustrated in a recent study that was done to compare the cooperative skills of wolves as compared to dogs (Marshall-Pescini et al., 2017). In this study, researchers taught the dogs and wolves how to pull a rope to gain access to food. For the social cooperation test, however, the object they had to pull to access the food was too large for one animal to pull alone. It had two ropes, one at each end, and needed to be simultaneously pulled by two animals to yield its goods. When they released one wolf into the yard with the contraption, the wolf immediately turned around and waited for his partner to arrive before even attempting the test. When they released the second wolf, she immediately ran to the other rope and both wolves started pulling their respective ropes simultaneously, to a successful end. The wolves had not been trained to collaborate like that; it's an ethological trait. Conversely, the dogs when tested were almost comical in their dysfunction. When the first dog was released she didn't wait for the second dog but immediately began trying to pull the rope. The second dog ran up to the first dog's rope or paced back and forth, but they never figured out how to work together to each pull on their respective ropes. This doesn't mean the dogs were dumber than the wolves; it simply means that collaboration with conspecifics is not a part of their ethogram. Again, that's not to say that they will never collaborate with each other! There is ample evidence that they can and will do so situationally. But when we're looking at social behaviors on the whole, dogs do not behave as pack animals the way wolves do.

If you think about it, this makes perfect sense: for so many millennia dogs have lived in a mutually beneficial relationship with humans. What function would a rigid social structure serve? They don't need one; humans are their social structure. So when dogs, a domesticated species, find themselves in a feral or sanctuary setting, they have to roll with it in whatever way works best. As scavengers and opportunists, flexibility and adaptability are critical to survival.

The concept of dominance

As we strive to meet our dogs' social needs through enrichment, a clear understanding of their social structures is paramount. The misunderstanding of these structures, and in particular the misuse of the term "dominance," hampers our ability to comprehend what our dogs are telling us about what they need and what they are currently getting from us. It also leads us to make well-meaning but misguided decisions about how to best meet their social needs.

Before we delve into the ways in which a dogs' social needs can be met through enrichment, let's talk about the concept of "dominance." It is important to understand that, just because dogs do not have a hierarchical social structure and there's no such thing as an alpha dog, doesn't mean there's no such thing as dominance. However, dominance (as it is) differs significantly from dominance theory (as it's understood in popular culture). In order to accurately discuss dominance and submission in dog behavior, we must understand it as a relationship dynamic between two individuals in a moment in time rather than as an intrinsic character trait that a dog possesses in relation to all other dogs, humans, and other living beings at all times. Think of dominance as something a dog *does* rather than something the dog *has*.

The problem is that dominance is such a deeply entrenched notion within our society and has so many varied definitions among laypeople and behavior professionals alike, its definitions have been loose and inconsistent at best and circular at worst (e.g., "dominance means behaving in a way to establish dominance over another individual"). Fortunately for all of us, some ethologists like Dr. Roger Abrantes recognized this problem and have taken measures to correct it. Dr. Abrantes' methodical and precise approach to discussing, differentiating between, and defining dominance and aggression is so dang helpful and clarifying that we highly recommend reading his articles on this topic in their entirety. For your convenience, they're listed in the Resources section at the back of this book. But for now, this is Dr. Abrantes' definition of dominance, which is by far the most accurate one the authors have seen (2017):

> *Dominant behavior is quantitative and quantifiable behavior displayed by an individual with the function of gaining or maintaining temporary access to a particular resource on a particular occasion, versus a particular opponent, without either party incurring injury. If any of the parties incur injury, then the behavior is aggressive and not dominant. Its quantitative characteristics range from slightly self-confident to overtly assertive.*

To help you understand what this definition means, we're going to tell you a little story about a light switch. The authors met each other when we were hired onto the behavior consulting team at an animal sanctuary. We shared an office with our other teammate, Ashley. Unlike Allie and Emily, who were hired as full-fledged behavior consultants, Ashley was originally hired as a junior consultant. It was her first real job out of college, and she had never been a behavior consultant out in public before working at the sanctuary. As the team member with the least experience, no one would characterize her as an authority figure over either Allie or Emily. But Ashley would get chronic migraines, during which she was sensitive to light. When experiencing a migraine, she would turn off the light in the office and work only by the natural light coming through the windows. Whenever either Allie or Emily came into the office and reached for the light switch, Ashley would cry out, "Don't touch the light switch! I have a migraine!" Allie and Emily would immediately leave the light switch alone, without any kind of resistance or argument. After a while, as the team got to know each other and our various quirks better, Allie and Emily got into the habit of asking Ashley, "Is it okay to turn on the light right now, or do you have a headache?" Then Ashley would tell us whether or not we could turn on the light. So what was going on there? We could accurately say that Ashley dominated over the light switch, and that Allie and Emily submitted—or deferred—to Ashley's dominance. But it certainly didn't mean that Ashley was the boss of Allie or Emily, or that she was intrinsically superior, or that Allie and Emily always submitted to her about everything. It simply meant that, in that situation, Ashley controlled access to that particular resource, and Allie and Emily deferred to her.

This definition will undoubtedly come as a surprise to a lot of people: we are so accustomed to thinking of dominance as an aggressive display of force and intrinsic superiority that to think of it otherwise may take a few moments to sink in. But here's the truly fascinating thing about dominance and submission: deference is always given, not taken. In the example above, Ashley never had to slap our hands away, or punch us, or taze us, or spray us with pepper spray. She simply told us that this resource was important to her, and we deferred. And this is not simply a case of anthropomorphization. When studying wolves in the wild, scientists have observed that the wolf who is deferring is the one who willingly rolls over; the dominant wolf never "alpha rolls" the submissive wolf by grabbing them and throwing them down. Likewise, when one dog stakes a claim on a resource through subtle body language signals, it is the other dog who offers appeasement signals and backs away, or licks the dominant dog's lips, or otherwise demonstrates their willingness to defer. In fact, aggression never occurs in stable relationships. Only in unstable relationships, where the animal attempting to achieve dominance lacks confidence and trust, does aggression occur between the two parties (Yin 2007, 2009). In other words, it is the individual who is insecure, lacking a solid, trusting relationship with the other individual, who is aggressive and tries to force the other dog to submit to their will.

Even more interesting is that even when a dog does control access to a resource, it isn't always for personal gain or superiority. In the study of street dogs in Rome mentioned earlier, one of the most fascinating observations the scientists made was that the dominant male dog controlled access to the centralized food resource, but not for himself. Instead, he enabled the pups from his youngest litter to eat first, then his older puppies, then he ate, then other adult dogs ate last.

Dominance between dogs and humans

Dogs aren't stupid; they know humans aren't dogs. They are not trying to incorporate us into their pack structure, even if such a thing existed (again: it doesn't!). Every interaction with humans that traditionally gets erroneously labeled as dominance has other, more scientifically sound explanations: impulsiveness, eagerness, affection, a strong reinforcement history, hyperarousal, an obnoxious play style, poor social skills, or resource guarding are some of the most common explanations for so-called "dominant" behaviors.

In fact, with the advent of functional MRIs, scientists have recently been able to get even better insight into what dogs are feeling toward their human families. What they found is that dogs have a stronger emotional response to their owners than to other dogs or other people (Berns et al.,

2015) and that their emotional response is similar to that of an infant's toward their parents. These findings made us giggle, because for decades professionals in our field have been chiding their clients about thinking of their dogs as their kids, and yet the evidence thus far suggests that dogs probably would beg to differ! Regardless, not only are dogs *not* trying to dominate us, they are looking to us for guidance.

This is an important point, because the authors hear many people, when presented with this information about debunking dominance theory and the myth of the alpha dog, say something along the lines of, "Well if I'm not supposed to dominate them, what *am* I supposed to do? I'm certainly not going to let them dominate me!" This is a false dichotomy. We are not suggesting that we should let dogs rule the roost and run roughshod over our houses and lives. Doing so wouldn't meet anyone's needs! The opposite of dominating your dog isn't submitting to them; the opposite of domination is teaching.

To summarize, we need draw a clear distinction between:

- **Dominance theory**: The outdated belief that dogs form rigid, hierarchical social structures in which they gain status through conflict

- **Dominance**: A relationship between two dogs at any given moment in time, in which one dog controls access to a particular resource and the other dog willingly defers.

Until and unless dominance theory loses its popularity among the general public, training methods based on dominance theory go the way of the dinosaur, and the accurate definitions of dominance and submission become common knowledge, we believe it is impossible to use those terms when speaking to the public about dog behavior without creating confusion and miscommunication. At this point in time, the words "dominance" and "submission" are inextricably linked with the false paradigm of dominance theory. For this reason, even though dominance and submission does exist in dogs, and there are accurate ways to use those terms, the authors choose to use other, equally accurate ways to describe those behaviors.

Understanding dogs' social needs

So what does all of this mean? And why does it matter? The implications are far-reaching indeed. First and foremost, the belief in dominance theory heavily skews how we read and interpret dog body language. If you believe in dominance theory, you might think that a dog is showing "respect" when in fact they are demonstrating fear or stress. You might think that a dog is being "submissive" when in fact they are attempting to defuse what they perceive as threats in order to prevent conflict. You might think that a dog is being "dominant" when in fact they are feeling joy, or excitement, or are attempting to bond with you. You might think that a dog is "calm and relaxed" when in fact they are in an extreme state of stress, or even learned helplessness. Understanding dogs' social needs necessitates understanding their social structure, and being able to gauge whether or not those needs are being adequately met necessitates accurately interpreting their body language and understanding their emotional states. We can't let dogs be dogs if we can't speak their language.

But also, believing that dogs are pack animals heavily influences how we might attempt to meet their social needs. The desperate, almost manic pressure people put on themselves to "socialize" their dog with other dogs is often unnecessary and counterproductive. Just like humans, different dogs have different social needs. Not every dog is or should be forced to be a social butterfly.

A dog's social needs and desires are influenced by multiple factors: genetics, prenatal environment, the primary and secondary critical socialization periods, sensitivity periods (more commonly known as fear periods), learning history, age, health, and reproductive status. An in-depth treatise on each of these contributing factors lies beyond the scope of this book (if you're interested in learning more, however, we've provided plenty of options in the Resources section at the back of the book). However, acknowledging the complexity of this topic is important, because so many people take an oversimplified "nature versus nurture" stance and end up promoting viewpoints that are as extreme as they are inaccurate: either you end up with breed-specific legislation and websites wholly devoted to demonizing specific dog breeds, or you end up with "it's all how you raise them" and interminable finger-pointing. The former unfairly judges the dog; the latter unfairly judges the owner. Either one is bound to create problematic approaches to meeting a dog's social needs.

The bottom line, however, is that all dogs are social animals, but the degree of their sociability toward humans and dogs varies among each individual, and those variations are not aberrant or unnatural. In other words: just because a dog may prefer the company of only a handful of humans and dogs, or only has one dog friend, or doesn't really want to be around any other dogs at all, does not necessarily mean that they are reactive, aggressive, or in some way defective. Conversely, a dog can be sociable and also contextually behave reactively or aggressively. For the purposes of this book, let's define **sociability** as "the desire to be around other individuals." Let's define **reactivity** as "an overreaction to a particular stimulus or stimuli (person, animal, or object)." Finally, let's define **aggression** as "an intent to inflict harm." Sociability is not mutually exclusive with either reactivity or aggression, and unsociability is not a synonym for either reactivity or aggression. With that understanding, let's talk about sociability as it relates to various species.

Sociability with humans

Most dogs are raised from birth around humans and, given the length of time they've spent as a domesticated species, many of them are highly sociable with all humans and solicit attention and interaction from everyone they meet. During their secondary critical socialization period (approximately 7 to 12 weeks of age), we can help to increase that tendency by allowing them to meet and interact with a variety of people in safe and fun ways, but more is not necessarily better. In order for socialization to achieve its intended purpose of helping a dog to feel safe, comfortable, and happy in the human world, it needs to meet these important criteria:

- The puppy needs to have the agency to approach or walk away from the new person as desired.

- The puppy needs to have safe, non-threatening interactions with a variety of outcomes (e.g., sometimes people provide food, sometimes they provide petting and praise, sometimes they will play with the puppy, sometimes they won't have anything to do with the puppy at all).

- If the puppy does feel scared or overwhelmed by a person, the handler must gradually change the way the puppy feels about that person incrementally, until the puppy is comfortable around the previously scary person no matter what they're doing.

Exposing puppies to large numbers of people in a situation in which the puppy is forcibly handled with no opportunity to escape is likely to have the opposite of the intended effect, and it has the potential to make the puppy more fearful of new people. Sadly, when people don't understand these concepts and they see a puppy reacting fearfully to humans, they often assume the dog is somehow defective or "naturally aggressive," which can then set that puppy down a doomed path. If, instead of blaming the dog, we recognize the part we play in their behavior and change how we interact with them, we can nip a problem in the bud and set them up to have better, safer relationships with humans for the rest of their life.

However, even well socialized puppies can still grow up to have preferences as to how many humans they're around and what they are comfortable with humans doing to them. There are many dogs who bond closely with just one or two people and feel neutral toward everyone else. Likewise, there are many dogs who don't find petting or cuddling to be fun and rewarding and, even though they like their human companions, would very much prefer if humans kept their hands to themselves. There is nothing wrong with these dogs; they are simply less sociable than the typical family dog everyone envisions when they think of who a dog should be. Like people, dogs should be allowed to have social preferences. As long as they don't behave reactively or aggressively toward anyone, their behavior is normal and healthy, and they should be allowed to be who they are.

This flies in the face of the traditional, dominance-based view of human-dog interactions most of us were raised with. We have been told from birth that we are the masters and we should be able to approach and handle any dog we see, and if they have a problem with that it's because they're challenging our alpha status, so we have to assert our alpha position. But when we've dispensed with those tired old myths and are able to look at dog behavior clearly, we see that letting dogs be dogs means accepting them as they are, even when they may be more aloof and uninterested in interacting with strangers. We realize that, instead, consent is important, and we need to first ask the dog's owner if we can approach and pet their dog, and then, if the owner gives consent, we must then ask the dog themselves if they want to be petted. Obviously we can't ask a dog with words, but we can ask a dog with our body language. Instead of reaching down and petting a dog, we can instead offer our hand a few inches from their head, chest, or shoulder and wait for a response. If a dog wants to be petted, they will physically move toward our hand, sometimes even pressing their head or shoulder into our hand. If they don't want to be petted, they will ignore the hand, or perhaps even move away from it. Eileen Anderson, on her YouTube channel *eileenanddogs*, has a fabulous video that demonstrates how to ask a dog for consent and how to gauge whether they are enjoying or merely tolerating being petted. The authors feel that everyone who interacts with dogs should watch that video.

To be clear, this is not to say that we can't teach a dog to enjoy petting or handling, or even grooming or medical procedures. We can! We should! That's not only possible, but important! Animals who actively choose to participate in their own husbandry are more likely to get more thorough and frequent care, will be much less stressed in the process, and as a result are more likely to live a longer, healthier, happier life. But the degree to which a dog will solicit attention from a variety of people will nevertheless vary, even among dogs who have been trained to be handled.

With all of this in mind, how can we meet a dog's social needs with regard to humans? This one's pretty easy: spend time with them, but let them have a say in how you interact with them. If you happen to have a dog who loves everyone they meet, they might be great candidates for outings to dog-friendly restaurants and coffee shops, pet stores, and pet-friendly events around town. If your dog prefers to keep their close circle of friends at home, let them be a homebody. Don't keep a social dog housebound, but conversely don't try to force your homebody dog to be a social butterfly.

Sociability with dogs

Because of the widespread belief in dogs as pack animals, most people believe that all dogs should absolutely play with other dogs. This belief is so prevalent that the authors have heard many trainers and shelter workers make such claims as, "Playgroups are a necessary part of canine enrichment." While we certainly agree that playgroups are a valuable and important part of a shelter enrichment *program*, and dog daycares and other dog social events are valuable resources to have at our disposal, it is extremely important to point out that they are not necessary—or even beneficial—for every dog.

Dogs can be broken up into four broad categories of sociability:

- **Dog-social**: dogs who enjoy being around all other dogs, enjoy playing in large groups, and will put up with almost any kind of behavior from other dogs.

- **Dog-tolerant**: dogs who enjoy being around most other dogs, may enjoy playing in groups for the most part, but will correct other dogs if they are annoyed by their behaviors and may dislike particular dogs.

- **Dog-selective**: dogs who enjoy a few specific dogs but have strong preferences—which may be based on age, sex, appearance, personality, health status, play style, greeting style, energy level, or any combination thereof—and require supervised, gradual introductions in order to meet and befriend new dogs.

- **Dog-aggressive**: dogs who don't enjoy the company of any dogs or may have a couple of dog friends but must still be supervised around them due to a low tolerance for behaviors they perceive as being rude or annoying. The authors feel that calling this category "aggressive" is a bit of a misnomer, since not all dogs in this category will actually display aggression toward other dogs, but simply prefer not to be around them. Among ourselves, our apprentices, and our clients we tend to refer to this category as "dog-solo."

One interesting thing to note: recently a group of scientists published a study indicating that some dogs may have **sensory processing sensitivity** (SPS)—wherein they are more easily overstimulated by their environment—like some humans do, and as with the humans there appears to be a genetic cause (Braem et al., 2017). Since there is a high association between SPS and introversion in humans, it is entirely possible that some dogs could, in fact, be introverts, too. While this line of research is in its infancy and is therefore far from concrete, we nevertheless should be aware that some dogs are genetically more sensitive than others, and trying to force them to be otherwise is a cruel exercise in futility.

Although genetics, prenatal environment, and the primary socialization period certainly set the stage for a dog's social tendencies, these categories are fluid, and dogs may transition between them over the course of their lives. What kind of social interactions we expose them to, what occurs during those interactions, and how we respond to those interactions will play a vital role in whether our dogs become more or less sociable as time goes on. But again, just as with humans, as long as a dog isn't reactive or aggressive toward other dogs, there's nothing wrong or unnatural about them preferring to eschew interactions with other dogs.

When dogs are anything less than dog social, the authors see a strong tendency for people to work very hard to "socialize" their dog. Let's be clear: there is no such thing as socializing an adult dog. That is impossible. The only time socialization can occur is during the critical socialization period of their puppyhood. After that period ends around 3 to 4 months of age, all we can do is either change the way they feel about stressful stimuli (using desensitization and counterconditioning), allow them to get used to the stressful stimuli over time (called habituation), or force them to interact with the stressful stimuli until they "get over it" (called flooding). When we put a dog into a playgroup, dog daycare, or dog park when they are uncomfortable with most or all other dogs, that is flooding.

Emily met a couple whose dog had been going to playgroups multiple times a week for five years. This dog still, after five years, had to be muzzled to be safe around the other dogs (and, it should be noted, had not been taught to love wearing her muzzle, either), and at playgroups showed clear signs of extreme stress and learned helplessness. The couple had spent many thousands of dollars over the course of those five years on these playgroups, but when she asked them why they were doing it and what they hoped to get out of it, they looked at each other quizzically and shrugged. They had no idea why they were doing it, other than that the trainers at the daycare facility told them it was necessary, and they had some vague sense that their dog needed to be "socialized." Emily asked them, "Ok, how's that working out for you? Is your dog more social now than she was five years ago when you started?" Clearly she wasn't. So Emily then asked them, "If the purpose of taking her to these playgroups is to make her more social, and after five years she isn't more social, is this approach working?" A look of dawning realization crept across their faces, then guilt and anger. Emily then had a long chat with them about how it isn't their fault, and they shouldn't feel guilty. We're all just doing the best we can with the information we have, and their intentions were wonderful. But moving forward, now they know: if a dog is stressed out by and doesn't enjoy being around groups of other dogs, don't put them in groups of other dogs. Doing so isn't meeting any of their needs and is more likely to create new problems than solve old ones.

Agency and management

Even if a dog does enjoy being in groups of other dogs, how we handle those situations can affect their sociability in the future. Again, agency should be at the forefront of our minds when managing groups of dogs. This means:

Giving them space to retreat when they need a break. We can do this either by hosting dog groups in a large enough space for an individual to be able to walk away from the group as needed, or watching for signs that they're done and removing them from the group so they can relax.

Intervening when one dog is bullying another. If a dog won't allow another dog to escape or move away, we need to do this for them. *There is no need to be harsh when we do this.* All it takes is simply leashing up the offending dog and walking them away. Better yet, use a hands-free approach by teaching a dog a strong recall first and using that to cue them to move away from the other dog(s). Anything beyond that runs the risk of the dog forming an unpleasant association with you or the other dog and acting aggressively later on.

Allowing them to give each other appropriate corrections. The authors know of many, many handlers, dog daycares, or playgroups who will punish dogs if they offer any kind of correction toward another dog, be that a growl, lip curl, bark, air snap, or nip. These dogs are punished with prong collars, shock collars, whips, citronella spray, an alpha roll, or even a kick to the ribs. It is often presented as ensuring a "safe, calm" experience. But this is, hands down, the worst possible way to handle that situation. Why? Because dogs need to be able to correct each other if one of them is being rude or inappropriate. Dogs don't have words; the only communication tools they have at their disposal are their voice and their body language. By punishing the communication we aren't improving the way the dogs feel about each other, or helping them to communicate their needs to each other more effectively, or teaching them how we want them to handle the situation instead. All we're doing is suppressing their only tool for navigating a social interaction with another dog. Certainly, that approach can keep those dogs "in line" in a group setting indefinitely. The authors know of many dogs who have been attending playgroups in that state of learned helplessness for years without any external incident. But it isn't helping them to improve their sociability, it isn't meeting their needs, and ultimately for most dogs it makes their social skills worse, not better. As soon as the threat of punishment from humans is removed, they will likely take their frustration out on each other. So in order to "keep dogs in line" we must constantly remind them that our threats are still there. What an unnecessary and unpleasant burden! Instead, we need to stop micromanaging dog interactions, let them navigate their own social interactions, and only intervene when it becomes apparent that the dogs aren't able to successfully do so on their own and need our *compassionate, humane, productive* help. To claim that dogs need more forceful or aversive interference than that simply isn't true; both authors have managed hundreds of playgroups and dog introductions at a variety of organizations, and have never needed any of those aversive techniques.

Even when an interaction between two or more dogs is clearly heading for a fight and intervention becomes necessary, we don't need to use harsh methods to do so. Choking a dog out, hitting them, kicking them, shocking them, or whipping them isn't necessary, and often it will make the problem worse rather than better—not to mention that many of these methods run the risk of causing severe physical harm to the dogs or causing the dogs to redirect aggression onto their handlers, or both. The authors have successfully used and recommended a least intrusive, minimally aversive (LIMA) protocol to break up dog fights for years, without incurring any damage to ourselves or the dogs we've worked with. This protocol can be found in the Shelter Playgroup Alliance's (SPA) guide-lines, which are included in the Resources section at the back of the book.

Our goal is to reduce the physical and emotional trauma of the con-flict as much as possible by trying the least intrusive, minimally aversive approach to breaking up the fight first, then escalating as necessary. As you can see in the SPA guidelines, though, even the most aversive, more forceful methods of breaking up a fight on that protocol still don't in-clude anything designed to hurt or scare the dogs. And of course, these methods are safest for both dogs and humans involved.

How to meet a dog's social needs

So, what *are* our goals for meeting the social needs of dogs? The answer depends on the dog.

If a dog is dog-social or dog-tolerant, taking them to places where they have the opportunity to play with other dogs is a great idea. When look-ing for a place to do that, make sure that the environment will provide, as much as possible, safe and fun interactions that are more likely to main-tain the dog's current sociability than damage it. Here are some ways to determine whether or not a specific resource is going to be a safe bet for your dog.

Dog parks

While dog parks are wonderful in theory, know that not all dog parks are safe in practice. Many well-intentioned people and sometimes less expe-rienced trainers will bring dogs who are inappropriate for this setting to dog parks in the name of "socialization." There is often a higher risk fac-tor at dog parks; it's up to you to keep your dog safe in these settings!

- Look for dog parks that have wide open spaces with plenty of oppor-tunities to escape. Small, enclosed spaces, where the dogs feel their options for escape are limited, are more likely to breed conflict.

- Don't take your dog when the park is overcrowded. Too many dogs in a big space can have the same effect as a small, confined space.

- Find out who owns/operates the park, and ask them if they'd be will-ing to post educational signs to help owners determine when their dog is either feeling stressed or causing other dogs to feel stressed. The International Association of Animal Behavior Consultants teamed up with Lili Chin to create excellent, easy-to-read signs that can be posted at dog parks; these are linked to in the Resources section. We highly recommend getting those for your dog park. Educated dog owners are more effective dog owners.

- Leave toys and treats outside the park. Even dog-social or dog-tolerant dogs may find themselves in a fight if another dog wants to vie for a valuable resource. If you want to play fetch or Frisbee with your dog, do it elsewhere or come back when the park is empty.

- The authors advise that dogs less than 6 months old should not go to dog parks.

Playgroups/dog daycares/boarding facilities
These facilities offer a bit more control than an open-access dog park, but care should still be taken when deciding to take your dog to one and selecting which one you'll use.

- Ask to take a tour of the facility first. Make sure the facility is (for the most part) clean. Elimination happens so the occasional mess here and there isn't a cause for concern, but if there are messes everywhere and the place smells bad, that may indicate an under-trained and/or under-managed staff, not to mention a general lack of concern for the comfort, health, and well-being of the animals in their care.

- Ask to observe a playgroup. Watch how the staff interacts with the dogs. They will be on their best behavior when an outsider is watching but knowing what they believe to be best behavior is valuable information. If, for example, they're still shouting at dogs when the dogs correct each other, that points to a lack of education.

- Ask the owner, point blank, what they do when a dog snarks (air snaps, growls, etc.) at another dog. Ask what they do when a dog is bullying another dog. Ask how they break up dog fights. Again, there's a chance they may not be honest, but learning what they believe to be appropriate responses is still enlightening.

- Make sure the facility has webcams you can access throughout the day. Even if the facility's owner is knowledgeable and implements good practices, every business runs the risk of a bad apple employee. Cameras keep employees accountable and will allow you to watch how the staff and the dogs interact with each other.

- Make sure the dogs are separated by size, personality/play style, or both. Allowing small breed dogs in groups with large dogs is a recipe for disaster.

- Ideally, at least one person on the staff will have a pet first aid certification, although in the authors' experience this is rare. Alternately, some vet clinics have their own dog daycare and boarding facilities, which is even better than a staff member certified in first aid. Either way, if you can find a place that meets all the criteria above and also has direct access to medical care for when accidents happen, that's ideal.

Dog-friendly events/group walks

Events like this can be found via shared interest websites, social media, or your local pet store. You can easily advertise within your community to start your own.

- Make sure everyone who brings a dog is required to sign a waiver, and that the organizer has a clear set of rules every participant is required to adhere to.

- Make sure the group has some way to signal to other participants that their dog needs space, so that dogs who are working on their social skills can do so at a safe and comfortable distance rather than being flooded by other participants. Some group walks give out yellow bandanas for dogs who need space, which we feel is a clever way to communicate with the rest of the group.

- Make sure the places where these groups meet provide plenty of space to move away as needed, as well as enough objects in the environment to provide visual barriers as needed.

Playdates with friends' and family's dogs

These are a great option, because you know the other dog and the other humans involved.

- Make sure all humans understand canine body language or have a professional dog trainer help with the initial meeting.

- Make sure the space is free from potential resources, including food and toys.

And, for any kind of dog social event, stay observant as to how your dog is behaving before, during, and after the play time. If at any point your dog is offering distress or avoidance signals, or is in a shut-down state, that may not be the best environment for your dog. Even if it's perfect on paper, that doesn't necessarily mean your dog will enjoy that particular mix of people, dogs, and environment! Again, if your dog is more stressed after an encounter than they were before, you haven't actually met their social needs.

If your dog might become aggressive

If a dog is dog-selective or dog-aggressive, the goal is to reduce their stress response in the presence of other dogs and teach them what we want them to do instead of behaving reactively or aggressively. Our goal is *not* to make them play with more dogs. Ever. If, during the course of training, they become more dog social and show an interest in playing with more dogs, then of course they can and should be allowed to play with those specific dogs. But remember: some dogs just prefer the company of humans better, and that's okay. As long as they are safe, their social needs are being met, and they know how to cope with being around other dogs, that's all they need.

An in-depth description of how we do that lies beyond the scope of this book, but the basic concepts are as follows:

- We change the way they feel about seeing and being near other dogs through desensitization and counterconditioning, and sometimes habituation.

- We teach them to check in with us whenever they see something potentially stressful, which gives us the ability to decide how to respond to the situation instead of the onus being on the dog.

- We teach them to walk away from stressful circumstances instead of engaging in conflict.

- We manage their environment to reduce the number of times they are exposed to stressors and to prevent them from being able to practice old, undesirable behaviors.

The Resources section of this book provides more information about the details of how and why we take this approach. However, if you have a dog-selective or dog-aggressive dog, we strongly recommend that you contact a qualified behavior professional (information about how to find such a professional can also be found in the Resources section at the back of the book) and hire them to help you through this process. As with anything, understanding the basic concepts by reading books or watching videos cannot and should not replace the years of hands-on experience that behavior professionals have.

Using play as a social activity

Regardless of what species or how many individuals a dog gravitates toward, the bottom line is that dogs, as social animals, need to have trusted friends. And more to the point, they need to be able to play. A veritable wealth of research exists demonstrating the physical, emotional, and psychological importance of play across species, so we can accurately say that play is a universal need. However, it is also a learned behavior. While play signals in dogs are innate (for example, puppies who are born blind and deaf still offer play signals), a dog may not play because they have never learned how or they are too stressed to do so. The authors often hear people say, "This dog does not like to play." But, like foraging, we respond: that isn't true. This dog simply doesn't know how to play.

When working with a dog who seemingly doesn't want to play, we must first make sure the dog is not too stressed to play. If the dog is shut down or hypervigilant, we need to take steps to help that dog become more relaxed in their home environment. Extreme cases may need the consultation of a veterinary behaviorist to make sure the dog gets an appropriate type and dose of anxiolytic medication. However, often we can achieve this simply by giving them a safe space filled with calming enrichment, removing as many stressors as possible from their environment, and building their confidence through training, which we'll discuss more in Chapter 9. When the dog becomes more relaxed and confident in their home environment, their personality will blossom and they'll begin to play. Nothing on earth is more thrilling to the authors than watching a formerly shut-down animal come to life.

When a dog simply doesn't know how to play, it is important for us to teach them how to do so. This can be accomplished in a variety of ways:

Role model dogs

If the dog in question prefers the company of other dogs over humans, we can use dogs to help them learn to play. Because of the authors' work at the animal sanctuary—where we worked with several dogs who were either feral or came from hoarding, puppy mill, or dog fight cases—we have had many cases where the best way to teach a dog to play was by pairing them with a dog social dog and letting them learn from that dog. Often the inexperienced dog expressed curiosity in the role model dog and would approach them or even offer a play bow, but when the role model dog reciprocated they would initially run away or tap out (quickly and stiffly roll on their back to expose their belly), or otherwise just be hilariously awkward. However, over time, they would catch on and start to offer real play behaviors: running away from or chasing the role model dog, wrestling with the role model dog, slap fighting, or playing games with toys, such as tug. The more interactions they had, the more proficient they became at playing with other dogs, until they could be paired with any dog and no longer needed a role model.

Observational learning

For dogs who are more human-oriented, we can teach them how to play by first showing them. We start by playing a variety of games with other dogs—chase, wrestle, tug, etc.—then, when the dog seems interested, we offer to play with them in the same way. Again, adult dogs will rarely learn to play after just one session. It usually requires several sessions, during which their skills, confidence, and interest gradually improve. But persistence pays off. Eventually, dogs will learn to play without needing prompting.

Shaping play behaviors

Shaping is a training method in which we first have a clearly defined end-goal behavior, then begin by rewarding the closest thing the animal can currently do to our goal—called an **approximation**. Once the learner consistently performs that approximation, we reward them for performing a slightly more difficult approximation. When the learner is proficient at that approximation, we once again increase our criteria. We continue to do so until they can fluently perform the end-goal behavior.

With some dogs, we can actually shape play behaviors. This is what shaping might look like, specifically with regard to play:

- Dog looks at toy ⇨ mark ⇨ treat

- Dog moves head toward toy ⇨ mark ⇨ treat

- Dog touches toy ⇨ mark ⇨ treat

- Dog puts mouth on toy ⇨ mark a treat

- Dog picks up toy ⇨ mark ⇨ treat

- Dog picks up and drops toy ⇨ mark ⇨ treat

- Dog picks up and tosses toy ⇨ mark ⇨ treat

Even though this is just a simple example, the concept remains the same: you reward the closest thing they are currently doing to playing, and then reward them for incremental advances in behavior until they are fully playing with toys. By pairing play with mark/treat enough times, the act of playing itself becomes its own reward, and dogs will begin to play just for the fun of it.

You will notice that we offer several options for how dogs can play. As with foraging, each dog has their own play style and will prefer some games over others. That's perfectly fine! We don't need to force dogs to play in every possible way. That is as silly as it is impossible. As long as a dog knows how to play and has opportunities to do so on a daily basis, who they play with, what their play style is, or how many individuals they play with is irrelevant. Our focus, when meeting a dog's social needs, should be on quality rather than quantity. And again, the only way to know what a dog needs is to observe their behaviors and adjust your enrichment plan accordingly. Don't let ideology get in the way of observation.

Chapter 9
MENTAL STIMULATION

Pet owners and professionals alike understand the importance of physical exercise for our four-legged friends. On a routine basis when the authors ask clients to describe their dog's typical day, it includes a discussion of number of walks and the respective distance, as well as play sessions including games like fetch. Very little discussion revolves around mental stimulation unless the dog is attending a training class. In the vast majority of these situations the authors recommend increasing mental exercise, and the request is often met with a look of confusion. "But I'm exercising her so much already! You mean I'm not giving her enough exercise?" As discussed before, walks *can* be a great source of mental exercise if we allow our dogs to stop and sniff and vary our route so they can explore new sights, sounds, and smells. But so often, people believe they must keep their dogs at a heel and make them walk at a rapid pace along the same route.

Mental stimulation is not often thought of within the pet community, or is thought of in a limited way. Such an emphasis is placed upon the well-being of the body—diet, exercise, and veterinary care—that the mind often takes a back seat. While the body is incredibly important to care for, the conversation often stops there without considering the mental needs of individuals. So too does this happen in humans, as the topic of mental health is still highly stigmatized or, at best, trivialized. The authors often find that dogs receive an appropriate amount of physical exercise, but their brains are not being exercised nearly enough. And, in the authors' experience, dogs who receive too little mental exercise are far more likely to exhibit annoying or problematic behaviors.

Foraging, while being important enough to have received its own chapter, is also an important part of mental stimulation. Much of the research involving mental stimulation and problematic behaviors looks at the impact of foraging on animals exhibiting stereotypies, which you will recall from Chapter 1 are a sign of distress in captive animals. Researcher Dr. Laura Price provides an answer as to why foraging is so important to welfare: "Species-specific behaviours may be restricted in captive carnivores due to feeding regimes that do not fulfil the specific needs of an animal, thus it may become inactive or prone to particular behavioural problems" (2010). Studies abound on the impact of foraging opportunities on decreasing stereotypies and other abnormal and unwanted behaviors in many carnivorous species like bears (Wagman et al., 2018), African wild dogs (Price, 2010), red foxes (Kistler et al., 2009), and of course the domestic canine (Schipper et al., 2008). While much study has taken place on the effects of foraging on behavior, researchers have also looked at other forms of mental stimulation, such as training. One study found that performing husbandry training with African wild dogs decreased stereotypic behaviors (Shyne and Block, 2009).

The lack of mental stimulation seen in pet dogs is equally apparent in the sheltering community, where enrichment programs, training, or any other type of mental exercise are treated as a luxury that should only be undertaken after the physical needs of the animals are met—if they have the time, money, and desire to do so. Ironically, most of the major challenges in the sheltering community could be more successfully addressed if everyone in the community understood that mental and physical needs are inextricably bound with each other, and the success of one is dependent on the success of the other. A healthy, well-adjusted animal is one whose needs are being met in their entirety. Those are the animals who will get adopted faster and will be less likely to be returned. A shelter full of animals whose needs are being met will be more attractive to the community and will receive more visitors, and therefore more adopters. A community that is educated in enrichment and understands how to best meet the needs of a dog is a community that will be more likely to adopt and less likely to surrender or return animals.

We need to understand that our dogs' mental and physical health are equally important, and we cannot wholly improve one without improving the other. So let's look at the various ways we can provide mental enrichment for dogs.

Training as mental stimulation

The best way to mentally enrich dogs through training is to find what motivates them—in other words, what they'll work to attain—and then teach them skills by rewarding them when they get it right. By doing so you'll end up with a dog who is an engaged, eager problem-solver.

Training basics: how to get a behavior

There are four ways to get a dog to learn a behavior:

Shaping. As mentioned earlier in the book, shaping is rewarding the closest thing to the end-goal behavior the dog can currently do, and then rewarding subsequent approximations until the dog can successfully perform the end-goal behavior.

Luring. Luring means using a lure—typically a food lure—to lead the dog into the behavior you want them to do. In many cases, we briefly use luring to start a behavior, and then use shaping to get the dog through the rest of the approximations. However, that is not always the case. For example, we might lure a dog onto their bed for a few repetitions, and then fade the lure into a pointing cue to teach the dog to go to their bed when we point at it.

Capturing. Capturing is when the dog performs the behavior on their own, we add the cue while they do it, and then reward them afterwards. For example, if a dog lies down for a nap we might say "down" as they lie down, then give them a piece of food or a scritch behind the ear afterward. After a few repetitions of that, the dog would learn that "down" is the cue for lying down.

Modeling. Modeling means applying physical or psychological pressure to get the dog to perform the behavior you want, for example, pressing on a dog's hind end to teach them to sit down. We do not recommend modeling as a training technique for two reasons: the first is that modeling makes the dog focus on how to escape or avoid something unpleasant instead of focusing on how to work to get what they want. The second is that it typically takes longer for the dog to learn how to do the behavior unprompted because we are the ones performing the behavior for them. We tell our clients, "You are doing your dog's homework for them." As such, it doesn't provide mental exercise for the dog.

Meeting a dog's needs for mental exercise through training

To use training as a tool to meet dogs' mental exercise needs, the behavior itself isn't as important as the process of collaboration and reward. Obviously it's a good idea to train dogs in basic manners such as watch me, sit, down, stay, come, target, stationing, and loose-leash walking. But after the dog knows those, then what? The sky's the limit! Here are some ideas:

- **Medical/grooming handling.** Teaching your dog to actively participate in their own care will make trips to the vet and groomer less stressful and more fun, but if you shape the behaviors it will also be great mental exercise.

- **Fun tricks.** There's no end to what kind of fun and silly tricks you can teach a dog. The easiest way to do this is to capture a behavior they naturally offer, then shape it into something fun. For example, Emily had a project dog at a shelter she worked with who liked to stretch out on the cool tile and scootch a few inches forward on his belly. Emily captured that behavior then shaped it into an "army crawl," where he'd scootch all the way across the room on his belly. Allie had a project dog, Castiel, whom she shaped to perform a "mic drop" by gradually increasing the duration he held a plastic microphone in his mouth before dropping it on the ground.

- **Shaping creativity.** Shaping creativity is shaping without an end goal behavior. Instead, you start by rewarding whatever behavior the dog offers, then shape it into whatever direction the dog takes it. The authors love to use this process for mental exercise because, in addition to the problem-solving skills that any free shaping provides, it also teaches dogs creativity and establishes a more collaborative relationship between the dog and their trainer. A great game involving shaping for creativity is 101 Things to Do With a Box. The Resources section at the back of the book will have more information about how to play this game.

Like any skill, science-based training requires practice to become proficient at it on both the human's and the dog's end. You cannot be expected to be highly skilled right off the bat, nor can you expect your dog to be an instant expert at learning in this manner. The Resources section will provide links to YouTube channels, books, and training organizations, as well as an article on how to find a good dog trainer so you can get some help learning how to successfully shape your dog's behavior.

Mentally stimulating dog sports

As we've already established, reward-based training is great mental exercise, but if time is at a premium and you'd like to find activities that simultaneously provide mental and physical benefits, some dog sports can be a good solution for you. We've already mentioned many of these sports in Chapter 4 because many of these sports do a great job of providing both physical and mental exercise.

Agility/degility. Agility is a timed event where dogs learn to run through an obstacle course. It is scored on speed, precision, and responsiveness to the handler. Because they are running through the course while also learning to navigate tricky obstacles, this is a great way to simultaneously provide both physical and mental exercise. Degility, also called "functional agility," is a slower-paced version of agility where the dog works on one obstacle at a time and there's more flexibility as to what can be done at each obstacle. It provides lower-impact physical exercise but the same amount of mental exercise.

Scent detection sports. A number of sporting activities, including Barn Hunt, field trials, Earthdog trials, hound trailing, K9 Nose Work, and retrieving, share the quality of asking the canine participants to use their noses to process information and achieve the intended goal of the sport. In the authors' experience, any kind of scent work has a profound effect on the dog's mental health and well-being. We often incorporate nose work into our therapeutic approaches to a wide variety of behavior issues, including anxiety, fear of people, fear of objects, compulsions, stereotypies, impulsiveness, hyperkinesis, boredom-based destruction, and even resource guarding. Though there admittedly is very little research explaining this phenomenon, we've collectively worked with thousands of dogs for whom a training plan and even psychopharmacology in combination weren't enough to help them become calm, focused, confident, and happy. Although the dogs were making some gradual progress beforehand, it wasn't until scent work of some kind was added to their routine that we saw significant improvement in their behavior. To be clear, we are not promoting scent work as a panacea for all problems. However, we do frequently use it as a huge piece to the puzzle of successfully helping dogs enjoy improved mental health and quality of life. Some fascinating research on this topic has come out in the past few years, but that research has only begun to scratch the surface. We would love to see further research on this subject. (Duranton and Horowitz published a study noting a correlation between scent work participation and "optimism" in dogs in 2019; Drs. Simon Gadbois and Catherine Reeve explore canine olfaction in depth in Dr. Horowitz's 2016 book.)

Dog parkour/dog surfing. Dog parkour is based on human parkour, and focuses on balance, core strength, and hind end awareness. Similarly, surfing requires balance, core strength, and hind end awareness, although the difference is that, in parkour, dogs learn to use a wide variety of objects in a variety of environments, whereas in surfing dogs need only to learn on a surfboard. However, the unpredictability of the waves provides plenty of variety!

Freestyle/freestyle disc dog. Freestyle is basically dancing with your dog: teaching dogs a variety of "tricks" or "dance moves" and then chaining them together into a choreographed piece. Freestyle disc dog incorporates a Frisbee into the choreography. Either way, just as for people, dancing provides dogs ample physical and mental exercise.

Herding trials/treibball. Herding trials allow herding breed dogs to do what they were bred to do in a competitive setting. It is great for both physical and mental exercise. The drawback to herding trials is that they're primarily accessible to dogs and people who live in a rural area. For that reason, Treibball was created. Also called "urban herding," treibball is somewhere between billiards and soccer: the dogs have to herd exercise balls into a goal. Due to the collaborative nature of the sports and the wide variety of behaviors that have to be learned, both sports are excellent physical and mental exercise.

Although many of these sports were designed for specific breeds in order to allow them to perform the behaviors they were bred for, any sport can be taught to any dog if you so desire. If something appeals to you, and your dog shows behavioral tendencies that would lend themselves to that sport, go for it!

Additional mental exercise ideas
In addition to the broad categories of shaping and dog sports mentioned above, there are a few other ways we can provide mental exercise to our dogs:

- **Foraging.** Since we already devote an entire chapter to this, there's no need to spend a lot of time explaining it. However, we should emphasize that, in order for foraging to be mental exercise, it must remain challenging. If your dog can finish their food puzzle in five minutes flat, it's time to graduate them to the next grade and give them another challenge!

- **Flirt pole.** When used correctly, a flirt pole can provide excellent mental exercise, in addition to the physical benefits we've already discussed. It can also be used to teach dogs valuable life skills such as "drop it" and "wait." A flirt pole basically looks like a gigantic version of the cat fishing pole toys (in fact, for miniature breed dogs and puppies, we do recommend using the cat fishing pole toys): it's typically made of a long piece of PVC with a nylon cord running through it. On one end of the pole the cord is tied into a handle; on the other end it runs the entire length of the pole and has one to three toys tied along the length of the cord. Alternately, a horse lunge whip can be repurposed into a flirt pole for dogs who won't break them, simply by tying one to three toys along the length of the whip. If there are multiple toys on the cord, ideally they are different types and textures. For example, Emily's flirt pole has a plush squeaky toy, a braid rope tug toy, and an empty water bottle. Allie, on the other hand, changes the attached toy based on that particular dog's toy preference test. The rules of the game are as follows:

- The dog must sit or lie down while you hold the pole in "resting position" (completely vertical, holding the cord flush against the pole).

- Then you give them the release word, and either run in one direction or in a circle so that the dog must chase the toy(s) on the cord. If the dog is physically mature so their growth plates are already fused, and they have neither joint disease nor a high risk for joint disease, you can also pull the handle to alter the height of the toys so the dog must jump to get them. Do so with care and caution, however! Protect their skeletal health!

- After a decent amount of time, let them catch the toy(s), and say "take it!" when they do.

- Play a good game of tug for approximately 90 seconds, then let the pole "die" by lowering it to the ground and holding it still. When dogs are new to the game they may continue to tug for a while, but eventually a dead toy is a boring one.

- When the dog drops the toy, say "drop it," then gather the pole up and return it to "resting position." You can opt to toss a treat on the ground to encourage the dog to leave the toy alone. The added bonus of this is that you're incorporating some scent work into the game as well.

- Give the dog about a minute to rest, then cue sit or down and start again. Whatever direction you ran in last time, run the opposite direction on the next round.

- Over time, dogs will learn the rules of the game and will "take it" and "drop it" as soon as they are cued. You can then begin to apply those cues to other objects.

- **Any play activity** you want to do with your dog that requires them to think, explore, and problem-solve can be great mental exercise. As we discussed earlier, off-leash hikes can work well for this. Playing hide and seek can also be good mental exercise (not to mention making recall a super fun—and therefore high-probability—behavior for your dog!). And of course, if your dog is already working in some way, this need is already being met. Well done!

Regardless of what type(s) of mental exercise you provide, remember: the old adage "a tired dog is a good dog" can only be true if both the dog's body and mind have been well-used that day. By meeting a dog's mental needs we can often overcome so many annoying behavior issues without even directly addressing them. Changing the environment so that the behavior is no longer possible, necessary, or desirable is called **antecedent arrangement**. If you'll look back at the Humane Hierarchy in Chapter 2, you'll see that it's one of the first stops! If we eliminate the cause for boredom-based destruction, excessive barking, excessive chewing, excessive digging, or any other behavior that is either caused or exacerbated by excessive mental and physical energy, wouldn't that make life easier for all of us?

Not all training methods are enriching
As we discussed in Chapter 8, the dominance myth often leads people to believe they need to dominate their dogs in order to avoid being dominated themselves. This in turn leads to rigid, often illogical rules enforced through coercive training techniques, rather than scientifically valid reward-based training.

In their Dominance Position Statement, the American Veterinary Society of Animal Behavior states:

> *Coercion and force generate passive resistance, tend to require continual pressure and direction from the leader, and are usually not good tactics for getting the best performance from a team (Benowitz 2001). Additionally, those [leaders] who rule through coercive power*

(the ability to punish) "most often generate resistance which may lead workers to deliberately avoid carrying out instructions, or to disobey orders" (Benowitz 2001). ... Leadership is established when a pet owner can consistently set clear limits for behavior and effectively communicate the rules by immediately rewarding the correct behavior and preventing access to or removing the rewards for undesirable behaviors before these undesirable behaviors are reinforced.

In other words: the best way to be a good leader to your dog is to teach them what you want them to do and prevent them from being able to practice undesirable behaviors, rather than setting them up to make a mistake and then punishing them for it.

There is a widespread paranoia that rewarding desirable behavior will make dogs then perform those behaviors to "trick" you into giving them something they want. People are advised against "letting their dogs train them." We should clarify that, technically, every interaction is a learning experience for both parties involved. Every interaction we have with our environment results in a consequence, and every consequence under the sun will either increase or reduce the likelihood of us repeating the same or similar interaction in the future. That's what learning is. We hate to break it to you, but our pets do train us, and we train them, and we train each other, and pets train each other. Training is a synonym for learning, and learning occurs during every interaction on earth, so it is literally impossible to train an animal or another person without also simultaneously being trained by them. That's just how the universe works. The notion of not being trained is as silly as the notion of not having weather. Weather is the condition of our atmosphere, and though it's always changing, it's never absent. Likewise, learning is the condition of sentience, and though it's always changing, it's never absent.

That being said, when we talk about training an animal, we are usually referring to structured sessions that are designed to teach them a skill, change an emotional state, or both. This is what most people think of when they talk about training, and training sessions are by far the most prevalent type of mental exercise.

However, as is implied by the leadership discussion above, not all training methods are created equal, nor do they all provide adequate mental exercise. As such, from an enrichment standpoint it is crucial to employ only science-based, positive reinforcement–based training methods. Without at least a basic understanding of behavior science, that can certainly sound like a horribly snooty, elitist thing to say. People will often argue that different dogs need different methods, so every method has validity. Or they will argue that science-based methods are completely out of touch with reality and end up coddling and spoiling animals. Or people will try science-based methods but lack both the expertise to do so successfully and the persistence to find someone who can help them learn, so they believe that either: a) "I can't train," b) "my dog can't learn," or c) "this method doesn't work for my dog." The authors have even seen people who barely scratched the surface of learning about behavior science and didn't continue their education to gain a deeper, broader understanding, then go on to write arguments against science-based training that sound quite compelling to a layperson but are laughable to behavior professionals who are educated on the topic.

Because here's the thing: all learning across species is composed of fundamental behavioral principles, which means that all of the training methods on earth—no matter how "secret" or "proprietary" they may be, or how fancy-sounding their names are, or how much funding has gone into marketing and promoting them—are merely functions of these basic principles. Nothing is new under the sun. Whether or not they realize it, no matter what a trainer is doing to get a dog to perform a behavior, they are bound by the laws of behavior science. For this reason, it's important to not get caught up in a cult of personality but instead look at the body of evidence behind any approach to training. It isn't about "my method versus someone else's method"; it's about what decades of research shows us about how all sentient beings learn.

In his 2014 article, "The Death of Expertise," which he later expanded into a book of the same title (2017), Tom Nichols says:

> *Having equal rights does not mean having equal talents, equal abilities, or equal knowledge. It assuredly does not mean that "everyone's opinion about anything is as good as anyone else's." … The death of expertise is a rejection not only of knowledge, but of the ways in which we gain knowledge and learn about things. Fundamentally, it's a rejection of science and rationality.*

As we discussed in our Author's Note (which, if you didn't read, please go back and do so now, since it's highly salient to this chapter), science matters. To become a competent behavior professional, we need both an education in the behavior sciences *and* real-world experience, and the two are not mutually exclusive. The argument that "I don't need to learn about behavior science because I've been successfully training dogs for decades" doesn't hold water. Decades of experience is not the same as actual expertise. So, what may seem snooty and elitist is actually a body of evidence debunking decades of long-held beliefs about the nature of human-animal relationships and how sentient beings of all species learn best. This isn't simply a matter of "differing but equal" opinions.

Let's stop here to acknowledge that what we just said may sound offensive or hurtful to some people. It may seem like a personal attack. This is not the case! *How we train is not who we are.* Everyone is doing the best they can with the information they have, and the vast majority of people who work with animals do so because they love animals and want to help them. To discuss the comparative merits of methodology is not to cast aspersions on anyone's character, intelligence, commitment to animals, or intrinsic worth as a human being. So that everyone understands that we're all coming from the same place, Emily was taught at a very young age about dominance theory and learned how to train using a combination of Koehler Method and the Monks of New Skete method—both of which are aversive, forceful, and based in dominance theory. Then in her mid-20s she learned a mixed method wherein both rewards and corrections were employed. Her journey through those various methods took a total of 16 years before she learned about the behavior sciences and a whole new world of possibilities opened up to her. So throughout this discussion, remember: this is not about judging or criticizing any person; it's about objectively evaluating methodology. We love this quote from Maya Angelou: "Do the best you can until you know better. Then when you know better, do better." With that in mind, let's continue.

An in-depth discussion about applied behavior analysis and its real-world application lies beyond the scope of this book, but if you'd like to learn more, there are many books and courses we recommend in the Resources section. In the meantime, this is all we need to know in order to discuss how training can be an excellent source of mental exercise if done well: any time an individual learns a skill by working to obtain something they want, they will be more mentally engaged and eager than if they learn that same skill by working to avoid something they don't want. Additionally, learning through corrections, threats, pain, fear, or psychological pressure runs a much higher risk of emotional and behavioral fallout and damage to the teacher-student relationship than learning through being rewarded for desirable behavior (Dr. Zazie Todd has a comprehensive, ongoing compilation of research on this topic on her website, which we will provide in the Resources section). Yes, absolutely, coercive methods can sometimes work with no adverse effects. If it didn't work at least some of the time, trainers wouldn't continue to train that way. But as behavior professionals it is our ethical duty to employ methods that have the least risk of fallout possible. Sure, surgeons back in the 18th century who were essentially just using a hacksaw and ether still had some successful outcomes. But why on earth would anyone practice medicine that way when we now have general anesthesia, antibiotics, and laparoscopic surgery? We do the best we can until we know better, and when we know better, we do better.

Building resilience: adversity, not aversives

In training, as in everything else, providing agency and reducing the amount of force we use is important. But why is it important to reduce the aversives we use in training? Life is hard; isn't it important to expose dogs to negative experiences to toughen them up in order to teach them resilience?

Actually, no. If you remember way back in Chapter 3, we talked about immunization training, which is essentially skill-building via positive reinforcement in incrementally difficult and stressful environments, until the learner is equipped to successfully navigate even extremely stressful situations. Throwing them to the wolves without any skill or confidence runs an extremely high risk of setting them up to fail. However, *giving* them skills will enable them to confidently handle whatever life throws their way. The kernel of truth in the belief that we need to add aversives to dogs' lives to toughen them up is that learners of all species do need *adversity* in our lives to help us overcome challenges and develop resilience. But those experiences occur throughout the course of being alive and interacting with the environment. Dogs trip and fall while trying to jump over a bush in the yard. They struggle to climb onto a chair to get food off the table, only to have the chair slide out from underneath them. They try to bring a tree branch into the house and the branch is too wide for the door, so they hit the door and come to a screeching halt in their progress. All of those are examples of naturally occurring adversity that a dog might encounter in their life, which teaches them important lessons and builds a resilient animal. The difference is that those consequences occur as a direct result of the dog's interaction with their environment: the dogs *chose* to perform those activities, and their environment is teaching them the finer points of failure and success. We aren't artificially adding them to the dog's learning environment as a well-intentioned but misguided attempt to "teach dogs a lesson."

Up until now, we have only talked about the deprivation of choice and the application of aversives in terms of the collateral damage they can cause: stress, avoidance, learned helplessness, increased aggression, and so forth. However, invariably when we have a conversation about this, someone pipes up with, "Well *I* used dominance/coercive methods with my dogs, and they're fine! They love me, they obey me, they're great. None of the stuff you're talking about has happened with my dogs." Setting aside the fact that most people fail to recognize the signs of stress, avoidance, or learned helplessness in dogs, the truth is that, yes, sometimes a dog is trained in forceful, aversive, dominance-based ways and still ends up a happy, healthy, productive dog. Why is that?

It's because if a dog is genetically sound, well-socialized, confident, and has a strong desire to work with humans, they will tolerate an enormous quantity of aversive stimuli in order to continue working with humans. Some fascinating research has been done on the correlation between the amount of control a learner has over the aversive stimulus and how aversive they perceive it to be: in other words, if they have a say in the matter, it won't feel as unpleasant as if they didn't. For example, Emily has a full backpiece tattoo that took six 6-hour sessions to complete. People often ask her, "Wow, did that hurt?" Well, yes, sometimes it did, and sometimes it didn't. But she *wanted* the tattoo, she *chose* to sit in the chair all day and deal with the pain when it occurred, because the end product was worth it to her. She was not traumatized at all by that experience and suffers no mental or physical damage as a result. It would be an entirely different story, however, if she didn't want the tattoo, but instead someone kidnapped her, tied her down, and forcibly gave her the tattoo. Her experience would have been much more painful, and there would be a high likelihood that she would suffer emotional, psychological, and possibly even physical damage as a result. This phenomenon is why dogs who are having fun can literally run until their paws are bloody without seeming to notice, whereas those same dogs will scream and writhe when undergoing a relatively minor medical procedure like a vaccination. Likewise, if a dog is choosing to remain engaged with a handler using aversive methods, their experience will be less traumatic.

Think about this, though: in order for forceful, aversive training methods to result in happy, confident dogs, those dogs must meet a whole constellation of criteria, including genetic propensity for resilience, confidence, and a strong motivation to work with humans, along with solid socialization during their critical period. If a dog lacks any of those advantages, they either end up in a state of learned helplessness—which can look like a successful training result to the uneducated eye—or their behaviors get patently worse. No wonder those methods have such a high fail rate. No wonder so many dogs are deemed by practitioners of those methods to be "too stubborn" or "too skittish" or "too unpredictable" or "too aloof" or "not drivey enough" or "untrainable" or "unfixable." No wonder so many dogs are recommended for rehoming or euthanasia.

Wouldn't it be better to train in such a way that *anyone* can successfully learn? A way that has a much higher success rate and a much lower risk of collateral damage?

Avoid fear, force, and pressure in your training

Aversive training methods tend to provide little to no mental exercise because of their reliance on fear, pain, intimidation, or force. When a learner goes over threshold, the fear center of the brain, the amygdala, literally takes over and essentially shuts off the learning, thinking, rational parts of the brain. The brain's primary concern at that point becomes survival. This is called the "amygdala hijack." When this happens, the brain physically cannot learn anything other than how to avoid the fearful stimulus. Learning for the sake of learning is not possible here.

Another method that has gained popularity over the last few decades is called "pressure-release training." While pressure-release training is usually less aversive than dominance- or punishment-based methods, it is no less forceful. Pressure-release training works by applying some kind of either physical or psychological pressure on the dog, and in response the dog performs the desired behavior, after which the pressure goes away. For this reason, it is also called "escape/avoidance" learning, because we elicit behaviors by creating a situation that a learner will work to avoid. Examples of pressure-release training include:

- Pressing on a dog's hindquarters ⇨ dog sits ⇨ pressure is removed.

- Leaning into a dog ⇨ dog backs up ⇨ you are farther away.

- Tightening leash to tighten collar ⇨ dog walks on a loose leash ⇨ pressure/pain around neck is relieved.

This type of training is also called "modeling," because when we train this way we physically (or sometimes psychologically) manipulate the dog into whatever position or behavior we want from them, like modeling clay. While modeling is usually less aversive than more traditional dominance-based methods like alpha rolls, hanging dogs at the end of leashes, whipping them, etc., it is no less forceful. The dog doesn't behave in a certain way because they *want* to; they do it to avoid something they *don't want*. As a result, they aren't truly doing any problem-solving during this kind of training; they're simply focusing on escaping or avoiding an unpleasant stimulus. The authors explain modeling to clients by telling them, "You're doing your dog's homework for them." Just as children don't learn a subject as thoroughly or expediently when their parents do their homework for them, neither do dogs. They aren't thinking it through; you're just telling them what to do and they're doing it. For this reason, modeling is also a poor form of mental exercise.

Be constructive, not combative

The thing about humans is that we have a strong tendency to focus on what we don't like, don't want, and don't have far more than what we want, like, and have. Learning how to think more constructively is a skill and, like any skill, becoming proficient at it takes time and practice. In training our dogs, we need to practice rewarding what we like and already have. Reward approximations. We also need to practice teaching our dog what we want them to do. Instead of thinking, "I want my dog to stop jumping up on people," ask yourself, "What do I want to teach my dog to do instead of jumping up on people?" In doing so, you are changing your mindset from viewing your dog as an opponent who must be defeated to viewing them as a collaborative partner with whom you are constructing new options, new possibilities, and new skills.

We also need to do this with ourselves! Another human tendency is to fall into the trap of false dichotomies. We tend to think our only two options are "expert" or "idiot," and if we acknowledge that we maybe aren't the expert we thought we were, that must mean we are an idiot. And who wants to feel like an idiot? No one. This right here is one of the reasons it's so hard to change: because our thinking about changing our own behavior is a false dichotomy. Change happens in approximations, and learning is a lifelong process with no end goal. You can simultaneously be good and successful at training dogs and also have plenty of room for more knowledge, more growth, more expertise. Reward your own approximations. Acknowledge how far you've already come, and how many skills you already have. Then ask yourself, "How can I learn an *even better* way to do what I'm already doing?" By doing so you may find that, in learning how to train your dog in a way that mentally enriches them, you also are mentally enriched.

Chapter 10
CALMING ENRICHMENT

Most discussions about canine enrichment focus on physical exercise, play, and, to a lesser extent, mental exercise. As we've seen, enrichment is so much more than that. Even so, calming enrichment is often over-looked or downplayed. This sort of enrichment is just as important as all of the others and deserves the proper recognition. Because large, pro-longed levels of any sort of stress can present behavior challenges and even permanently alter brain chemistry, being able to relax is essential for every dog.

Calming enrichment simply refers to activities that help your animal to calm themselves down and relax. For some humans, this could be yoga, meditation, deep breathing exercises, or soaking in a bubble bath. For others this could be repetitive tasks like coloring, knitting, or woodwork-ing. Each individual is different, and therefore what relaxes them is differ-ent. This is true for our animals as well. As such, the authors recommend experimenting with activities that cover most of the senses (Chapter 6) as well as other instinctual needs based in safety and security (Chapter 5).

Keep in mind, however, that this is a niche that is ripe for scientific in-put. While this area has extensive human research, there are few studies looking into relaxation and calming enrichment in our canine friends. We have more to learn! Because of this, the best way to provide the ide-al calming enrichment for your pet includes experimentation and doc-umentation. Experiment with only one therapy at a time, and docu-ment your dog's body language before, during, and after each exercise.

Continue utilizing and documenting this therapy for two weeks before deciding to add to or discontinue it (if you see undesirable effects, discontinue immediately). While more tedious, this ensures that the exercises you're using truly work for your dog instead of doing something needless or even detrimental.

Scent enrichment

As we discussed in Chapter 6, olfactory enrichment is one of the more important types because smell is a dog's predominant sense. When it comes to calming scent enrichment, we can explore aromatherapy for our canine friends just as humans do for themselves. While many alternative therapies are looked down upon by aficionados of science-based medicine, there's actually a growing amount of peer-reviewed research in support of some—although certainly not all—alternative modalities. Aromatherapy is no exception. For example, different aromas have been shown to decrease anxiety and increase alertness (Diego et al., 2009). And while only preliminary research has been conducted on the effect of aromatherapy on dogs, the findings are, so far, in line with that of humans. Wells (2006) found that lavender increased time spent resting for dogs with travel-induced excitement. That said, the authors recognize that this study included a small sample size, and not all dogs got the memo that lavender is supposed to be relaxing. Emily had one client whose dog disliked lavender so much that he ripped the diffuser out of the wall, took it outside, and pushed it under the fence! His owner got the message loud and clear: no more lavender. As we've said so many times, only the learner decides what they like and don't like.

Many opt for pre-made options like "Calm Balm" from Blackwing Farms. You can also go the more traditional route of regular essential oils such as cedar, vetiver, lemon balm, rose, ylang ylang, bergamot, chamomile, sage, jasmine, or sandalwood. If there's one on that list that you don't like, don't try it! You're not expected to suffer for the sake of your dog's relaxation (plus, remember that your stress will likely negate any beneficial effect!).

Most aromatherapy or essential oil vendors will provide you with a free sample of their products. This is a great option for figuring out what your dog prefers! Also bear in mind that many dogs prefer scents that we humans wouldn't think of as being particularly relaxing: the scent of grass, one of your old, sweaty t-shirts, or even a blanket their dog-friend has lain on may send your pup into the zen zone. Think outside the box when coming up with different scents to test out with your dog. When you have a variety of samples, do a scent test by spreading all of your sample scents out and letting your dog explore them. Ideally, do the test a few times to verify. They like best the one(s) they return to most often.

You can use these aromatherapies around the house, apply them to your dog's coat if it's safe to do so, apply them to your hands before you interact with your dog, and apply them to wherever your dog sleeps. The great thing about this enrichment is that it's so easy and takes virtually no additional time out of your day. Spritz and walk away! Just remember that dogs have an extraordinary sense of smell, so don't use a highly concentrated amount. The scent should be so faint that we humans can barely smell it. Just a whiff! That way it won't overwhelm their nose. Additionally, it is possible to overdose an animal on essential oils. Be wary of the concentration and type; ask your vet if you're unsure if the amount or type you're using is toxic. A quick note for those of you with cats in the house: cats are more sensitive than dogs to certain essential oils, and there are some types that are dangerous to our feline friends. Check with a qualified veterinarian prior to using aromatherapy with your dog to ensure that it's also safe for your cat (they will be exposed to it too, after all!).

Pheromones for scent enrichment

We are frequently asked about products that mimic the pheromones produced by nursing mothers. The most recent double-blind studies on these products do not show enough efficacy for us to recommend them. These fall into the "it doesn't hurt to try, but can be expensive" category.

Sound enrichment

Humans have long known certain sounds and music to be calming: light rainfall, lullabies, etc. In addition to our intuition and anecdotes telling us that sound enrichment can be soothing, there's quite a bit of research to back this up in both humans and non-humans. Studies suggest that music can reduce agitation (Sung et al., 2010), promote sleep (de Niet et al., 2009), and lower stress in humans (Cooper and Foster, 2008). Studies attempting to show the same in animals have found similar results in carp (Papoutsoglou et al., 2007), chickens (Gvaryahu et al., 1989), and western lowland gorillas (Wells et al., 2006). Sound enrichment is a favorite of the authors because it soothes the whole household! That said, know that sound enrichment in dogs specifically is a newer field of study, and while specific musical elements, such as consonance versus dissonance, melody alone, tempo, etc., have been studied in other species, the effects of each specific element have not been studied in dogs at this point. This means that the studies we do have are testing for several variables at once, thus making their results more vulnerable to contradiction.

The type of music does appear to matter. Wells et al. (2002) explored different types of auditory stimulation, using genres of music and human conversation, in shelter dogs. The dogs who listened to classical music spent more time relaxing and remaining quiet than any other genre. Kogan et al. (2012) put classical music to the test against heavy metal and music tailored to dogs and it still won out. Additionally, Kogan explored different beats per minute in four different classical music pieces (ranging from 100 to 143 bpm). Time spent sleeping did not differ significantly between each piece, though time spent vocalizing did, and not in the way you may think. The piece that created the most relaxing environment was the fastest classical music piece! Brayley included an audiobook reading in a 2016 study; the male voice audiobook reading had more of a calming effect than the music included in said study.

We previously discussed habituation to different types of enrichment, and the same is true of auditory enrichment (really all of them!). Knowing this, in a recent study, Bowman et al. (2017) looked further into different genres of music and if switching between several helped to negate habituation. They found that switching between genres did help curb habituation and that dogs also enjoy reggae and soft rock.

We have yet another option when it comes to sound enrichment for our dogs: dog laughter. Simonet et al. presented at the 2005 International Conference of Environmental Enrichment regarding the effects of listening to dog laughter on shelter dogs. Simonet describes dog laughter as "a breathy pronounced forced exhalation." It sounds a bit like panting, but louder and more purposeful. The authors have also observed that when dogs are laughing their tongues tend to be resting in their mouth, whereas when panting the tongues are more likely to loll out of the mouth. In Simonet's study, she found that shelter dogs relaxed more when listening to a recorded playback of dog laughter than when there was no playback.

Sound enrichment is just as easy as scent enrichment. Once you know what your pup likes, just press play and walk away! For even more options you can explore Tibetan singing bowls, white noise machines, or pre-made CDs (however, the studies including music specifically made for dogs have not shown this particular music to have a significant effect). A word to the wise: don't leave music playing all day for your dog. Anything gets old after a while.

A common sound enrichment used in shelters is volunteers reading to the dogs. There are many fabulous programs across the nation that invite children, especially those learning to read or who have speech impediments, to read to shelter dogs. Win-win! While classical music showed more calming effects on shelter dogs than human communication, for those people who love to read and spend some relaxing time with their dog, this is a great option.

Tactile enrichment

While there is no research (to our knowledge) on the effects of tactile stimulation on canines, our personal experience leads us to believe this is a worthwhile topic to discuss. Tactile enrichment can take multiple forms. The first is that of full body pressure, such as a Thundershirt. This vest applies gentle, constant pressure around most of the dog's torso. A similar product is the Anxiety Wrap. While not all dogs benefit from these products, they can fall into the "it doesn't hurt to try it" category, especially since the Thundershirt company offers a money-back guarantee. The authors have known several dogs who visibly relax when wearing products that apply constant pressure. A word to the wise: do not only use these products in times of stress. If you only pull out the Thundershirt before a vet visit, your pup can associate the two, thus nullifying the vest's effects. Have your pup wear their vest during periods of calm, too.

Tactile enrichment can also come in the form of petting or massage. Massage therapy has been touted for years for its palliative and therapeutic benefits. While little research exists for the effects of massage therapy on animals, the human research is abundant. For example, Field et al. (1992) found that regular back massages decreased anxiety and depression and increased sleep in child and adolescent psychiatric patients. Field et al. (2005) found that regular massages decreased anxiety and stress hormones in adults while increasing alertness.

Canine massage therapy is a growing field. While it is currently an unregulated field, finding a canine massage therapist who has gone to school and taken a national exam is recommended. Tellington Touch (TTouch) is another form of animal massage; this program certifies practitioners who are experienced with their method. Jin Shin Jyutsu is yet another modality for those seeking other options.

One word of caution about using massage to help dogs relax. There are certain training methods that have grown in popularity recently because of their deceptively appealing claims that they teach dogs to relax by "guiding" them through the massage process until the dog "chooses" to relax and "allows" people to touch them. Videos abound of trainers and laypeople bringing their dogs to a mat and touching or massaging them. In these videos, the dogs at first are growling or flailing around while the humans in the videos continue to touch, pet, or massage the dogs. Eventually the dogs stop growling or flailing and lie still. Usually the people in the video talk about the dogs' behaviors as if they are in some way bad or defective. They may say that the dog is "addicted to growling" or that we "can't let them get away with" thrashing around and we must "work them through it." They usually also incorrectly label this technique as counterconditioning and desensitization. It looks impressive because the dogs do eventually lie still, and the humans aren't doing anything overtly abusive to them. However, remember that a fundamental criterion of emotional and behavioral health—not to mention enrichment—is agency. Forcing a dog to receive petting or massage against their will is the opposite of giving them control over their environment and outcomes. To the educated eye, the body language and behaviors being exhibited by those dogs are not bad or defective; they are communicating discomfort and stress in healthy, appropriate ways, and those signals are being ignored by the humans. Eventually the dogs learn that nothing they do changes their outcome, so they give up and lie still. That is the very definition of learned helplessness, *not* counterconditioning and desensitization, much less relaxation. When it happens to humans, being forced to allow someone to touch you against your will is called "assault." The double standard for animals only exists because of our cultural attitudes toward non-human species. For this reason, the authors strongly recommend that you watch your dog's response to being touched by you, and only attempt to use tactile enrichment *if the dog actually solicits and enjoys being touched by you.*

Licking and chewing

In Chapter 6 we discussed that chewing is a natural, instinctual behavior. Research does not currently explore the effects of non-compulsive licking and chewing on relieving stress in our canine friends, so this section is anecdotal. However, anyone who's watched their pup lick a Kong for an hour and fall asleep for the next hour is inclined to agree that licking seems to have some sort of calming effect. Getting creative with raw, dehydrated, or canned food is great for dogs who love to lick: any of these foods can be stuffed into a Kong or marrow bone, smeared into muffin tins, or spread onto cookie sheets and then frozen before being given to the dog. If the dog is on a weight-loss plan, calorie-conscious alternate options include: canned pumpkin (alone or mixed with a spoonful of peanut butter for flavoring), mixed vegetables blended with sodium-free chicken broth, plain yogurt, or even blended fruits. Just experiment to find out what your dog likes best! Raw bones and antlers, bully sticks, or Himalayan Chews are just a few ideal options for dogs who prefer chewing.

Naps and safe spaces

Recall from Chapter 6 that dogs are crepuscular: most active at dawn and dusk. They typically sleep throughout the day and at night. That means that they need midday naps! And, like a toddler who's missed their nap, our dogs are often cranky when they miss theirs. Some dogs (especially adolescents) have trouble taking naps in households that are active in the day. They just don't want to miss the action! In those cases, it can often help to separate the dog into another room for a couple hours in the day with other calming enrichment so they can relax and nap.

We discussed in Chapter 5 the need for creating a safe space for your dog. This space is a great place to provide calming enrichment to create an all-in-one location for your dog. It's the place they feel comfortable, take a nap, and get to calm down. For dogs who have trouble deciding when they need to relax, many people will put this space on a cue: place/ crate. That way, when an owner sees their dog getting overtired or overly aroused, they can cue the dog to go to a safe space. When the dog has a relaxing association with the space, it can be a great reminder to them that they need to take a break.

Relaxation training

When we feel stressed or anxious we often hear "Relax, take a deep breath." It's such a part of our culture that we may not even know why we offer up this advice; it just seems like the thing to do. In fact, controlling your breath is shown to affect the autonomic nervous system (the fight or flight system) which can decrease heart rate (Jerath et al., 2006). Deep breathing is a way to physiologically change your stress levels, and any person who knows that can reap the benefits. Allie has even cured her fear of flying by doing deep breathing exercises during take-off and landing.

If only we could tell our animal friends about relaxation techniques like this! The good news is, through training we can. Many trainers advocate relaxation training exercises. You can capture the sighs and deep breathing your dog does when they're relaxed, and reward them for those. Put it on cue and you can tell your dog "Relax, take a deep breath." You can capture any of the calming signals that a dog naturally offers that seem to calm them down: shaking off, yawning, stretching. Put them on cue and you have a way to encourage your dog to relax.

Dr. Karen Overall has developed an in-depth exercise for relaxation. This technique takes mat work to a new level by rewarding your dog for increasingly difficult tasks while they lie on their mat or blanket. Dr. Overall splits this protocol into different days, with each day focusing on different tasks to perform, all while your dog lies on their mat: jog in place, clap your hands, touch the doorknob, and sit calmly, to name a few. When looking at the later days it can seem daunting. "My dog is supposed to lie there when I ring the doorbell?" Through training and rewarding successive approximations it can be done! Essentially, by teaching dogs to perform a behavior—lying down in a settle—that relaxes the dog, and then having them practice that behavior while a variety of distractions happen around them, we are teaching the dog to relax in any environment.

Suzanne Clothier also has a relaxation protocol involving a dog lying on a mat. This protocol focuses on the handler's energy, relaxing after play, and increasing duration of lying on the mat. It is not as focused on remaining on the mat in an increasingly distracting environment as Dr. Overall's technique. Both have merits, and some dogs do well with one over another. The important thing is that both focus on teaching your dog to truly relax by giving them the agency to choose where, when, and how to do so.

Nutritional therapy

We talked a bit about the importance of nutrition in Chapter 2. There is preliminary research on the effects of nutrition on behavior; however, much more research is necessary to make determinative claims. Preliminary research detailed in Lindsay's *Handbook of Dog Behavior and Training, Volume I* suggests that corn, often used as a protein in commercial dog foods, may have an undesirable effect on behavior. As such, many in the field often recommend a lower-protein diet. However, it's uncertain whether it's the reduction of protein or the reduction of corn specifically that affects behavior. Conversely, some veterinary behaviorists are noticing a correlation between the percentage of carbohydrates in a dog's diet and the dog's tendency toward hyperarousal, so that needs to be explored as well.

There is still much yet to be researched in the field of canine nutrition, and as discussed in Chapter 2, significant variations among individual nutritional needs further complicate this issue. For these reasons, we caution our readers to avoid hanging your hat on any one nutritional therapy to "fix" any kind of behavior issue. But diet certainly can have an influence on behavior, so nutritional therapies are worth exploring. Just be sure to do so under the advisement of a trusted veterinarian or veterinary nutritionist.

Medication and supplements

For those dogs who are so anxious or otherwise suffer from maladaptive behaviors that it is impossible for them to relax—and attempts at enrichment and training have had little-to-no effect—anxiolytic supplements and/or medication may be necessary. Several holistic veterinarians suggest trying nutraceuticals prior to trying medication, as they typically have fewer side effects. That can certainly be true, but nutraceuticals are also less likely to be as effective as we need them to be, in which case medication may be appropriate. While some people are tentative about or completely against trying medication, in many cases it is truly necessary for dogs who have abnormal brain chemistry. Just as we wouldn't deny insulin to a person with diabetes, so too should we not deny these dogs medication. Our bodies can have a deficiency in any number of neurotransmitters just as easily as they can have a deficiency in any other body chemistry for which we would take medication. The only difference is that mental health is much more stigmatized in our society than physical health is, so people have this misconception that medications that help to regulate neurotransmitters are "toxic" or are simply a "crutch."

If you or your behavior professional suspect that your dog may benefit from any kind of behavior modification drug, we strongly recommend that you consult with a veterinary behaviorist, or at least have your veterinarian consult with a veterinary behaviorist. You can find the list of board-certified veterinary behaviorists at dacvb.org/about/member-directory. Alternately, every vet has access to a veterinary behaviorist through their laboratory services, such as Idexx or Antech. This is important because veterinarians are not required to take any courses on nutrition or behavior in order to graduate from vet school, so even though they may be highly competent and skilled veterinarians, they aren't necessarily knowledgeable about psychopharmacology. For this reason, the authors have seen many cases where the client's vet put their dog on an inappropriate medication or an ineffective dose and/or the dog was on medication but wasn't working through a solid, science-based training plan, and then the client thought that medication "didn't work" for their dog. Specialists exist for a reason: if your dog needs that expertise, utilize it!

Seeing the results

Calming enrichment is incredibly important to creating an ideal environment for your animal. It helps to lower those stress hormones, getting the animal further away from threshold, and helps reduce a variety of behavior problems. The authors often see specific cases in which calming enrichment is needed, and it often happens with adolescent dogs who have not yet learned how to calm themselves.

For example, Allie saw a client, Peanut, who fit this description. Peanut was a 7-month-old puppy when she first came to Allie. Her human mom was fabulously committed to her and provided her with plenty of mental and physical enrichment throughout the day. However, Peanut was still mouthing the children. Plus, her mom noticed that it was worse on days that she received more exercise! This is normally the opposite of what we see, as that behavior is often boredom-based, so more mental and physical enrichment usually curbs much of it.

What made Peanut different? A few things: Peanut had some underlying anxiety, likely from her history prior to being adopted by this family, and she had no idea how to calm herself down. Essentially she became an overtired, cranky toddler. Even in the 90 minutes that they spent together during their first appointment, Peanut just couldn't settle. She was always up and moving. Allie gave her a stuffed Kong and, while it distracted her, it by no means relaxed her. The only time she got close to relaxing was when her mom sat with her and gently massaged her, and even that was only for a few minutes. These observations, plus her history, led to a multi-pronged approach for treating her anxiety and inability to relax, a large portion of which included calming enrichment. Peanut is now not only capable of calming down but is able to choose this option without the guidance of her humans. Both Peanut and her family are grateful for the shift in energy!

Bear this in mind, if you are working with a dog who can't seem to calm down no matter how much exercise you give them: sometimes less is more. Sometimes, instead of trying to burn off more energy, we need to teach them how to monitor their own stress levels and choose to relax instead.

Chapter 11
INDEPENDENCE

Independence can be defined in several ways. The online Merriam-Webster Dictionary defines independence as "not subject to control by others," "not requiring or relying on others," or "not looking to others for one's opinion or for guidance in conduct." As defined, it is impossible for our pets to be 100% independent. After all, we have the opposable thumbs and money for dog food! In modern-day society, the overwhelming majority of pet dogs rely on us to meet their basic needs. They will always need our help in some capacity.

So when we talk about independence as a facet of enrichment—by which we mean a basic need that every dog has and that we must strive to meet—what exactly do we mean? And what's the difference between agency and independence? Aren't those synonyms? Not quite.

If you recall, agency is defined as the ability to have some level of control in our environment and be able to make choices that will result in a desirable outcome. As we referenced above, independence is defined as not requiring or relying on others, and not looking to others for guidance. So for example, a dog can be working with a person in a training session and have agency as to which behavior to perform, but in that instance would not be independent because they are in the midst of a collaborative process with their trainer. Conversely, a dog who is chained to a post in a yard and only periodically fed and watered by humans may have to scrounge around for whatever food and water they can find within the radius of their chain, in which case they would be quite independent but have very little agency in their life. They certainly didn't choose to be chained up and neglected! Who would? So we can see that independence is the ability to do things without guidance or instructions but, as with every facet of enrichment, agency is an important criterion for humanely meeting a dog's need for independence.

The notion of independence is easy to grasp when thinking of human examples. We understand the difference between the child who moves out at 18 and the one who moves out at 30. We enjoy working with the colleague who requires minimal direction more than the one whose hand we have to hold through the entire project. In general, our society values independence in our human counterparts. It's something we have come to expect of an individual who is old enough, healthy enough, and with average or better mental faculties.

While there is a societal norm for independence in adult humans, the same cannot be said of our pets. In fact, there's a broad spectrum of what people believe is appropriate when it comes to their dogs. One person complains that their dog is too aloof when they don't come when called but then immediately complains that they are too clingy for seeking comfort during a thunderstorm. Another person doesn't seem to care whether their dog responds to cues but expects their dog to live in their purse and go everywhere with them, and gets upset if the dog ever tries to leave their side to explore. Yet another person owns dogs specifically to do a job, and wouldn't dream of letting them into their house, let alone carrying them everywhere in a purse! Those two constructs at the extreme ends of the independence spectrum, aloof and clingy, are diametrically opposed. So, which is it? And, in terms of enrichment, which should it be?

The answer, as usual, is: it depends. At the bare minimum, a dog should be comfortable being left alone during parts of the day, and preferably be able to perform at least a couple of tasks without human supervision. But there is nothing wrong with working dogs spending the majority of their life making decisions on their own and spending relatively little time interacting with humans. Remember: as long as all of their needs are being met in some way, they are still living an enriched life.

Independence is not found in a magic pill. It is a skill set that must be taught, just like any other. We can't wave a magic wand and instantly make a dog independent. Creating a healthily independent dog requires time, patience, understanding, and work. Let's discuss how the authors go about creating a more independent dog in a mentally healthy way.

Comfort with exploring/being in the environment

This is one of the first components to focus on if your dog is stressed in a temporary or permanent living situation. If your dog is uncomfortable in the space you're working in then it's hard to teach them anything else! We've already discussed the notion of security: the feeling that you are safe. Setting up a secure space complete with calming enrichment is a great way to do this.

Once a dog is comfortable in their secure space it's time for them to branch out. Placing treats just outside their secure space encourages them to explore just a hair farther but also rewards them for said exploration. When that distance is comfortable you can place treats a bit farther and farther, even creating a treat trail if desired, until the dog is eventually exploring the entire space. You do not need to be involved in this exercise other than placing the treats and walking away. The point is for the *environment* to provide the reward, not you.

For a dog who is uncomfortable not in a living environment but a new space, asking them to perform already known life skills can be quite helpful. Play is another great option here. Our dogs, like us, feel more confident when they're asked to do something they know how to do well. For instance, say you're at a party where you don't know anyone aside from the host and are feeling a bit shy. Someone asks you what you do for a living and you find it much easier to open up. Why? Because you know your job inside and out, and thus feel confident talking about it.

Exploring is a wonderful exercise to build independence. Your dog gets to make their own decisions, problem-solve, and have fun without being glued to your side. If your dog does not have a bite history, off-leash exploration is a great option. Your dog absolutely must have a solid recall before they are allowed off leash. If off-leash exploration is not an option, either because of training, safety, or liability reasons, you may opt for a long leash that allows the dog to explore but still keeps them tethered to you.

Comfort being left alone

Part of having an independent dog means they're content when you're not there! We can help build this independence by providing a party for them when we leave: put out food puzzles, chewies (that you know are safe for your dog), items they can destroy (again that are safe), and fun toys they only get when you're away. This encourages them to play, explore, forage, and have fun while you're gone. When you come home, quietly pick up the party.

Foraging in particular is a great way to build independence, as it provides agency and problem-solving components. An easy way to have your dog forage when you're gone is to place small piles of their kibble around the house like a treasure hunt. You can use food puzzles that your dog already knows how to use as well. With this component of providing independence, make sure that all of the food is coming from the floor. If only the floor pays, your dog isn't as likely to explore higher up (like the table or counters).

If your dog has true separation anxiety that has been diagnosed by a veterinary behaviorist, these tips will likely not help you. Please work with a qualified, science-based behavior professional to help you work through this issue ethically and effectively.

Learning and being able to implement life skills

This section is key for pet dog independence! Part of being independent means understanding how to act in the world. We need to teach our dogs how we expect them to act in our human society if they are ever going to have a chance at fitting in. Most pet owners know that on a basic level: they take their dogs to training classes. That's a great first step! The next step is **proofing** those behaviors: practicing the same behavior in varying contexts so your dog can generalize the cue to any situation. Many trainers talk about the 3 Ds in proofing: duration, distractions, and distance. The authors like to bump that up to the 5 Ds and include different locations and different handlers. Proofing allows you to teach your dog what behavior is appropriate in what situation, thus allowing them to choose it on their own. No more micromanaging on your end!

Another crucial skill for our dogs to have is some sort of **default behavior**. This is a behavior that your dog does when they don't know what else to do or are awaiting further instruction. Sits and downs are common in pet dogs; in the zoo world stationing behaviors (like go to your rock) are more common. These behaviors can be quite strong. For instance, Allie taught Oso a default sit well before adopting him and has continued to use it now. When moving back to the Midwest, Oso encountered his first squirrel, which of course he wanted to catch! He tried screaming at it in the tree, but no luck. When he realized that that didn't work, he looked at the squirrel for a moment, and then sat down and looked expectantly at it. Sitting worked for everything else, why not try this?! Allie could then reward him for sitting and looking at the squirrel. To teach a default behavior, reward your chosen behavior profusely whether or not you ask for it. A default behavior is one of the only behaviors that we want them to perform whether or not we cue them to do it. Additionally, ask your dog to perform this behavior for anything they want: going outside, eating dinner, playing a game, etc. Once they realize that this behavior seems to work for everything, they'll be more apt to try it in new situations, like Oso did. Think of default behaviors as habits.

One extremely useful exercise that teaches a super useful default behavior is Dr. Karen Overall's relaxation protocol, which we discussed in Chapter 10. The authors find that those dogs who have started going through this protocol develop default downs and are able to choose that behavior in more difficult situations. It is also an example of immunization training, discussed in Chapter 3, which means that it helps boost confidence and therefore independence. This exercise provides a lot of bang for its buck!

Each household is different, and useful life skills will vary depending on the situation. For example, for some dogs, stationing away from the door when the doorbell rings is a valuable skill, while other pet parents want the dog to be right at the door when it opens. The skill itself is not the important part: it's that your dog knows what to expect and can perform. Some other common life skills include watch me, targeting, and stationing.

Ultimately, when deciding what skills to teach your dog, your goal should be helping them to build habits that enable them to make the choices you want them to make without needing prompting from you. Instead of thinking of what skills you think your dog "should" have in terms of what behaviors are "good" or "bad," think about what behaviors you *want* your dog to be able to perform automatically in order to most seamlessly fit into your household. In other words, think of their behavior in terms of *desirability* rather than *morality*. Teaching your dog these skills not only helps them to become more independent, it also enables your entire family—human and non-human—to live together more harmoniously.

Chapter 12

PROVIDING THE RIGHT ENVIRONMENT

Humans have known for a long time how important the "right" living environment is. We describe ourselves as city or country folk. We compare our hometowns to every other town we've lived in. We devote TV shows to finding the right home. Sometimes we move solely because we dislike how small or busy or unfriendly or industrial our town is, regardless of all the redeeming qualities it offers. And, we know that what's right for us is not right for the next person.

On a basic level, many pet owners understand the importance of the right environment for their pets. Time and again the authors hear that people don't want a big dog in an apartment in the city (which can be misguided, as many large breed dogs are more sedentary than smaller breeds!). Many pet owners also understand that environment is not solely location, that lifestyle is also part of the equation. The authors often hear that someone has opted for a cat, stating that they're not home enough for a dog (which can, again, be misguided, as cats require almost all of the same enrichment components as dogs). Some pet owners also understand the importance of finding a pet who matches their lifestyle: the marathon runner looking for an active dog, or the workaholic looking for a dog who is content to entertain themselves for several hours a day. Many people intuitively understand the effect of environment on their pets.

This chapter is dedicated to taking that intuition one step further. Environment can play a large role in a whole host of behavior challenges and can sometimes be a roadblock to solving them. It's impossible to list every factor that goes into the catch-all category of environment. Just as only the learner decides what's reinforcing, so too do they decide what's important or unimportant when it comes to environment. For instance, both authors grew up in green, lush areas of the United States. After living in the desert for several years, each realized how important greenery was to them. The absence of green plants and trees was actually mildly stress-inducing. On the other hand, both have met people who grew up in the desert and only feel comfortable when surrounded by rocks and sand. Those people would feel more stressed in the areas the authors prefer. While there are an infinite number of specifics that could fall under the environment umbrella (like the presence of greenery versus sand), there are several underlying general principles that can be discussed.

Reducing environmental stress

Different environments have different noises and noise levels, amounts of space, smells, sights, and activity levels. Cities, suburbs, and rural areas each come with their own typical surroundings, but environment is so much more than simply location. It's also the people in the household: how many, how old, their personalities, and their expectations for their pet. Other pets fall into this category, too! It's the social life of both the humans and the animals in the house: two- and four-legged visitors, parties, and dog parks. It's the routine and schedules. Allie even has a client whose dog's barking behavior changes depending on whether or not there's carpeting and rugs down! Environment is really an umbrella category for so many things in our dog's life. Just as specific things about our household and environment stress us out, so too does that happen with our dogs.

We've mentioned before that not all stress is bad stress. Eustress, or good stress, also exists, usually in the form of excitement. And while eustress is, well, good for the individual, it produces some of the same stress hormones as distress. What that means in terms of behavior is that eustress can add to behavior issues just as distress can. A dog who undergoes an inordinate amount of eustress may present as jumpy, mouthy, anxious, and/or reactive. A dog who undergoes an inordinate amount of distress may present as reactive, anxious, fearful, and/or aggressive. Thus, when we're talking about environmental stressors, keep in mind that we're talking about *all* stressors and not distinguishing between "good" and "bad."

While some dogs can thrive in any environment they're thrown into, many have trouble in certain types. Simply living in a certain environment can create or exacerbate a host of behavioral problems. While the authors have yet to see any research on this topic, trainers and behavior consultants typically anecdotally agree that there are trends. Leash reactivity runs rampant in parts of the country with an abundance of free-roaming dogs running up to on-leash dogs. Working breeds in apartments often display anxiety-based behavior such as stereotypies and destruction. Herding breeds often end up nipping in homes with kids. Dogs prone to anxiety tend to escalate in households with anxious people and erratic schedules. Note: while environmental factors are a component of behavior issues, they are not the only cause. We should not expect that all behavior issues will immediately disappear by simply changing environments.

How can we know if a dog will do well in a certain environment?

While trends exist, it can be difficult to accurately predict what sort of situation a dog will do well in. Many dogs surprise us, whether it be in desirable or undesirable ways. Or what sometimes happens is they choose a survival strategy when they are over threshold that we weren't expecting them to choose—fight when we expected flight, or flight when we expected freeze. For instance, Allie has a good friend who adopted a dog with a bite history against people; the behavior was fear-based and only presented with strangers or when the dog was startled. A few weeks after being adopted, he was having diarrhea and needed to see a vet. The trip was much earlier than his owner anticipated, and she hadn't yet started desensitizing him to the vet clinic. She was understandably concerned how he would do with the techs and vet. That's a lot of new people in a small space! He was fully muzzle trained and came into the clinic with his basket muzzle on. However, the dog surprised his new mom by choosing to freeze instead of fight. While we've discussed the implications of learned helplessness, it merited a sigh of relief in the moment.

That being said, people are constantly asking professionals to predict how their dog will do in a certain environment. What kind of dog should they adopt, can it meet the grandkids, is this truly a dangerous dog and are you willing to appear in court to testify one way or another? These are questions that can cause tension between professionals and their clients because the answer is rarely straightforward. We can never 100% predict how a dog will do in a certain environment. Behavior can absolutely never be guaranteed.

History, breed, age, and overall behavior should be taken into account when assessing whether a dog is appropriate for a certain environment. Various evaluations and temperament tests exist, and each has its own pros and cons. These typically test for sociability, responses to handling, excitement, startling, and resource guarding. To an expert who has performed hundreds of evaluations, these can help to predict future behavior based on past experience. However, recent research has spurred debate in both the shelter and behavior realms as to how much stock we should put in these tests. When studied, the results from these assessments were not as predictive as we would hope in terms of how tested dogs later behaved in their homes. It is not yet known whether that is due to the change in environment, relationship with the handler, or another factor. Additionally, while these tests can be quite useful for someone who has a large enough "database" to compare cases against, think about the mistakes someone with less experience will make along the way.

How can we offset the effects of existing environmental stress?

The obvious, least practical choice is to change the entire environment: move! While you may laugh at the prospect, it's not unheard of for people to move with their pets in mind. Allie was originally living in a townhouse without a yard when she adopted Oso. The complex housed many leash-reactive dogs and was in a town with a large occurrence of off-leash dogs. She knew before taking him home that this was not the right environment for a leash-reactive dog, but was moving to a more suitable environment a few months later. Since then she has only moved to single-family homes with fenced-in yards. Unsurprisingly, the behaviors got drastically better with the move, and it was easier to work on the remaining reactivity. Emily had a client living in the city with a leash-reactive herding-breed dog and had explained to her that it can take a while to see progress when there are so many triggers on walks. After several months Emily got a follow-up email. The client and her husband recognized that the environment was a large part of the issue, and decided that, instead of going through all the management and training necessary to reduce their dog's stress and meet his needs in the city, they preferred to move to a more rural area on some land. The dog has been great since!

Moving is not an option for the majority of situations. In those cases we need to decrease stressors as best we can. That can be accomplished through management, training, or both. Either way, the first step is to determine what your dog's stressors are, which a qualified, science-based behavior professional can help you with.

For example, some dogs are prone to stress during inclement weather. These dogs will likely display heightened stress signals for triggers that were previously minor. Other dogs, often with underlying medical distress, are more prone to stress at certain times of the day. For instance, those dogs who get upset tummies in the morning may show an increase in handling sensitivity at that time of the day.

Avoid trigger stacking

This phenomenon of stressors compounding upon one another is called **trigger stacking**. Trigger stacking happens to every individual, humans included. For example, let's say your alarm clock doesn't go off in the morning and you wake up late. Then you find that your dog was having digestive issues during the night, and you have to clean up diarrhea. After that your car doesn't start and you have to get it towed, only to find that it will cost $400 for a new alternator. You finally make it to work, at least an hour or two late by now, and your boss asks you why you're late. Normally, the two of you could have a rational conversation and you could explain reasonably what sort of morning you had. However, because all of those things happened prior to this stressful encounter, you explode and end up yelling at your boss. It was the straw that broke the camel's back. We've all been there, regardless of how long our fuses are.

Trigger stacking is not pleasant for anyone involved, including the individual experiencing it, and it takes a while to come back down from it both emotionally and hormonally. In fact, those stress hormones will be floating around your system for a while, making it more likely to have an impact in upcoming stressful situations.

This phenomenon is why managing environmental stress is so important. Every stressor your dog encounters throughout the day stimulates the production of even more of those stress hormones, making your dog more likely to go over threshold faster than before and take even longer to return back to their baseline. When working with dogs with behavior issues, it becomes even more important. The authors work with a large number of leash reactivity cases. In almost all cases the dogs also display reactivity through a window or door. Part of the training plan for these dogs requires managing or modifying their behavior inside as well, not just on a walk. Every time the dog sees a stressor through a door or window, the trigger stacking process continues to occur. The leash reactivity rarely improves completely without also addressing the exposure to stressors happening in the home.

The next step in offsetting environmental stressors is determining which triggers are avoidable and unavoidable. Life is rarely so black and white as that, so many people develop their own "scale of avoidability." This helps to prioritize which triggers can be managed and which need modification.

Using environmental management to reduce stress

Managing triggers involves avoiding or diminishing them. There are as many ways to manage behavior as there are behavior consultants in the world. Below are common management techniques for common undesirable behaviors:

- Reactivity at windows: put up blinds, curtains, window film, or wax paper

- Reactivity toward the doorbell: ask guests to knock, or take the dog outside prior to guests' arrival (so they can't hear the doorbell)

- Reactivity toward people entering the house: crate the dog away from the action or put them in a bedroom or bathroom with the door closed

- Resource guarding toward other dogs: feed in separate rooms (with the door closed), pick up toys, bones, etc., and only give separately

- Resource guarding from humans: don't take things away from your dog, toss a treat away from them if you need to get something out of their mouth

- Fearful of new places: keep them at home

- Fearful of new people: don't require them to meet every person who comes to the house, avoid going places where there are a lot of people

- New dog attacking older resident dog: rehome new dog or keep them separated until you can hire a behavior professional to help you improve their relationship

- Sound sensitivity: dampen upsetting noises by playing music, turning on the TV, or using a white-noise machine

This list could go on and on. Some people choose to manage certain triggers for the remainder of their dog's life—and that's okay! There are several triggers that are far easier to manage than modify, and if everyone in the household is content with this, then far be it for us to argue. Some triggers are also safer to manage rather than modify. For instance, a dog with a bite history against other dogs should never be a candidate for dog parks. Or expecting a severe resource guarder to share their food bowl with another dog is unrealistic. That environment is just not ideal for that dog.

When management isn't an option

Counterconditioning is required for unavoidable triggers, environmental and non-environmental. We discussed this form of behavior modification in previous chapters. Let's say that your dog really dislikes the mail carrier. We can countercondition to the mail truck and the person. Or your large apartment-dwelling dog is fearful of the stairs or elevator. We can countercondition to both or either.

Habituation

Many animals get comfortable with mildly stressful environmental triggers through **habituation**. This includes the diminishing of an emotional response through frequent, repeated exposure. In college, Allie lived in an apartment near train tracks, and there were several horse pastures adjacent to them. The adult horses were unfazed; the train had never hurt them and it became just something that happened near them. In the spring when the newborn foals were in the pasture, though, they would kick and buck and run away when the train went by. After a few weeks the foals habituated to the train and would join their elders in ignoring the locomotive. Habituation is effective and happens on a daily basis, and it can be a good strategy for some environmental triggers. However, it should only be used for mild stressors, and know that it will usually take longer to habituate than to countercondition.

Stressors take many forms in our dogs' environment, and it's up to us to determine what they are and fix them in some capacity, either through management or modification. When working with dogs with behavior challenges it is imperative to factor in the environment. There are likely stressors adding to or causing the issue that must be resolved in order to resolve the behavior.

Creating the ideal environment

As the old adage goes, "The best defense is a good offense." This applies to our pets' environment as well. While we've discussed how to mitigate stressors that already exist in our dogs' lives, we should focus on creating an ideal environment for every pet, not just those with behavior issues. By providing an ideal environment we will help to prevent behavior problems before they start.

The human factor

Humans are one of the biggest factors in our pets' environment. Recent studies indicate that dogs seem to think of their owners similarly to how human children think of their parents (Horn et al., 2013). Any adult will tell you how influential their parents were in their early development. Thus, we have the same obligation to create a loving, nurturing environment for our pets as we do for our children.

Dogs and human children both see the adults in their lives as a "secure base" from which they can interact with their environment. Horn et al. found that dogs stuck with a problem-solving task longer when their owner was present, regardless of whether the owner was silent or encouraging. Whether the person was their owner or a stranger mattered as well; results were dissimilar when testing with an unfamiliar human. What does this mean? Our dogs like us to be around! Recall as a kid that it often felt encouraging to work on your homework with a parent close by, even if they weren't helping you. Just knowing that they were there if you needed them provided a sense of comfort. From an environmental standpoint, this means that we should factor ourselves into the mix. Our dog is going through a new experience? We should be there! Our dog is going through training for the first time? We should participate! Being present in your dog's life is important.

We behavior professionals commonly say "Our stress adds to their stress." This is entirely true! A dog's sense of smell is amazing, and we are still exploring the many uses of our canine friends' noses. We're now using dogs to sniff out cancer, diabetes, and migraines. A less well-known profession for our dogs includes cortisol and adrenaline detection (aka stress hormones!). Dr. Nicholas Dodman is quoted in the *New York Times*, saying "Canines can detect rising cortisol levels in our sweat and breath" (Hollow, 2014). These dogs are going to work detecting the onset of panic attacks and fear. One dog, Cali, is even employed by a New Jersey special needs school to help their students.

While the majority of us don't have service dogs, that doesn't mean that they can't smell our stress. That, coupled with the fact that they see us as a secure base, means that when we're stressed about something, our dogs get stressed too. Allie experienced this just a few weeks after adopting Oso. While he was reactive on leash to other dogs and fast-moving humans when she first adopted him, he had no problem with vehicles passing. While on a walk one day Allie noticed a slow-moving vehicle. Growing up near Chicago, which has some of the highest crime rates in the country, including a higher-than-average incidence of drive-by shootings, she put her guard up. The vehicle passed her, then turned around and was now moving in her direction. Her heart started beating faster as she watched it approaching. What she didn't expect was Oso's reaction. He yelled at the truck—loudly. It was something she hadn't seen and wasn't expecting, and the only explanation she could think of was that he was feeding off of her stress. A few days later another truck slowed to a stop near them while Allie wasn't paying attention. The gentleman remarked how handsome Oso was and asked Allie about him. Similar scenario, but Oso stood calmly beside her while they conversed. No stress, no reaction!

Some dogs are more prone to this than others. Oso was highly sensitive to any person's emotional state when Allie first met him. Other dogs, it seems, couldn't care less when their owner is upset or stressed. A scenario that the authors often see, however, is the anxious dog paired with the anxious human. These cases can be difficult because they require the client to address their own anxiety in addition to their dog's. And, because they can smell our stress hormones, it's not enough to simply "fake it 'til you make it." Your dog knows when you're stressed, no matter how good you are at hiding it from other humans.

For this reason, the authors are cognizant of how their emotions might influence an animal they're working with. On days in which they're personally trigger stacked, the authors typically forego working on difficult tasks with their own animals. When managing dog playdates and playgroups they make sure that every human involved is truly comfortable. If any person thinks that it won't go well, they're kindly asked to watch from a distance. There have even been times when the authors struggled with separating past experiences with a dog from the upcoming playdate and have asked to remove themselves. Avoid self-fulfilling prophecies whenever possible! A large part of being "good with animals" means setting them up for success, even if that means setting aside your own ego and admitting that you're not the right person for the job.

Another reason it's important to be cognizant of your emotions when working with an animal is so you can avoid your frustration turning into punishment. Only the learner decides what's reinforcing and punishing, so even the common side effect of raising our voices when we're upset can be seen as aversive to many dogs. This phenomenon of redirecting our frustrations onto someone else is so common that we all likely know the phrase "taking it out on someone." We should avoid this with our animals! While still not ideal with humans, we can at least go back after the fact, apologize, and explain why we acted the way we did. We never get that chance with our animals. Our animals simply see it as "unpredictability." And as you will recall from Steven Lindsay in Chapter 3, "Family dogs habitually exposed to unpredictable/uncontrollable punishment are at risk of developing disturbances associated with the learned-helplessness disorder."

When we're talking about setting up the ideal environment for our dogs, we need to keep in mind that we are one of the biggest factors. Our behavior and emotions have the potential to make our animals feel safe, but also to elicit or magnify behavior problems. We need to be just as diligent about the human factor as we are about all other factors.

Predictability and control

There are many facets of dog behavior that are similar to human behavior. In Chapter 3, we explored in depth a need all species share: agency. As we discussed then, agency is a requirement for every facet of enrichment, environment included. We need to be mindful and proactive in building agency into our pet's environment.

Predictability and routine is another facet in which dogs and humans are similar. Both are creatures of habit. The presence of predictability and routine has long been touted by some of the best minds in the animal behavior field, especially for anxiety cases, and rightly so: they decrease stress hormones. Remember the 2009 study by Lefebvre et al. that looked at the effects of routinely given enrichment and sporadically given enrichment in 14 military working dogs we discussed in Chapter 5. Each set of dogs was given roughly the same amount of enrichment; the only difference was how predictably it was given. Unilaterally, the dogs who received their enrichment on a set routine were less stressed than those who received it sporadically. Because eustress and distress rely on the same hormones, it's unclear as to which is the culprit, but recall that an excess of both can lead to behavior problems.

Therefore, we should try to adhere to a routine with our animals as much as possible, not only with their daily schedule but also with their enrichment. This is easier for some households than others, but is not impossible for any household. Even if you can predictably provide just one or two things for your dog every day, that's better than nothing!

Multi-pet households

Multi-pet households are incredibly common in America. With that comes another type of behavior problem the authors often see: issues with other pets in the household. This is a complex issue that we can't address in any great detail in this book, but fortunately there are many other books written on the topic. What is applicable within this topic, however, is that a multi-pet household brings another layer to an animal's environment.

Adding another pet to your household is usually stressful for everyone. Because of this, the majority of professionals advocate management and slow introductions for new family members. This isn't just for your new pet to become adjusted (which usually takes months, not days); it's also because it takes time for the resident pet to adjust. Suddenly, and without their consent, a new animal is sharing the original dog's people, their space, their toys, their water, and in some households their food. It's equivalent to your college roommate getting a significant other. No one asked you, but now a stranger is sleeping over almost every night and drinking all the milk.

Management and slow introductions help to create a better environment for all pets when you add a four-legged family member. Additionally, management throughout the remainder of their lives together may be necessary for an optimal environment, depending on the relationships among the animals. This involves separating animals during feeding (regardless of resource guarding), setting up separate safe spaces, and giving them alone time. Even if you live with your best friend, you still need some time and space to yourself!

What else?

As we said earlier, environment is really an umbrella category that so many facets of enrichment fall into. In addition to what we've already recommended to create an ideal environment, remember to include the other aspects of enrichment as well. They are just as important! Providing your dog with agency, safety, security, mental stimulation, and physical exercise are all part of providing them with the proper environment.

Chapter 13
THE HUMAN ELEMENT

In the world of animal welfare, the most neglected animal is the human animal. We are so focused on making sure our companion animals' needs are being met, and that we are doing what's best for them, that we forget we are animals, too, and we also have needs. This is true across the board: from veterinarians to dog trainers to shelter and rescue workers to pet owners, and everyone in between. In putting the needs of our pets above our own, we aren't doing anyone any favors.

Those of us who work in animal welfare, or even those of us who volunteer, foster, or have pets with medical and/or behavioral special needs, are at a high risk for any of the occupationally-related stress response syndromes (OSRS) such as secondary traumatic stress disorder—also known as compassion fatigue—and burnout. These syndromes can cause, among other things, depression, fatigue, increased illness, nightmares, feelings of worthlessness or helplessness, feelings of being overwhelmed or trapped, and even suicide (Thomas and Wilson, 2004). In fact, the animal welfare professions are among the highest risk for suicide (Tiesman et al., 2015). In addition to the harm we do ourselves, when we suffer from one or more of these syndromes and don't take measures to heal ourselves, we aren't the only ones who suffer; the animals suffer, too. People suffering from one or more of the OSRS syndromes are more likely to make mistakes that can adversely affect the animals in their care. Research indicates that compassion fatigue can also cause caregivers to commit ethical violations when interacting with their charges (Gentry, 2007). Even though so far this research has only looked at caregivers of humans, this pattern is consistent among caregivers of non-humans as well. Feelings of frustration, powerlessness, and the inability to effect change frequently cause caregivers to handle animals roughly, ignore their emotional states, and become calloused to their misery. But how we treat animals isn't the only way their well-being is affected by ours. Most companion animal species, but especially dogs, are also masters at reading and responding to our body language and physiological states. In other words, when we suffer from one or more of the ORSR syndromes, so do they.

In addition to the pressures that are built in to animal care, as well as the ones we put on ourselves, we also put an enormous amount of pressure on each other. We all have strong opinions about what is best for our pets, and those opinions are often in conflict with others', which means that tribalism, divisiveness, and judgmentalism run rampant in the animal welfare community. As caregivers we want what's best for our wards, and due to our past experience and the information we have acquired over the years, we all think we have a pretty good grasp on what that may be. As a result, when we encounter people who do things differently, or do things in a way that we perceive as being dangerous or harmful, our natural impulse is to jump in and criticize and correct, and to try to protect the animals in their care. Even though that impulse is entirely understandable, the result is that everyone is criticizing and correcting everyone, all the time. A person can't post a picture online or ask a question without getting lectured, which creates an incredibly hostile and intimidating environment. If we, instead of criticizing the things we think everyone else is doing wrong, looked for and honored the things they are doing right, made learning a safe and fun endeavor, and made desirable behaviors easier and more enjoyable, we could make our lives and the lives of our comrades in animal welfare so much easier and better.

Meeting needs at both ends of the leash

In the meantime, this is our reality: when we are looking for ways to improve the lives of our pets, we not only have our own internal critic to contend with, but those online and in the real world as well. For this reason, it is crucial that we learn to treat ourselves with utmost patience and compassion. Otherwise we feel overwhelmed, we believe we are failures, and we end up quitting our animal-related jobs or rehoming our pets because we feel like we just can't do it anymore. By *feeling like* we're failing these animals, we end up psyching ourselves into *actually failing them*. If, instead, we use what we've learned about training to train ourselves, we can look at our behavior objectively and compassionately. We can figure out what our end goal is, and then shape our behavior toward our end goal.

The authors often say to our clients during behavior consults, "I can write the best training plan in the world, but if it isn't sustainable for you, it's worthless." This is where most people get overwhelmed: we try to do too much at once, feel frustrated and disillusioned when we can't do it all, and ultimately give up. Throughout this book, we've provided a lot of ideas and information about how to provide an enriching life for your dogs. While reading this, you may very well have felt overwhelmed, and perhaps thought to yourself, "Well, yeah, that all sounds nice, but how on earth can I possibly do all of this? With what spare time?" The rest of this book is devoted to practical and sustainable ways to provide the enrichment we've been discussing, but for now, let's focus on the mental games we play with ourselves. Winning the mental game is half the battle.

Behavior science applies to people, too!

Behavior science is a natural science just like physics and chemistry: it is universal. No one is immune to it. There are no exceptions. As sentient beings in this universe, we all follow the laws of behavior science just like we follow the laws of gravity. In order to better understand and change our own behavior, therefore, it's helpful to understand some of the most basic principles of behavior science.

Classical conditioning

Classical conditioning is the involuntary association between a stimulus (that is, a person, place, thing, or event) and a physiological response of some kind—in this case, emotional states. When we are trying to incorporate new habits into our lives, we are dealing with both the cognitive and the physiological types of learning, and believe it or not, the emotional learning is often the larger challenge. It usually isn't very difficult to learn *how* to perform the new habits, but it can be extremely difficult to *want* to do them. For this reason, our primary focus should not be changing what we do but changing how we feel. The easiest way to do this is to make the learning process easy and fun for ourselves—by pairing the act of providing enrichment with the feeling of enjoyment.

A good example of this is when Emily was trying to get the members of her local parrot society to start making more fresh foods and toys for their birds in order to improve their overall health and well-being. When Emily first started teaching classes and workshops about parrot enrichment and husbandry, a lot of people were understandably resistant to the idea of adding all this extra work to their already full schedules. So she and the other two co-founders began to organize social events centered around providing enrichment: toy making workshops, food making parties and co-ops. Several of the members would get together, eat, drink, and chat while making food, toys and other enrichment items for their birds. Before long, people started making parrot enrichment items on their own at home and organizing their own parrot parties with their friends. After a couple of years, avian vets in town started to tell Emily that they were noticing a clear difference in the health and well-being of their parrot patients as a direct result of the parrot society's efforts.

These changes didn't occur as a result of teaching people how to make toys and food. That part is easy; anyone can figure it out. They occurred as a result of changing the way people *felt* about making toys and food for their birds. And everyone won: the parrots, their owners, and their vets.

Make it fun for yourself. Start with things that are easy for you to incorporate into your existing schedule and pair them with activities you already enjoy. Organize your own enrichment parties or turn movie nights into movie-and-toy-making nights, or simply make your doggy quality time into doggy enrichment quality time. Take pictures of your enrichment efforts and share them online, so that your friends and colleagues can admire your hard work and ingenuity. Aside from enrichment parties, one of Emily's favorite ways to make enrichment fun for herself is to end her weekly house cleaning day by sitting down with some chocolates and a glass of wine and making toys while she watches a movie. Toymaking becomes her reward for cleaning her house. One of Allie's favorite ways to make enrichment fun for herself is to take her dog on a fun adventure hike so they both get to exercise and explore together.

Operant conditioning

In addition to classical conditioning, the other half of learning is operant conditioning: the cognitive process most people think of as learning. And as we've discussed previously, shaping is the process of rewarding the closest thing to the end-goal behavior that the learner can currently do. Then, when they're fluent at that, rewarding the next closest thing, until the learner can fluently perform the end-goal behavior. A good example of shaping in humans is learning how to play an instrument. First, you learn how to use the instrument. Then you learn the scales. Then simple songs. Then more advanced songs. And so forth. No one would put a brand-new violinist into the London Symphony Orchestra and expect them to succeed. It would obviously be much too difficult for them to perform at that level. We would start them with hand position, then when they were competent at that we'd teach them bowing, then we'd teach them to play the scales, then simple melodies, then more advanced melodies, then the finer points of bowing, and so on. It would be years before they could successfully perform with a professional orchestra.

While intelligence and other genetic factors may come into play, most learners who are of sound mind and body are perfectly capable of learning any task if they are skillfully shaped. Research has shown that learners who have been labeled as "stupid," "stubborn," or other such unpleasant characteristics are merely the victims of poor teaching methods and have been able to quickly master what they previously had not when placed in the hands of a skillful shaper (Chance, 2014). Many animal trainers are well aware of this and are perfectly capable of shaping animals of all species, personalities, and learning styles, and yet have difficulty applying the same principles to their own species, much less themselves. And certainly, anyone who works in animal welfare but has not been taught the art of shaping has no idea how to shape themselves. In our line of work, the authors frequently hear people say that they "just can't be trained" or they "are stuck in their ways." We submit that they simply haven't been taught how to teach themselves.

Learning how to provide our dogs with a more enriching life is just like any other skill: we will have more success in the long run if we teach ourselves how to do it through shaping. Make it easy for yourself. Start with things that are easy for you to incorporate into your existing schedule and practice doing them daily until they become a pleasant habit. Then, when that feels easy and painless, add a different or additional element of enrichment to your routine, and practice doing that daily until it, too, becomes a pleasant habit. And so forth. If you are patient with yourself and allow yourself to take on one new habit at a time, instead of trying to *all of the sudden* do *all of the things*, you will end up with a schedule that you can both sustain and enjoy, wherein both you and your pets have a happy, enriched life.

Training plans
A training plan is a step-by-step plan for how you are going to achieve your end goal. It is like a road map to your intended destination. While a training plan is just a guideline and shouldn't be adhered to too strictly—we do, after all, need to be flexible enough to go with the flow of each individual's learning process—it can be a powerful tool for setting ourselves up for success. Not only will you be able to map out a clear plan to get you where you want to go, you'll also be able to look back on how much you've already achieved. This can be enormously helpful on days where you feel overwhelmed and like you're failing. By looking at your training plan and seeing how much you've accomplished, you will be able

to silence your inner critic and receive a much-needed dose of reinforcement for a job well done.

Balance in all things

The authors have an adored and respected colleague who often jokes about having a made-up disorder that he calls Canine Partner Under-Enrichment Perception Syndrome, or CPUPS. He talks about his chronic anxiety that he isn't doing enough to enrich his dogs' lives, and often if we invite him to a social event he will say, "Sorry, I can't. I have to do XYZ with my dogs. You know...because I have CPUPS." While he is mostly kidding and is a generally happy, well-adjusted person, the authors have certainly encountered people whose "CPUPS" does adversely affect their well-being. Often, people who are in reality doing a stellar job of providing their dogs with a life abundant in enrichment feel constant, unmitigated guilt and anxiety that they are not doing enough. Sometimes they can put so much pressure on themselves to do more that they end up psyching themselves into compassion fatigue. We have even encountered people who unnecessarily rehomed their pets for fear of not being good enough owners.

Don't fall into the CPUPS trap. When writing your enrichment training plan, take into account the realities of your environment, schedule, and budget. Figure out a reasonable amount and type of enrichment you can provide. If you get to the end of your training plan and realize that you can realistically add more, then do that. Otherwise, observe your dog's behavior and body language in their daily lives to determine whether you are meeting their needs. If they are happy, well-adjusted, and engaging in all the species-appropriate behaviors they are designed to perform, you're doing a great job. Be happy with that. Be proud of that. Be content with that. Also bear in mind that providing enrichment for your pets isn't a "keeping up with the Joneses" situation. Some people may need to and be able to do more for their dogs than you do for yours, and that's okay. Likewise, other people might need less. Because the authors own their own businesses and have a lot of other projects as well, we regularly work more than 70 hours per week. With that work schedule, we can't provide as much enrichment as some people can, but we have found ways to provide enough enrichment and incorporate it into our busy schedules that our dogs' needs are being met, and they are happy and well-adjusted.

While there are certainly cases of a mismatch between dog and human, often it's more of a matter of bad perception than bad ownership. Yes, a person who lives in a high-rise condo and works 80 hours a week probably isn't going to provide the best home for a border collie puppy. But in

most cases, it's simply a matter of working smarter, not harder, and figuring out how to provide the most sustainable and effective enrichment
possible in your environment. Which is what we're going to discuss in
the next chapter.

Chapter 14

WORK SMARTER, NOT HARDER

Throughout the course of this book you have probably thought to yourself at least once, "This is all fine and good, but how on earth am I supposed to be able to *do* all of this? I have a life, you know!" In fact, the number one concern we hear from the shelters, rescue groups, veterinary hospitals, and individual clients we work with is whether or not enrichment (although it's usually couched as "enrichment-and-training") is sustainable. "Our staff is already stretched thin as it is." "I'm a single mom with a full-time job." "We're run by volunteers; all our dogs are in foster homes. We can't expect foster homes to do a bunch of extra stuff." "I suffer from a chronic illness and have trouble taking care of myself some days, let alone going above and beyond for my dog." "I travel a lot." Those are all valid concerns. So let's address them for these differing circumstances.

The average busy household, rescue, vet clinic, and foster home

The best place to start is by looking at what you already *have* to do for dogs in order for them to survive, and finding more enriching ways to do those activities. Earlier in the book we talked about the fact that every interaction is a training session; we all learn from every interaction we have with our environment. So the big question is, what do we want our dogs to learn from their interactions with us? By asking that question, we can often find ways to improve our dogs' lives without significantly increasing our workload.

Tweaking what you already do

For example, you already have to feed your dogs every day, which is why food puzzles are one of the first things we recommend to people who are trying to enrich their dog's life. You have to feed your dog anyway. It isn't that much more difficult or time-consuming to put food in a foraging toy or scatter it out on the lawn than it is to put it in a bowl. So why not start there? By simply changing your feeding method, you're already well on your way to enriching your dog's life.

Likewise, you have to provide your dog with exercise. That's already taking up a portion of your day. Why not incorporate mental exercise into the physical exercise you're already providing? What that might look like depends entirely on you, your routine, and your dog's preferred type of exercise. But given the many options described in previous chapters, there's almost always a way to simply add an extra element to what you're already doing to make it more of a mental challenge for your dog. For example, if walks are your thing, simply let your dog stop to smell the interesting smells. Trying to keep your own heart rate up? No problem. Simply walk in place while your dog sniffs. Or if your dog is more of a fetch fan, you could add a drop of diluted essential oil or other scent your dog enjoys to their ball to add that extra olfactory element to the game. Use a different scent each day of the week to mix things up and keep it interesting for them. If your dog prefers to wrestle and tug, teach "start" and "stop" or "take it" and "drop it" cues to turn their regular exercise routine into a de facto training session. Use a flirt pole to exercise all the muscle groups *and* teach self-control. No matter how you exercise your dog, adding these little twists will get you more bang for your buck without taking up any more of your time.

Your dog already needs a place to rest, such as a bed or a crate. Why not make that space as calming and comforting as possible by making that the place from whence all good things, such as meal time and chew time, flow? It takes no greater effort to put their food puzzle and chew toys on their bed than it does in the kitchen or wherever you typically offer those items.

What else is a regular part of your dog's routine? Can you think of ways to make what you're already doing more fun, challenging and species appropriate?

What You're Already Doing	How You Can Tweak It
You're already training your dog.	Try shaping and rewarding in successive approximations.
You're already feeding your dog.	Use foraging instead of a bowl.
You're already feeding your dog.	Teach the dog to wait before eating.
You're already letting the dog in and out of the house.	Teach the dog to wait before going through the doorway.
You're already walking your dog.	Let them stop and sniff things that interest them.
You're already walking your dog.	Take them on new routes and to new locations they've never been before.
You're already taking your dog on excursions.	Use that time to proof behaviors they already know.
You're already playing fetch or tug.	Use those games to teach "leave it," "take it," and "drop it."
You're already playing fetch or tug.	Add some kind of scent enrichment to the toy.
You're already providing a bed or crate for your dog.	Use that as their safe space and provide calming enrichment there.
You're already vegging out in front of the TV.	Use that time to make toys or prepare frozen licky treats.

Adding tiny extras

After you've gotten comfortable tweaking what you were already doing, the next simple step is to add quick and easy things to your schedule—nothing overwhelming, just simple little steps. Again, what this looks like from household to household will vary wildly; we all have vastly different lifestyles, and our dogs have different needs and personalities. However, here are some common strategies we recommend to clients on both an individual and organizational level:

- **Frozen licky treats.** Whether that is frozen stuffed Kongs or marrow bones, pupsicles or simply frozen cubes of low-sodium broth, this does require some extra prep work, but not an untenable amount. We recommend that pet owners have a minimum of three frozen items per dog to keep on rotation: one in use, one in the freezer, and one being washed.

- **5- to 10-minute training sessions.** Whether you're working on something practical, fun tricks, or free shaping, short little training sessions here and there can pack a powerful punch. They don't take up much of your day, but animals tend to learn faster when that learning happens in short bursts. Plus, you'd be amazed at how much 10 minutes of shaping wears a dog out!

- **Find it.** Set aside a handful or two of your dog's kibble. When you first come home after work, or when you let them outside to play, say "Find It!" and toss some of the kibble out as far and wide as you can. They'll spend a good 15 minutes *at least* on an Easter egg hunt looking for each piece of kibble, wearing themselves out in the process while giving you time to get settled.

- **Stinky t-shirts.** Wear a ratty old t-shirt you don't care about when you work out, then put that t-shirt on your dog's bed. It's a bed cover that smells like you: what a treat!

- **Scent of the day.** Create a spray bottle with a different scent for each day of the week, and quickly spritz your house before you leave for work. Every day will smell different!

- **Sound of the day.** Use the same concept with music or TV, so that every day your dog has something different to listen to and/or watch.

Of course, as has been discussed throughout this book, there are many ways to provide enrichment that are more elaborate or labor-intensive than these ideas. And certainly, if you can and want to pursue those options, that's fabulous. But even if you did nothing but these few simple exercises, you would get—and give—so much more for minimal effort.

You work long hours

For those who work long hours we can break up our enrichment into two categories: make the most of the time you have with them, and enrich them when you're gone.

Make the most of the time you have with them

We've talked about several forms of enrichment that will give you more bang for your buck. For training sessions, that would be shaping instead of modeling. For exercising, that could be flirt pole instead of walking. If you only have a few hours of consciousness with your dog, go for these activities instead. Getting the most out of those activities will give you more cuddle time, which is also important for the dogs who enjoy it!

Enrich them when you're gone

The great thing about much of the enrichment we've talked about is that you don't need to be there for it. Remember the "passivity" of some enrichment that we talked about in Chapter 6? Don't feel bad if you need to use more of those than types where you're involved! The great thing about our crepuscular canine friends is that they typically rest a lot in the middle of the day anyway. Great options here include saving some or all of their breakfast (in a food puzzle) for when you leave, leaving a "treasure hunt" of treats around the house, leaving a CD of calming music on, and spritzing some of their preferred scents on their bed. All of these will enrich your dog and take up very little of your morning routine.

Many people are worried about the extra time commitment required to leave enrichment for their dog in the morning. It doesn't have to be this way! For instance, Allie has a plastic drawer system so she can enrich her dog and get out the door quickly. One drawer is stocked with different chewies, one drawer with toys, and one drawer with items for him to destroy like crumpled up newspapers or egg cartons with treats inside. In the morning all she has to do is open each drawer and take something out for him. For an extra bonus, Allie feeds Oso part of his breakfast in a slow-feed bowl with his supplements and veggies, and the other part she puts in a food puzzle, which she then hides for him to find. This adds less than five minutes onto her routine and he's typically sleeping soundly by the time she gets home.

Another option for people who are gone an extra-long time is bringing in a dog walker throughout the day. This is recommended if your pup is home alone for more than eight hours. While they may be able to hold their bladder for that long, it's not that healthy to do so. This person could be a paid professional, a family member, or the neighbor kid down the street. Get this person involved with your enrichment plan and ask them to do something extra with your dog or simply leave more passive enrichment activities for your dog when they depart. If this person is willing to work with you and your dog, it means they care about both of you and want to help! Many people jump at the chance to do something more.

Some people choose to go the doggy daycare route. This can be a great option for dogs who enjoy playing with other dogs! Your dog is enriched while you're gone and you get to reap the snuggle time after. It's a win-win. This is only an option, however, if your dog already enjoys playing with dogs. This is not an appropriate option if your dog merely tolerates other dogs, only enjoys some dogs, or "needs to be socialized." Additionally, make sure that the doggy daycare you choose meets your standards when it comes to group size, how scuffles are taken care of, and any behavior modification practices, as outlined in Chapter 8.

You travel often

Enrichment for travelers will differ depending on whether or not you can take your dog with you. If you are able to bring your dog along, they are already getting lots of enrichment with all the new sights, sounds, and smells! You likely won't have to do as much mental exercise during these trips, but make sure to keep up the physical exercise. Additionally, while traveling can be exciting, it can also be stressful for your routine-oriented dog. Try to stick to your regular routine as much as you can and pump up the calming activities. This can be as easy as playing calming music from your phone and covering your dog's bed or crate tray with a smelly you-shirt on the trip.

Sometimes, though, you will not be able to travel with your dog. As we mentioned earlier with dog walkers, your pet sitter will likely be happy to help with your dog's enrichment! Show them how the food puzzles work and create a stockpile of items like Allie's drawer system for them to use. Leave simple instructions for very easy enrichment items; don't go overboard. Again, this is a great chance to use those more passive forms of enrichment. You can ask the same of a boarding facility as well, though they may provide their own enrichment. It never hurts to ask!

You are your own special-needs patient

In full disclosure, both authors suffer from chronic illnesses and know full well how difficult it can be to go above and beyond with their animals on days when they don't feel well. The first part of tackling enrichment in this category is tackling the voice in your head. Skipping a day or two of enrichment is not something to beat yourself up over! Your dog will be okay if you can only do the minimum some days. In fact, they may enjoy the extra cuddle time.

The next part of tackling enrichment in this category is figuring out what works for your abilities and your dog's needs. You can't run but you have a four-legged athlete? Try flirt pole from a swivel chair. You have a brainiac but can't get out of bed? You can shape from anywhere! Creativity shaping exercises are a great game for days when you're incapacitated. Your non-dog-savvy significant other is taking care of the dog today while you rest? Stockpile frozen Kongs and items for destruction on days you feel well to prepare for these instances. On days when Allie is too tired to work with her dog but he's raring to go, she plays a modified form of "find it": she grabs the bag of treats from the table next to the couch (her usual perch), takes a few treats, and chucks them onto various areas of the floor. Oso has a blast and is tired after a few rounds, and Allie never has to get off the couch.

Providing enrichment for your dog doesn't mean your quality of life has to suffer. It's all about finding the right balance in a way that's enjoyable for both of you. Keep in mind, though, the importance of truly working smarter. The authors so often find that people try to make their dog's routine complicated or convoluted because "it's what they're supposed to do." They often hear of people taking hours at a time to walk their dog several miles when a much shorter flirt pole session would do the same thing. Or trying to train for an hour at a time when their dog only needs 10 minutes. Don't do something just because you think it's what you're supposed to do. Monitor your dog's behavior to determine if they like the activity, if it is beneficial, and how much of it is necessary to achieve that benefit. Chances are you're doing more than you need to in some categories and could pare down some activities and devote that time to others—or to yourself!

Chapter 15
PRACTICAL ENRICHMENT FOR SPECIAL NEEDS DOGS

When going over all the various types of enrichment with clients, colleagues, shelter workers, and boarding facilities, the most common troubleshooting questions that crop up have to do with how to apply these concepts to dogs with special needs. These dogs experience a broad range of limitations—either physically or psychologically—so that what might be safe for a healthy, neurotypical dog may go horribly awry otherwise. To be honest, this topic is so vast it could fill its own book. However, in this chapter we will briefly touch on the most common issues we encounter and different ways to navigate through them.

Dietary restrictions

By far the most common medical issue that the authors encounter is food allergies. Many clients tell the authors, "My dog has to be on a special diet, which they don't like very much, so I can't use food in training or enrichment."

Fortunately, that isn't true! In fact, we can use training and food puzzles to help increase a dog's taste for their prescribed diet. How do we do this?

First, we need to get a list of approved foods from the dog's vet. Even if a dog is on a strict food trial, the vet or veterinary nutritionist overseeing the case can recommend a small list of foods that are still okay for the dog to eat while on the food trial.

Once we have that list of foods, we can offer small pieces of the food to the dog and observe their response. Dogs are not like adult humans: they don't save the best for last. Whatever they eat first is what they like most. If they eat all the food indiscriminately, then congratulations! You've got lots of options. Otherwise, reserve the food(s) the dog ate first for your enrichment plan.

Using the Premack Principle to encourage eating

Once we've identified the dog's preferred food, we can then employ the Premack Principle, which is a behavioral phenomenon where high-probability behaviors are used to reinforce low-probability behaviors. In other words: "If you eat your veggies, you get to eat dessert." Although in this case, when the dog eats a piece of the prescription food, they then get the high-value treat. If a dog really doesn't like the prescription food, you may need to start further back than that: if you sniff the food you get the treat. Or, if you touch the food you get the treat. Or, if you lick the food you get the treat. But eventually, eat the food, get the treat. You can then play a nose work game: find the kibble, eat the kibble, get a treat.

By doing this with dogs, they can actually learn to enjoy their prescribed food. You can then use it for regular training sessions, reserving the treats for high-distraction or high-stress training scenarios. Additionally, you can use food puzzles just as you regularly would, perhaps sprinkling in a few treats to keep it extra engaging.

Emily had a client whose dog, Charlie, had extreme allergies and had been put on a prescription diet. His vet said he could only have the prescribed food and a list of certain fruits and veggies. As it turned out, one of the veggies on the list was sweet potatoes, which Charlie loved. So we cut up sweet potato into tiny pieces the size of almond slivers and used those for training, nose work, and food puzzles. His owner couldn't believe how much Charlie loved dried sweet potato, and was even more surprised when Charlie started to love and work for his prescription food as well!

Allie had a client with a dog named Coolio, who also had severe food allergies. The owner didn't want to feed her dog a kibble diet, so she worked with a veterinary nutritionist to come up with a whole-food diet that was both nutritionally balanced and appropriate for the dog's allergies. Allie showed her how to use frozen food puzzles so the wet whole-food diet wouldn't gunk up foraging toys: frozen Kongs, frozen stuffed marrow bones, pupsicles in muffin tins, and frozen smeared cookie sheets became the dog's primary means of eating. Allie also showed her an article by Eileen Anderson on how to make dog treats in a pyramid pan. Riffing off of this idea, the client ran some of Coolio's food through a food processor to make it smooth, then baked it as indicated. Coolio loved meal time and training time, his medical needs were met, *and* the client was able to avoid using kibble as she desired.

When food is not an option

So yes, we can absolutely still use food in an enrichment plan, even for dogs with severe food allergies. But what about when food isn't an option?

Emily had a client who was extremely ideologically opposed to using food in training. From the first moment they met, Emily could tell that this was an emotionally charged topic for the client. Rather than arguing with him or trying to change his mind, Emily worked with him to meet the dog's needs. This dog also had severe food allergies and liked his prescription food just fine, but the owner was vehemently opposed to using it in training, or even in food puzzles. Fortunately there are so many other ways to meet a dog's needs, and they worked around it. They used the dog's favorite ball as a reward in training and also incorporated as many functional rewards as possible. For example: go to your mat and sit-stay for one minute in order to get your meal. Wait at the door in order to go outside. If you keep the leash loose we get to keep walking; if you pull, we stop walking; if you voluntarily check in you get copious verbal praise. And so forth. For nose work, we used diluted animal urine (which can be purchased online) as the scent and his favorite tug toy as the reward for finding the scent. We also used the flirt pole for mental and physical exercise and self-control training. The dog got to go on lots of greenbelt hikes and had a blast. He had plenty of doggy friends and structured playdates. Even though we know that food is a powerful and efficient training tool and working for food is an important factor for a learner's well-being, our primary goals are to meet the dog's needs and the client's goals, *not* to proselytize. At the end of the day, both the dog and the client were happy, and the dog now has a high quality of life *and* lots of important life skills. That's what matters most.

Restricted activity and limited mobility

Another medical challenge the authors frequently encounter is dogs who either have advanced arthritis or some kind of paralysis or paresis (partial paralysis), or need to temporarily be on restricted activity due to a medical treatment of some kind, such as heartworm treatment. For these dogs, especially if they're young, we often see increased irritability, restlessness, vocalization, and mouthiness because their physical exercise needs aren't being met. They have so much pent-up energy they're climbing the walls! So how can we help them?

For dogs with paralysis or paresis, physical therapy is super important. A veterinary physical therapist can guide their client on how much and what types of exercise will best meet the dog's needs. They'll often recommend swimming, core strengthening exercises, specific types of obstacle course work, and sometimes even massages. In the meantime, these dogs can still do scent work, food puzzles, tug games (if vet approved), training sessions, and structured relaxation time. We also like to send these clients to balanceit.com to get a recipe for reduced activity, to make sure their dog's nutritional needs are being met without giving them extra energy that would be difficult to burn off.

For dogs who temporarily need reduced activity, the challenge is getting through those months with no exercise more strenuous than short potty walks. Again, they could benefit from a dietary adjustment, but the name of the game for these kids is a metric ton of mental exercise. They need to work for every single piece of food they get through food puzzles, training, and nose work. If we can't wear out their bodies, wearing out their minds is a must. Structured relaxation time with scent and sound therapies can also be hugely beneficial, ideally at predictable, consistent times of day. And finally, the sudden reduction in physical activity can make their muscles stiff and uncomfortable. Anyone who has been hospitalized or has taken a long road trip knows what prolonged inactivity feels like, and how uncomfortable it can make us. Daily massages can help to alleviate this discomfort. Information on how to provide dog massages can be found in the Resources section in the back of the book.

Emily had a client who is an actual saint. This man found a juvenile Rottweiler mix on the side of the road who had been hit by a car. When he took this dog in to his vet clinic, he learned that he had no microchip, was unneutered, had four broken legs, a broken pelvis, and to top it all off, three different kinds of intestinal parasites and heartworm disease. To his unfailing credit, he decided to adopt the dog and pay for his treatment. He named the dog Roscoe. The treatment and recovery process was extremely difficult for Roscoe, particularly because of his size. As time wore on he became increasingly loud, extremely mouthy, and super cranky. When Emily first met him, he had a manic look in his eye and he grabbed a nearby blanket and shook it out of redirected frustration. Emily taught her client about shaping for creativity, but since the dog couldn't move around she picked up a toddler activity center from Goodwill and brought it to her client's house. In addition to the other enrichment activities mentioned above, Roscoe and his owner played shaping games on the activity center. Roscoe learned to slide wooden pieces around, flip lids up and down, hit the light-up buttons in a variety of patterns, pick up the phone part and hang it on one of the bars, and all kinds of other tricks. By shaping behaviors on this activity center, he was able to use his brain in countless ways without ever needing to move any part of his body other than his head and neck. Roscoe's owner saw a dramatic improvement in his behavior once he had his daily routine of free shaping, food puzzles, massages, and structured relaxation time with calming scents, sounds, and lickable treats. Almost a year later, when Roscoe was finally given a clean bill of health by his vet and could resume normal physical activities, he and his owner already had such a deep bond and excellent communication skills that basic manners training took no time at all.

Neurological movement disorders
Some dogs will have movement disorders—such as ataxia, dystonia, or myoclonus—most often as a result of a disease like distemper or a traumatic brain injury like being hit by a car. Although the authors don't often see these cases in private practice, we worked with a large number of them at the sanctuary where we met. Since this sanctuary took in many feral dogs from the desert, it wasn't uncommon for some of them to have survived distemper and been left with some type or combination of movement disorders. For the most part, these dogs could be treated like any other and could do everything a neurotypical dog could do. However, in the more severe cases we'd often notice that these dogs would get frustrated at the difficulty of controlling their limbs and would sometimes give up during training sessions, while working on food puzzles, or while playing with toys. So what to do? The solution wasn't just to not have them do any of those things. If you'll remember from the discussion on constructive discontent in Chapter 7, the key is to make it challenging enough that they must put forth an effort, but not so challenging that they get discouraged and give up. What's the solution here? Since movement itself is already a big challenge, make everything easier.

Emily worked with a dog named Bentley who was the sweetest, cutest 50-pound lovebug of all time. But his puppyhood battle with distemper left him with severe movement disorders, which caused him a great deal of frustration. The name of the game for him was making things easier. Instead of leaving toys on the ground for him to try to pick up, we'd hand him a tug toy and hold the other end still. Emily would give him bigger-than-usual treats to get off the ground, since they were easier targets. She would ask him to perform more realistic behaviors: instead of expecting him to target to two fingers as she does with most dogs, he could target to anywhere on her thigh. But also, when he seemed to have a really bad day, Emily loved to sit on the floor of his run with him and give him some deep pressure massage. She loved to watch him visibly relax after a few minutes of touch therapy.

Compulsive behaviors

Compulsions are repetitive behaviors performed to an unhealthy extent, such as licking oneself to the point of injury, tail chasing, or incessant barking. In the overwhelming majority of cases, compulsive behaviors have an underlying medical cause. As such, our top priority is to take the dog to the vet to get a diagnosis. If the veterinarian is unable to find a medical cause, the next step is to have the vet consult with a veterinary behaviorist, who can help them to do more thorough sleuthing.

Regardless, it is imperative that you not punish your dog for exhibiting these behaviors. Even though compulsive behaviors can be extremely annoying or even embarrassing for the dog's owner, it's important to remember that the dog isn't doing these behaviors for fun or out of stubbornness. They are doing these behaviors because they already feel pain or distress. Adding more pain and distress may indeed stop the external behaviors in the short term, but it isn't solving the problem and, more often than not, it increases the dog's distress. Driving a problem further underground where we can't see it externally isn't the same thing as fixing the problem. We should always strive to fix problems rather than suppress them.

Because the compulsive behavior(s) occupy most of their time, these dogs lack behavioral diversity. So, in addition to addressing the underlying medical cause, we should focus on teaching them a wide variety of other behaviors to perform: foraging, trick training, any kind of dog sport—it really doesn't matter. As long as they're busy behaving in other ways, they won't have time to fall back on their compulsions. Depending on the type and severity of compulsion, we may also need to manage their environment to prevent the compulsive behavior(s) from occurring, but veterinary care and a smorgasbord of desirable behaviors are the pillars of addressing compulsions.

Emily belongs to a local Facebook group for dog trainers of all methodologies. Because she doesn't believe in cramming unsolicited information down people's throats, she typically chooses to lie low in the group and doesn't intervene in conversations about behavior and training unless asked. However, she was tagged into one conversation where a new trainer posted about her dog Millie, who was compulsively licking her paws, and the woman didn't know how to stop the behavior. Multiple people suggested that she use an electronic collar to shock the dog every time she licked her paws. At that point, Emily informed the woman that compulsions usually have a medical cause and recommended that she take Millie to the vet instead of shocking her for already being in pain. The woman did as Emily suggested and, sure enough, Millie has a food allergy. The woman ended up hiring Emily for a consult after she and her vet had isolated the allergens, changed Millie's diet, and treated the secondary bacterial infection. They worked together on teaching Millie some life skills to better cope with her health issues, and because the underlying medical cause had been addressed first, progress was rapid. Although Millie will always struggle with allergies so treatment and management will be an ongoing journey for the rest of her life, for the most part she is now a happy, healthy, skilled dog, and her owner has become a compassionate, knowledgeable dog trainer in her own right.

Anxiety and other behavioral disorders

Just as in humans, anxiety is an extremely common mental illness in dogs. Many people scoff at the idea that dogs can have mental illnesses, but we have reached a point in medical and technological advancement where the evidence is irrefutable: mental illnesses exist, and they exist across species. The cultural stigma against mental illness with regard to humans is exponentially magnified with regard to non-humans, but if we are to be both effective and humane in our approach to behavior modification, we must come to terms with the reality that our bodies are chemical factories, and those chemicals can be imbalanced. No one bats an eye if they hear that an imbalance of chemicals being produced by the pancreas or thyroid needs to be treated medically. We call those imbalances diabetes and hypo- or hyperthyroidism, and we receive medical treatment for them. And yet, when the imbalances occur in the brain or the adrenal glands, why is it so much more difficult to acknowledge that these, too, are diseases that must be treated?

The vast majority of problem behaviors—reactivity, aggression, anxiety, phobias, extreme shyness, and hyperkinesis, for example—are rooted in some type of mental illness. Just as some cases of diabetes or heart disease can be addressed with lifestyle changes alone, so too can some of these behavior disorders be addressed solely with an enrichment plan that includes training and environmental management. The specifics of how we'd address each behavior disorder lies beyond the scope of this book, but this, at its heart, is what behavior consulting is: determining the underlying function of the problem behaviors, assessing the dog's environment and history to analyze which of the dog's needs are and are not being met, and creating a treatment plan that ensures that all of their needs are met. We treat the whole animal, not just the problem behavior.

That said, just as there are some cases of diabetes and heart disease that cannot be addressed with lifestyle changes alone, and require medication either temporarily or for a lifetime, so too is that true for mental illnesses. Sometimes behavior disorders cannot be resolved without medication. Sometimes medication isn't necessary but makes the treatment process faster, easier, more humane, and more sustainable for the owner. Sometimes medication temporarily helps until the completion of the treatment plan renders it unnecessary. Sometimes medication is necessary for the lifetime of the animal due to structural abnormalities or permanent insufficiencies. In any case, if the treatment plan alone isn't yielding desired results, rather than blaming the dog, or yourself, or the client, or the training method, seek the guidance of a veterinary behaviorist. The intersection of medicine and behavior is their specialty; no one is better suited to address these cases.

These are just some of the many medical and behavioral issues that may create additional challenges when it comes to enrichment, but the best way around this is to focus on what the needs are and then get creative about how to meet those needs given the challenges present. If you're out of ideas, that's what community and colleagues are for. Don't be afraid to reach out and ask for help. And as always, work in conjunction with the dog's vet to ensure you don't make any recommendations that conflict with theirs!

Chapter 16
PRACTICAL ENRICHMENT IN SHELTERS AND RESCUES

Early in this book we discussed that much of the research done on enrichment comes from the zoological world. Caretakers saw the need to provide more for those animals kept in captivity, in order to care for their mental and emotional needs in addition to their physical needs. While this has long been known in the zoological community, those trends are now making their way into the animal sheltering community. The authors work with many shelters and rescues and, indeed, this community is where their passion lies. A common question from the organizations they work with is: "How do we provide enrichment quickly, easily, and cheaply within the time and budget constraints we have?" This chapter is devoted to answering that question.

How important is enrichment to shelter animals?
Hopefully by now you understand how acutely necessary enrichment is for the well-being of all animals in our care. Shelter animals are no different. In reality, an argument could be made that shelter animals require *more* effort to provide enrichment than their domestic family counterparts; their environment typically provides less social interaction, less agency, fewer opportunities to use their minds or truly, fully relax. This increases their chronic stress. Aside from caring for these animals' mental, emotional, instinctual, and physical needs, enrichment can, in theory, provide for a better adoption and retention process. Meeting an animal's needs typically creates a more confident, calmer animal who is usually a more appropriate member of our society and exhibits fewer undesirable behaviors. This is what adopters want to have in their homes!

We can use enrichment to help these animals to reach their potential, thus allowing for a smoother adoption transition and creating an animal adopters want to keep.

Few studies exist on the efficacy of enrichment on shelter animals. Graham et al. (2005) looked at olfactory enrichment in the form of different essential oils and found that dogs rested more, were less active, and were less vocal when stimulated with lavender and chamomile scents. Allie performed a study on enrichment in shelter dogs for a senior thesis and found that stuffed Kongs increased rest and decreased vocalization (Bender et al., 2013). Herron et al. (2014) looked at the effects of food puzzles and training on shelter dogs and found that the program being studied increased desirable behaviors and decreased typically undesirable behaviors. Gunter et al. (2019) found that short-term fostering in the form of overnight sleepovers reduced stress in shelter dogs. While the research is currently limited, it seems to point to enrichment decreasing stress and increasing behaviors that adopters find desirable.

The authors collectively have thousands of personal anecdotes regarding the efficacy of enrichment in aiding shelter adoption. A favorite of Allie's is Fillmore. Fillmore had a habit of mouthing—*hard*. Needless to say he was not a caregiver favorite in the beginning and needed help before he would be ready to go home. Fillmore had an ally in his caregiver, Jacquie, who worked with Allie tirelessly to meet Fillmore's needs and teach him a more appropriate way to interact with humans. Fillmore was adopted thanks to his growing team of human confidants and has been perfectly behaved from day one in his forever home. One of Emily's favorite anecdotes is a Harrier named Freedom. Freedom had been at his shelter for a year, being either overlooked or adopted but then immediately returned. People accused Freedom of being stupid, stubborn, aloof, and annoying. He would spend hours pacing or running around in circles, baying at the sky. He didn't make eye contact with people, didn't enjoy being petted, had a hard time standing still, and even had a hard time learning to sit. His caregivers, who were fairly proficient at dog training, and the volunteer dog trainers who helped out at the shelter, could not figure out how to get him to sit—by luring, shaping, or even modeling. They couldn't even capture the behavior, because Freedom never sat on his own; he was either standing or lying down. Emily got Freedom started on nose work to give that scent hound a job, and free shaping to get his brain working on something other than his repetitive patterns; she also shaped eye contact so that he would look at people when they called his name and built the duration so he could stay focused on them. She also recommended structured daily relaxation periods with scent and sound enrichment and a frozen licky treat. Everyone but Emily was shocked to discover that Freedom was neither stupid nor stubborn nor aloof, but was actually a smart, affectionate, engaged dog once his needs were being met. And after a few weeks of free shaping, once he had learned "how to learn," teaching him to sit was a breeze. He learned it in under five minutes. He was adopted a short time later and he and his family adore each other.

Our favorite shelter enrichment techniques

The authors are continually astounded by how similar shelters and rescues are throughout the country. Each deals with the same issues on varying scales and levels, has similar programs, set-ups, and even personalities. However, each organization also has its own quirks, and the details vary, especially with the day-to-day operation. As such, it's impossible within the span of a single book chapter to directly apply a practical guide to every shelter's operations perfectly. And in reality, most of the options we've discussed within these chapters can be applied to a shelter and especially a rescue setting. Instead we'll discuss unique practices that can be applied to most situations (sometimes with a bit of ingenuity) with a concentration on easiness and getting the most bang for your buck.

Scent work, described in Chapter 6, is one of those exercises that really does give you the most bang for your buck. Most dogs tire after 10 to 15 minutes of searching, and the authors have used scent work in conjunction with other activities to help alleviate stress and resulting stereotypic behavior. With the short time frame needed, small space requirements, and the incredibly cheap budget requirements of some cardboard boxes and smelly treats, this activity is a "must" in shelters as far as the authors are concerned.

Food puzzles, especially DIY options, typically offer another great return on investment. Choose sturdy options like PVC pipes, Buster Cubes, and Kong Wobblers. These can all be sterilized and reused for the next dogs who come along. DIY options can be made out of disposable items for often no money, and you don't need to sterilize them. You need to feed the dogs in your care anyway, so this is a great option to provide enrichment within the confines of daily routine! Emily created a DIY toy-making instruction manual for the sanctuary she worked at so volunteers could make food puzzles for the shelter dogs according to the unique specifications of the organization. That way the onus wasn't on staff to make food puzzles for all their dogs; volunteers could make a large volume of safe and appropriate toys with minimal supervision from the staff. Each organization could do something similar and incorporate it into their volunteer program. Pro tip: invest in a funnel. It will make filling food puzzles so much easier.

Playdates and playgroups allow you to mentally and physically exercise and socially enrich multiple dogs at once. They also give you more information about the dogs in your care so you can more effectively place them in adoptive homes. Definitely a win-win! There is a common misconception that running playgroups is hard or requires a special program or a large investment with a professional. Save your money! All you need are a few people skilled in reading dog body language who have the confidence to start trying dogs together. There is no one "right way" that works for every single dog or human. Additionally, many groups get bamboozled into purchasing lots of "management" tools that can increase the cost of operating a playgroup program. The authors' favorite tools are a bucket of water and a carabiner. Chances are you already have those lying around your shelter; no need to purchase fancy equipment if your playgroups are run efficiently, ethically, and safely. More information about how to run safe and healthy playgroups can be found in the Resources section at the back of the book.

Games like fetch, tug, and flirt pole are fantastic for physical exercise and will help to get your dogs adopted! Dogs who do not respond to play solicitation from potential adopters are not likely to be adopted by those people. Figure out each dog's favorite game and toy (it takes just a few minutes) and ask volunteers to play that game with them. The dog will be more willing to play their special game with an adopter if it's a regular part of their routine!

Training for shelter enrichment

Training is huge for shelter enrichment. Training can provide agency, independence, mental stimulation, and confidence. Many choose not to train because it seems hard or because they think they need a lot of time to do so. Both are untrue! "Click for quiet" is an incredibly easy and quick exercise that truly anyone can do and will make a big impression on potential adopters walking into a quiet shelter. Training can come in the form of individual sessions, but many shelters choose a group class setting if they have access to a willing trainer to lead those classes. These classes allow you to capitalize on the trainer's time and knowledge base by having multiple dogs worked with at one time. More information about easy training options are found in the Resources section at the back of the book as well.

Often the authors hear something along the lines of trepidation from shelter staff when it comes to letting volunteers train. "They'll mess it up!" That's valid. Volunteers and inexperienced staffers could scare a sound-sensitive dog with the clicker; frustrate a dog by not setting up clear criteria, having a low rate of reinforcement, or poor mechanics; overly arouse a dog; or even poison training in general. All of that could happen. However, in our experience, the worst things we've seen volunteers do is teach something that we didn't want that then had to be untrained. In reality, much of basic manners training is quite simple, and most people can muddle through and make progress even if it's not as fast or clean as an experienced handler could do it. It doesn't need to be perfect to be effective enrichment! That said, being selective about which dogs you offer to volunteers as training candidates, creating a solid volunteer training program, and providing clear direction for your volunteers goes a long way toward having this modality be successful.

The authors have created several "training how-to" resources for volunteers, including quick info guides to clicker training, simple training plans for basic manners, and more in-depth training plans for more complicated training. They've also compiled several binders full of information that can easily be given to a volunteer to do—some coordinated by the volunteer's skill level! An esteemed colleague created dog-walking "training lanyards," which have simple tasks volunteers can do while walking the dogs. Never underestimate the power of simple, physical instructions that volunteers can refer back to while working.

Tips for working within your budget

The biggest tip that the authors can provide in this category is so simple it's often forgotten: ask for help! Often the authors see organizations that, for whatever reason, choose the hardest route when trying to implement enrichment programs. They try to purchase brand-new food puzzles and the latest no-pull harnesses for every kennel, and hire experienced training staff right off the bat. There is nothing wrong with these actions— if you can afford them! But when you're first starting out a new program, ask your community for help. The authors often hear excuses for this like "They won't understand why we need this," "No one will give us that," or "They'll just get us the wrong thing." We get it. We've been there. And, luckily, we've learned from our prior mistakes that caused those statements to be true at that time. To be successful you will need to make your benefactors understand *why* you need something and how it will help the animals, and then make it incredibly easy for them to donate exactly what you want.

Allie created a daily enrichment program for the dogs and cats at one of the shelters she worked for. She kept costs down by centering it on foraging (as many of the other aspects of enrichment were already covered) and by using garbage as the main form of food puzzles—things like empty water bottles, toilet paper rolls, and paper bags. She set out to ask their volunteers and benefactors to donate their trash. Knowing that she would need to convince them that it was worth it to save those items and make a trip to the shelter, she created videos and took pictures of the animals using their enrichment items and shared them on Facebook and the shelter website. The animals were clearly having a blast, and Allie included commentary about how important these foraging options were to their mental health. Soon Allie had more items than she knew what to do with, a growing social media audience, and some of the program's aspects were being included in the Karen Pryor Academy shelter course. Allie made it easy to donate by literally asking for garbage and repurposing it, explaining how it helped the animals, and showing potential donors what their contribution meant to the animals. And for the time constraints associated with DIY? She asked volunteering groups to make up items for the next two months (which was all the storage area allowed for).

When it comes to purchased items, the authors are huge fans of online wish lists that link to easy-to-use online purchasing sites. We hear many shelter staff hesitating to ask for enrichment items because they're afraid donors will get them the wrong item and staff will spend more time disposing of, donating, or repurposing said item. If you want something, ask for exactly what you want and provide a link to the item for easy purchasing. You will get what you want the majority of the time (some people will still go rogue and buy you things you don't want or need) and you've made it easy for your donors, as they can usually choose to ship it right to your shelter! Throw in a "thank you" video of an animal using the item and you're bound to get more shipments.

Items are not the only things you can ask your community for. Many professionals are willing to donate their time and expertise to your cause. If you're (unfortunately rightfully) worried about the quality or experience level of those donors (though we'll also remind you that beggars can't be choosers), seek out relationships with respected area professionals and ask for their help. Chances are, if your shelter is large enough, that you already have some professionals volunteering for you who you may or may not know of. Trainers, groomers, vet techs, and even canine massage therapists often choose to volunteer at their local shelter. Both authors do! Some professionals will choose to keep their profession quiet so as to enjoy just spending time with the animals and "not working," but their skills will often give them away. Asking never hurts, but be understanding and respectful if a volunteer chooses to remain at their current level instead of helping more within their profession. Many professional schools are now opting to have their students work with shelter animals as a way of gaining experience. Inquire about partnering with those programs.

Our second tip is to be creative. This goes for donation requests, DIY items, programs, anything! You know your community and shelter best. If your community is active, ask a local running group to get your dogs out for a run. If your community is artistic, ask local artists to donate items for a silent auction with the funds going toward agility equipment. So often we confine ourselves to what's been done or how a "normal company" would operate. While in many ways non-profits should operate like a for-profit company, they have the advantage of being able to ask for donations, sponsorships, grants, and acts of goodwill, and they generally have their community wanting to help and wanting to see them succeed.

Recruiting and optimizing volunteers

The authors could devote an entire book to incorporating volunteers into your programs. Volunteers, while so widely wanted and requested, are so often underutilized or underappreciated. Many organizations have a culture of "staff versus volunteers," in which volunteers are seen as ignorant and unhelpful and staff are seen as cold and uncompromising by their respective other sides. The authors have held almost every role imaginable in various non-profits, and while they understand where this divide comes from, it's time to say enough is enough! We need to band together to complete our goal of helping the homeless animals in our care. And that starts with incorporating our volunteers more.

Of the whole book this section may be the scariest for shelter staff. Let's take a moment to address the all-too-common elephant in this room. Giving your volunteers more duties, especially important duties, can be scary. "What if they do it wrong? They can't possibly do that!" We get it. We, too, have had volunteers let dogs escape, start dog fights, break very clearly set protocols involving aggressive dogs or those with zoonotic diseases, and generally be detrimental to daily operations while under our watch. It's easy to become jaded to the whole prospect of volunteers, and it's easy to make blanket rules that affect everyone due to those incidents. But realistically those volunteers comprise such a small subset of your overall population. We cannot blame the actions of the few on the many! Nor should we impede the responsibilities of the many because of the misguidance of the few. That's a good way to frustrate your great volunteers, make them feel inadequate (when most are not), and ultimately have them find a new place to volunteer where they feel more respected.

The authors are not saying that we should allow everyone a free-for-all. On the contrary! In working with and traveling to many shelters, the authors have found that objective, tier-level, skill-based systems that have a large base of volunteer training opportunities, and take responsibility for volunteer actions, are typically the most effective.

These systems allow volunteers to move up through the different tiers or levels by proving they have the skills necessary to complete those tasks. Tiers or levels are typically based on the types of dog (who the staff categorize into each tier level, usually after a formal or informal evaluation), and/or by what activities the volunteer can do with the animal. Each shelter does this advancement a bit differently, but the authors have observed that the most effective systems require an objective handling and skills testing portion. An objective test diminishes the effects of playing favorites or not passing a volunteer because you don't mesh with them. The test makes it obvious if the volunteer is ready to handle dogs at a higher skill level or perform more advanced skills. Many of these advancement strategies also require attending a certain number of volunteer continuing education events. That's something we can definitely get behind!

Allowing your volunteers to perform duties based on their skills addresses the largest concerns the authors hear about volunteer involvement: safety, competency, ability, knowledge, and taking advantage of the skill set you have available. The objectivity allows the staff to be seen as impartial when making advancement decisions. The inclusion of additional training quenches the thirst for knowledge that so many volunteers have and helps them to feel like they're gaining more from their position.

Within the most successful tier systems are usually quite varying roles, and that too makes sure that you are using everyone to their utmost potential. There are volunteers who (willingly!) will file your adoption contracts, answer basic phone calls, clean kennels, and input data. Indeed some of the most helpful volunteers the authors have had were those who never touched the animals and were happy to not do so! There are a myriad of different roles a volunteer can participate in regarding enrichment, depending on their skill level. These are just a few that the authors have successfully implemented in different organizations:

- **Storyteller**: A volunteer sits outside a dog's kennel or in a room with a dog and reads aloud to them. Great for kids, less able-bodied volunteers, one-time volunteers (like those with company volunteer groups), and those with developing handling skills.

- **DIY enrichment master**: A volunteer creates DIY enrichment items based on diagrams, instructions, and materials provided to them. Emily has created several binders with step-by-step instructions complete with pictures for these roles and we've even seen short videos created! Great for kids, less able-bodied volunteers, one-time volunteers (like those with company volunteer groups), and those with developing handling skills.

- **Enrichment distributer**: A volunteer distributes daily enrichment items. Great for volunteers who have just a few minutes to spare but really want to make a difference.

- **Kennel manners trainer**: A volunteer works on desirable kennel presentation such as standing quietly at the front of the kennel through the gate. Great for volunteers who are interested in training and are still developing their handling skills.

- **Dog walking liaison/kennel concierge**: A volunteer coordinates and handles taking dogs in and out of their kennels for other dog walking volunteers. This is a wonderful solution for shelters who struggle with their dog walkers putting on walking equipment, routinely have dogs escaping, or are working with in-kennel manners. Great for more experienced volunteers looking to get into more of a leadership role.

- **Playgroup coordinator**: A volunteer is in charge of running playgroups, including choosing the dogs, finding other experienced volunteer handlers to help, and making decisions within the group. Great for experienced volunteers who are looking to do something more with their volunteer shift.

- **Scent work trainer**: A volunteer is in charge of playing scent work games with different dogs. Great for volunteers who are looking to do something more with their volunteer shift and may be working on their training skills.

- **Shy-dog class trainer**: A volunteer is in charge of running classes designed to benefit the shelter's shy dogs.

- **Behavior helper**: A volunteer helps work through a training plan set up by an experienced behavior professional. Great for experienced volunteers who are looking to do something more with their volunteer shift.

Because enrichment has such a wide array of components, we can get quite creative when finding ways to recruit volunteers to help with implementation. We can also use volunteers to solve problems, such as the dog walking liaison above. Instead of focusing on what a volunteer can't do, ask what they can do for you instead. You'd be surprised by what helpful volunteer tasks you can think of once you shift your mindset! And while it may take a bit of work in the beginning to train and support volunteers on a new task, it will more than make up for itself in the long run.

Chapter 17
PUTTING IT ALL TOGETHER

When first presented with all of this information about enrichment—the history of it, the science behind it, and all the various aspects of its implementation—it's not unusual for people to feel a bit overwhelmed. At a recent workshop the authors gave, one of the attendees approached Emily after the enrichment presentation with a dazed look on her face. "I feel so guilty," she said. "I've had dogs my whole life and I don't do any of this stuff with them. I've never had food puzzles or toys or done any training. They've always seemed happy, but now I feel bad! Have I been a bad dog owner this whole time and didn't even know it?" Emily asked this woman more about her life and routine with her dogs. The woman lived out in the country on a couple of acres. She had goats, horses, and chickens. Her dogs had always had unlimited indoor/outdoor access, so they came and went as they pleased. They liked to sleep inside when the weather was cold, but on warm nights they preferred to be outside with the goats. The dogs liked to keep an eye on the goats and chickens as the unofficial herd guardians, but also accompanied the woman when she took her horses out on trail rides. They wandered off the trails to explore, but generally stayed close by. She had always fed her dogs a good diet and taken them to the vet, and only bathed them if they got caked in mud or sprayed by a skunk. Sounds like the idyllic life for a dog, right? That's because it is! After walking through all the aspects of enrichment with this woman and learning that all of her dogs' needs are being met, Emily's advice to the woman was: "If it ain't broke, don't fix it." The woman felt so relieved and walked away with a huge smile on her face.

If you have a lifestyle that already lends itself to meeting all of your dog's needs, you don't need to add a bunch stuff to their routine for the heck of it. What matters is *that* their needs are being met, not necessarily *how* they're being met.

On the other end of the spectrum, however, was a client of Allie's who had two American Bulldogs named Mork and Mindy. With such comedic names you'd expect the dogs to be total goofballs, but when Allie first met them she was struck by how serious they were. They didn't engage much with either Allie or their owner. They were both very obedient, following every command as soon as it was given, but seemed aloof. The woman had sought Allie's help because both dogs performed compulsive behaviors to the point of self-injury: fly biting, licking the sides of their crates until their mouths were raw, and licking themselves raw. This poor woman had gone through the wringer trying to figure out why both of her dogs had these issues. Thousands of dollars at multiple vets yielded no obvious medical cause. Two years' worth of food trials and diet changes proved equally fruitless. She bought each dog as a puppy from two different but equally reputable breeders, so a genetic basis was less likely.

Finally one of her vets referred her to Allie. Allie learned that the woman had been raised to believe that humans should establish themselves as the alpha and have complete control over the dogs at all times. They slept in their crates at night, and during the day while the woman was at work. She took them out in the morning for walks on both a prong collar and an e-collar. Any attempt on the dogs' part to explore their environment or greet humans or other animals was swiftly and consistently corrected, so they learned from a very young age to not engage with their surroundings. When they got home they ate from their bowl, then went back in the crate. In the evenings, the same walk and feeding routine occurred, then they spent the evening obediently lying on their designated mats until bedtime, when they went back to their crates for bed. It was immediately apparent to Allie that these dogs had no idea how to use their brains. They had spent their entire lives being told what to do and where to go, and any attempt to explore or problem-solve had been punished. The woman loved her dogs very much and had done the very best job she could to raise them right and take good care of them, and she thought that by teaching them strict obedience she was being a responsible dog owner. But it was that complete lack of agency in their lives that caused them to engage in the self-destructive behaviors. Allie gently explained that dominance theory is a myth, and about all sentient beings' need for enrichment and agency. She worked with her client to put together an enrichment plan that included teaching the dogs how to problem-solve, how to use their noses, how to explore, and how to make choices. She taught her client how to reteach the dogs all of their basic manners, but this time in a way where the dogs were the ones choosing to do the behaviors instead of being commanded to do them. The client was amazed that she could get the same level of obedience from her dogs while still letting them choose! By the end of their time together, the dogs were no longer performing any of their old compulsions and had developed the big, goofy personalities that American Bulldogs are known for. A few months later, Allie received a touching email from the client thanking her for her help. She said she had always loved her dogs, but she realized now that she hadn't ever actually *known* them before. She didn't know that such depth of communication and mutual understanding was possible between humans and non-humans, and getting to see their personalities blossom and their minds come alive was one of the most joyful experiences of her life.

The message here is clear: it's important that we not just *think* that dogs are living happy, fulfilled lives. We must objectively assess the various aspects of their lives to *know* whether or not all of their needs are being met. We can do this by creating an enrichment chart for our dogs like this:

Aspect of Enrichment	Is This Need Being Met?	Agency?	Priority	Plan of Action
Health/ Veterinary				
Hygiene				
Diet/ Nutrition				
Physical Exercise				
Sensory Stimulation				
Safety				
Security				
Instinctual Behaviors				
Foraging				

Social Interaction				
Mental Exercise				
Independence				
Environment				
Calming				

To use a chart like this to greatest effect:

- In the "Is This Need Being Met?" column, write out the specific ways in which it is being met.

- In the "Agency?" column, be honest with yourself in answering this question: "Does this dog have some modicum of choice and control in this aspect of their life?"

- Look at the areas on your chart that could use improvement. Figure out the priority of which ones you want to focus on improving and which ones can wait until later. In the "Priority" column, assign those aspects a number, 1 being most important.

- In the "Plan of Action" column, write down the ways in which you intend to improve that category.

- After you've filled out your chart, objectively assess the outcomes of your efforts. One way to do this is to use the SPIDER protocol that was developed for zoos. You can use it as casually or comprehensively as you want! The SPIDER protocol is provided in the Resources section.

To give an example of how this chart might be used, Emily created this one for her dog, Brie. Let's give a little background on Brie before we get started. You'll recall from earlier in the book that Brie was a feral dog living on a Native American reservation in the Arizona desert for the first year of her life. She was then brought to the sanctuary where Emily worked, and Emily adopted her a few months later. At the time, Emily lived on three acres that backed up to Bureau of Land Management land. For the first year and a half, Emily had to do an extensive amount of training with Brie to address her resource guarding, reactivity, counter surfing, predatory behaviors toward Emily's parrots, and boredom-based destruction, as well as to teach her a solid recall, since Brie would hunt and kill wild rabbits and birds as she had on the reservation for survival. Brie eventually became a mostly-normal pet dog, proficient at living in a home, and a few months later Emily moved to a major city to go back into business for herself again. With this background in mind, here is her enrichment chart, which we're presenting outside of the table format for ease of reading:

Health/Veterinary
Is This Need Being Met? Yes: daily medication for autoimmune disorder.
Agency? Yes: trained voluntary participation in medical treatment; go to low-stress handling vet.

Hygiene
Is This Need Being Met? Yes: no baths unless muddy, but ear cleaning as needed.
Agency? Yes: trained voluntary participation in ear cleaning.

Diet/Nutrition
Is This Need Being Met? Yes: special nutritionally balanced whole-food diet to reduce incidence of autoimmune flare-ups.
Agency? Yes: rotate through proteins when she gets bored with current flavor.

Physical Exercise
Is This Need Being Met? Yes: she and Copper run around and play to the point of panting for at least a couple of hours per day.
Agency? Yes: play is instigated by dogs, not me.

Sensory Stimulation
Is This Need Being Met? Yes: outdoor sights/smells/sounds; leave TV on for dogs when they're home alone; toy textures.
Agency? Yes: outdoor play is instigated by dogs, not me; toys are left for dogs to find and select at will.

Safety
Is This Need Being Met? Yes: house and yard are dog-proofed; dogs are not left outside when we aren't home.
Agency? No: if Brie had her druthers, she'd have unmitigated access to the trash can and the world at large.

Security
Is This Need Being Met? Mostly: while certainly more confident than she used to be, she still has fear responses to certain people and situations.

Agency? Yes: with the exception of rare situations at the vet, she is never flooded; escape is always an option and I have taught her to leave a stressful situation on cue.
Priority: 1
Plan of Action: Continue working on her reactivity training.

Instinctual Behaviors
Is This Need Being Met? Yes: she is allowed to bark at the neighbor's outdoor cat for short periods of time during certain hours of the day in accordance with local sound ordinances; she is provided with chew toys and gnawable snacks.
Agency? Yes: all engagement is self-instigated.

Foraging
Is This Need Being Met? Mostly: due to my schedule I'm not always consistent with setting up her treasure hunt.
Agency? Yes: foraging opportunities are left for dogs to find and select at will.
Priority: 3
Plan of Action: Get a separate freezer for animal enrichment only so I can prepare a month's worth at a time for greater consistency.

Social Interaction
Is This Need Being Met? Yes: she has lots of human friends and, being dog selective, has a select few dog friends.
Agency? Yes: with the exception of the occasional new staff member at her vet's office, she is never forced to interact with people or other dogs.

Mental Exercise
Is This Need Being Met? Mostly: foraging and reactivity training, but since moving and going back into business for myself I've really slacked off on shaping and nose work sessions.
Agency? Yes: she always has choice and control in training and foraging.
Priority: 2
Plan of Action: Create space in my schedule to regularly work on shaping and nose work.

Independence
Is This Need Being Met? Yes: homegirl is a strong, independent woman! She also has several default behaviors.
Agency? Yes: see foraging, social, and play above.

Environment
Is This Need Being Met? Yes: window film on front windows reduces her stress; sound therapy when home alone; structured relaxation midday on Emily's office days and days off; enrichment throughout house and yard.
Agency? Yes: see above.

Calming
Is This Need Being Met? Yes: our home environment allows and encourages Brie to rest midday.
Agency? Yes: she decides when to take her siesta.

Of course, writing out these details in a chart isn't necessary. We can do this in our heads if we prefer to. But for anyone who is feeling overwhelmed or unsure, this can be a clear, objective way to look at our dogs' lifestyle, make sure their needs are met, and create a priority list and plan of action that feels manageable.

Charts can also be a helpful guideline for shelters, boarding facilities, and board-and-train facilities. While too labor intensive to do for each individual dog, it can be helpful to use this to assess the efficacy of the facility's enrichment program and look for areas of improvement. And of course, if an individual dog poses a particular challenge, this chart could be helpful for objectively assessing how well their current schedule is meeting that dog's needs.

But remember: sustainability is key! As we discussed in Chapter 12, one of the most common reasons people give up and fail is they take on too much at once, get overwhelmed, and decide this is too hard and they can't do it anymore. That's why the priority column is crucial. Focus on improving one thing at a time. When your current project becomes a well-integrated part of your routine, then you can tackle the next thing on the list.

And finally, remember to revel in your success. As previously discussed, as a species we humans tend to only notice the things that aren't working well, that aren't succeeding, that aren't going exactly as we planned. We take for granted the things we do that are gloriously successful, the ways in which we've really improved, the miles of progress we've made. If we spend all our time punishing ourselves for the areas of remaining growth opportunity without ever reinforcing ourselves for all the areas of existing success, we are far more likely to give up altogether. Why? Because, by definition, the only behaviors that continue or increase are those that are being reinforced. That's the other benefit of creating enrichment charts: not only can you identify potential areas of improvement, you can also have a visual record of all the ways in which you're already doing a stellar job. Positively reinforce yourself every step of the way and you'll experience a lifetime of success at enriching yourself and the dogs in your care.

REFERENCES

Abrantes, Roger. Critical reasoning—on aggression and dominance. (February 22, 2017) Retrieved from https://ethology.eu/critical-reasoning-on-aggression-and-dominance/ April 2018

Barlow-Irick, Patricia. *How 2 Train A ___*. CreateSpace, 2012

Beals, Katherine. Email interview with the authors, October 12, 2017

Bekoff, M. et al. "Life History Patterns and the Comparative Social Ecology of Carnivores." *Annual Review of Ecology and Systematics*, Volume 15 (1984)

Bender, Allison J. Independent Study 490H: "The effects of environmental enrichment during the holding period of shelter dogs on rate of adoption." Retrieved from https://lib.dr.iastate.edu (published January 25, 2013)

Berns, Gregory S. et al. "Scent of the familiar: a fMRI study of canine brain responses to familiar and unfamiliar human and dog odors." *Behavioral Processes*, Volume 110 (2015)

Bland, Sondra et al. "Stressor controllability modulates stress-induced serotonin but not dopamine efflux in the nucleus accumbens shell." *Synapse*, Volume 49, Issue 3 (2003)

Bosch, G., Hagen-Plantinga, E., and Hendriks, W. "Dietary nutrient profiles of wild wolves: Insights for optimal dog nutrition?" *British Journal of Nutrition*, Volume 113, Supplement (2015)

Bowman, A. et al. "The effect of different genres of music on the stress levels of kennelled dogs." *Physiology & Behaviour*, Volume 171 (2017)

Bradshaw, John. *Dog Sense*. New York, NY: Basic Books (2012)

Braem, Maya et al. "Development of the 'highly sensitive dog' questionnaire to evaluate the personality dimension 'Sensory Processing Sensitivity' in dogs." *PLOS One*. 12(5): e0177616 (2017)

Brayley, Clarissa and Montrose, V. Tamara. "The effects of audiobooks on the behaviour of dogs at a rehoming kennels." *Applied Animal Behaviour Science*, Volume 174 (2016)

Brown, Joel S. et al. "The ecology of fear: optimal foraging, game theory, and trophic interactions." *Journal of Mammology*, Volume 80, Issue 2 (1999)

Cafazzo, Simona et al. "Dominance in relation to age, sex, and competitive contexts in a group of free-ranging domestic dogs." *Behavioral Ecology*, Volume 21, Issue 3 (2010)

Camacho, E.M. et al. "Association between socioeconomic status, learned helplessness, and disease outcome in patients with inflammatory polyarthritis." *Arthritis Care and Research*, Volume 64, Issue 8 (2012)

Carlstead, Kathy and Shepherdson, David J. "Alleviating stress in zoo animals with environmental enrichment." *The Biology of Animal Stress*. Ed. G.P. Moberg and J.A. Mench, CAB International (2000)

Chance, Paul. *Learning and Behavior, 7th Edition*. Belmont, CA: Wadsworth, Cengage Learning (2014)

Channel 4. "Patrick Speaks" YouTube, November 12, 2014. https://youtu.be/AHfC6jqBhkk

Chaouloff, Francis. "Effects of acute physical exercise on central serotonergic systems." *Medicine and Science in Sports and Exercise*, Volume 29, Issue 1 (1997)

Ciribassi, John and Kelly Ballantyne. "Compulsive Disorders: Have You Considered GI Involvement?" *Veterinary Medicine*. April 1, 2013. http://veterinarymedicine.dvm360.com

Cooper, Laura and Foster, Irene. "The use of music to aid patients' relaxation in a radiotherapy waiting room." *Radiography*, Volume 14, Issue 3 (2008)

Curio, E. "Proximate and developmental aspects of antipredator behavior." *Advances in the Study of Behavior*, Volume 22 (1993)

De Niet, Gerrit et al. "Music-assisted relaxation to improve sleep quality: meta-analysis." *Journal of Advanced Nursing*, Volume 65, Issue 7 (2009)

Delaney, Sean. "FAQs" Balanceit.com, Davis Veterinary Medical Consulting, https://secure.balanceit.com/info/helpfaq.php

Delaney, Sean. Email interview with authors, October 25, 2017

Dey, Sangita. "Physical exercise as a novel antidepressant agent: possible role of serotonin receptor subtypes." *Physiology & Behavior*, Volume 55, Issue 2 (1994)

Diego, M.A. et al. "Aromatherapy positively affects mood, EEG patterns of alertness and math computations." *International Journal of Neuroscience*, Volume 96, Issue 3-4 (2009)

Diener, Carol I. Dweck, Carol S. "An analysis of learned helplessness: Continuous changes in performance, strategy, and achievement cognitions following failure." *Journal of Personality and Social Psychology*, Volume 36, Issue 5 (1978)

Dillitzer, N. et al. "Intake of minerals, trace elements and vitamins in bone and raw food rations in adult dogs." *British Journal of Nutrition*, Volume 106, Supplement 1 (2011)

Dodman, Nicholas et al. "Effect of Dietary Protein Content on Behavior in Dogs." *Journal of the American Veterinary Medical Association.* Vol. 208, No. 3 (1996) https://europepmc.org/abstract/med/8575968

Duranton, Charlotte and Horowitz, Alexandra. "Let me sniff! Nosework induces positive judgement bias in pet dogs." *Applied Animal Behaviour Science*, Volume 211 (2019)

Eilam, David. "Threat detection: behavioral practices in animals and humans." *Neuroscience and Biobehavioral Reviews*, Volume 35, Issue 4 (2011)

Erickson, Kirk I. et al. "Exercise training increases size of hippocampus and improves memory." *PNAS*, Volume 108, Issue 7 (2011)

Field, Tiffany et al. "Massage reduces anxiety in child and adolescent psychiatric patients." *Journal of the American Academy of Child and Adolescent Psychiatry*, Volume 31, Issue 1 (1992)

Field, Tiffany et al. "Cortisol decreases and serotonin and dopamine increase following massage therapy." *International Journal of Neuroscience*, Volume 115, Issue 10 (2005)

Gentry, Jack E. "The Effects of Caregiver Stress Upon Ethics at-Risk Behavior Among Florida Licensed Marriage and Family Therapists." Florida State University Libraries (2007) Available at: https://diginole.lib.fsu.edu/islandora/object/fsu:168465/datastream/PDF/view

Graham, Lynne et al. "The influence of olfactory stimulation on the behaviour of dogs housed in a rescue shelter." *Applied Animal Behaviour Science*, Volume 91, Issues 1-2 (2005)

Grohmann, Kristina et al. "Severe brain damage after punitive training technique with a choke chain collar in a German shepherd dog." *Journal of Veterinary Behavior*, Volume 8, Issue 3 (2013)

Gunter, Lisa et al. "Evaluating the effects of a temporary fostering program on shelter dog welfare." *PeerJ*, Volume 7 (2019)

Gvaryahu, G. et al. "Filial Imprinting, Environmental Enrichment, and Music Application Effects on Behavior and Performance of Meat Strain Chicks." *Poultry Science*, Volume 68, Issue 2 (1989)

Hammack, S.E. et al. "Overlapping neurobiology of learned helplessness and conditioned defeat: Implications for PTSD and mood disorders." *Neuropharmacology*, Volume 62, Issue 2 (2012)

Handelman, Barbara. *Canine Behavior: A Photo Illustrated Handbook*. Wenatchee, WA: Dogwise (2008)

Herron, Meghan E. et al. "Effects of environmental enrichment on the behavior of shelter dogs." *Journal of the American Veterinary Medical Association*, Volume 244, Issue 6 (2014)

Hillman, Charles H. et al. "Be smart, exercise your heart: exercise effects on brain and cognition." *Nature Reviews Neuroscience*, Volume 9 (2008)

Hollow, Michele. "Stressed? This Dog May Help." Retrieved from http://www.nytimes.com (Published October 22, 2014)

Horn, Lisa et al. "Dogs' attention towards humans depends on their relationship, not only on social familiarity." *Animal Cognition*, Volume 16, Issue 3 (2013)

Horowitz, Alexandra. *Being a Dog: Following the Dog Into a World of Smell*. New York, NY: Simon & Schuster (2016)

Inglis, I.R. et al. "Free food or earned food? A review and fuzzy model of contrafreeloading." *Animal Behaviour*, Volume 53, Issue 6 (1997)

Jensen, Glen D. "Preference for bar pressing over 'freeloading' as a function of number of rewarded presses." *Journal of Experimental Psychology*, Volume 65, Issue 5 (1963)

Jerath, Ravinder et al. "Physiology of long pranayamic breathing: Neural respiratory elements may provide a mechanism that explains how slow deep breathing shifts the autonomic nervous system." *Medical Hypotheses*, Volume 67, Issue 3 (2006)

Joffe, Justin M. et al. "Control of their environment reduces emotionality in rats." *Science*, Volume 180, Issue 4093 (1973)

Kistler, Claudia et al. "Feeding enrichment in an opportunistic carnivore: the red fox." *Applied Animal Behaviour Science*, Volume 116, Issues 2-4 (2009)

Kogan, Lori et al. "Behavioral effects of auditory stimulation on kenneled dogs." *Journal of Veterinary Behavior*, Volume 7, Issue 5 (2012)

Krontveit, Randi I. et al. "Housing- and exercise-related risk factors associated with the development of hip dysplasia as determined by radiographic evaluation in a prospective cohort of Newfoundlands, Labrador Retrievers, Leonbergers, and Irish Wolfhounds in Norway." *American Journal of Veterinary Research*, Volume 73, Issue 6 (2012)

Larsen, Jennifer, et al. "Evaluation of Recipes of Home-Prepared Maintenance Diets for Dogs." *Journal of the American Veterinary Medical Association*, Volume 242, Issue 11 (2013)

Larson, Greger et al. "Rethinking Dog Domestication by Integrating Genetics, Archeology, and Biogeography." *Proceedings of the National Academy of Sciences of the United States of America*, Volume 109, Issue 23 (2012)

Lauten, S.D. et al. "Computer analysis of nutrient sufficiency of published home-cooked diets for dogs and cats." *J Vet Intern Med*, Volume 19, Issue 3 (2005)

Lefebvre, Diane et al. "Cortisol and behavioral responses to enrichment in military working dogs." *Journal of Ethology*, Volume 27 (2009)

Lindsay, Steven. *Handbook of Applied Dog Behavior and Training Volume 1*. Ames, IA: Iowa State Press (2000)

Line, S.W. et al. "Evaluation of attempts to enrich the environment of single-caged non-human primates." *AGRIS* (1989)

Maier, S.F. and Watkins, L.R. "Stressor controllability and learned helplessness: The roles of the dorsal raphe nucleus, serotonin, and corticotropin-releasing factor." *Neuroscience & Biobehavioral Reviews*, Volume 29, Issues 4–5 (2005)

Markowitz, Hal. *Enriching Animal Lives*. Mauka Press, 2011.

Marshall-Pescini, Sarah et al. "Importance of a species' socioecology: wolves outperform dogs in a conspecific cooperation task." *PNAS*, Volume 114, Issue 44 (2017)

Mason, Georgia J. et al. "The use of techniques from human economics to measure what animals value, illustrated by experimental work on the American mink, *Mustela vison*." *Proceedings of the 4th International Conferences on Environmental Enrichment* (2002)

Mech, L. David. "Leadership in wolf, *Canis lupus*, packs". *Canadian Field Naturalist*, Volume 114, Issue 2 (2000)

Meeusen, Romain and De Meirleir, Kenny. "Exercise and brain neurotransmission." *Sports Medicine*, Volume 20, Issue 3 (1995)

Mugford, R.A. "Where to put your choker." *International Journal for the Study of Animal Problems*, Volume 2, Issue5 (1981)

Neuringer, Allen. "Animals respond for food in the presence of free food." *Science*, Volume 166, Issue 3903 (1969)

Nichols, T. "The Death of Expertise." Retrieved from https://thefederalist.com (published January 7, 2014)

Nichols, Tom. *The Death of Expertise*. Oxford, England: Oxford University Press (2017)

Osborne, Steve R. "The free food (contrafreeloading) phenomenon: a review and analysis." *Animal Learning & Behavior*, Volume 5, Issue 3 (1977)

Owen, Megan A. et al. "Enclosure choice and well-being in pandas: is it all about control?" *Zoo Biology*, Volume 24, Issue 475 (2005)

Papoutsoglou, S.E. et al. "Effect of Mozart's music (Romanze-Andante of 'Eine Kleine Nacht Musik', sol major, K525) stimulus on common carp (*Cyprinus carpio L.*) physiology under different light conditions." *Aquacultural Engineering*, Volume 36, Issue 1 (2007)

Petruzzello, Steven J. et al. "A meta-analysis on the anxiety-reducing effects of acute and chronic exercise." *Sports Medicine*, Volume 11, Issue 3 (1991)

Price, Laura. "A preliminary study of the effects of environmental enrichment on the behaviour of captive African wild dogs." *Bioscience Horizons*, Volume 3, Issue 2 (2010)

Radosevich, Paul M. et al. "Effects of low- and high-intensity exercise on plasma and cerebrospinal fluid levels of ir-beta-endorphin, ACTH, cortisol, norepinephrine, and glucose in the conscious dog." *Brain Research*, Volume 498, Issue 1 (1989)

Salmon, Peter. "Effects of physical exercise on anxiety, depression, and sensitivity to stress: a unifying theory." *Clinical Psychology Review*, Volume 31, Issue 1 (2001)

Schenkel, Rudolph. "Expressions Studies on Wolves." University of Basel (1947). This publication is available as a set of downloadable PDFs from http://davemech.org/wolf-news-and-information/schenkels-classic-wolf-behavior-study-available-in-english/

Schipper, Lidewij L. et al. "The effect of feeding enrichment toys on the behaviour of kennelled dogs." *Applied Animal Behaviour Science*, Volume 114, Issues 1-2 (2008)

Seligman, Martin E. and Maier, Steven F. "Failure to escape traumatic shock." *Journal of Experimental Psychology*, Volume 74 (1967)

Shyne, A. and Block, M. "The effects of husbandry training on stereotypic pacing in captive African wild dogs." *Journal of Applied Animal Welfare Science*, Volume 13, Issue 1 (2010)

Simonet, Patricia et al. "Dog laughter: recorded playback reduces stress related aggression in shelter dogs." *International Conference of Environmental Enrichment* (2005)

Stewart L., et al. "Citizen Science as a New Tool in Dog Cognition Research." *PLoS ONE*, Volume 10, No. 9: e0135176 (2015)

Stockman, J. et al. "Evaluation of recipes of home-prepared maintenance diets for dogs." *Journal of the American Veterinary Medical Association*, Volume 242, Issue 11 (2013)

Sung, Huei-Chuan et al. "A preferred music listening intervention to reduce anxiety in older adults with dementia in nursing homes." *Journal of Clinical Nursing*, Volume 19, Issue 7-8 (2010)

Thomas, Rhiannon B. and Wilson, John P. "Issues and Controversies in the Understanding and Diagnosis of Compassion Fatigue, Vicarious Traumatization, and Secondary Traumatic Stress Disorder." *International Journal of Emergency Medicine Health*, Volume 6, Issue 2 (2004)

Thompson, P.D. et al. "The acute versus the chronic response to exercise." *Medicine and Science in Sports and Exercise*, Volume 33 (2001)

Thorpe, W.H. *Learning and Instinct in Animals*. Cambridge, MA: Harvard University Press (1956, reprint 1966)

Tiesman, Hope M. et al. "Suicide in U.S. Workplaces, 2003-2010: a comparison with non-workplace suicides." *American Journal of Preventive Medicine*, Volume 48, Issue 6 (2015)

Tomasello, Michael and Kaminski, Juliane. "Like Infant, Like Dog." *American Association for the Advancement of Science*, Volume 325, Issue 5945 (2009)

Varela, Juan A. et al. "Control over stress induces plasticity of individual prefrontal cortex neurons: a conductance-based neural simulation." *Nature Precedings* (2011)

Volpicelli, Joseph et al. "Feedback during exposure to inescapable shocks and subsequent shock-escape performance." *Learning and Motivation*, Volume 15, Issue 3 (1984)

Wagman, Jason D. et al. "A work-for-food enrichment program increases exploration and decreases stereotypies in four species of bears." *Zoo Biology*, Volume 37, Issue 1 (2018)

Wallace, F.R. et al. "Stimulus change contemporaneous with food presentation maintains responding in the presence of free food." *Science*, Volume 182, Issue 4116 (1973)

Watson, John S. and Ramey, Craig T. "Reactions to response-contingent stimulation in early infancy." *Merrill-Palmer Quarterly of Behavior and Development*, Volume 18, Issue 3 (1972)

Wells, Deborah. "Aromatherapy for travel-induced excitement in dogs." *Journal of the American Veterinary Medical Association*, Volume 229, Issue 6 (2006)

Wells, Deborah et al. "The influence of auditory stimulation on the behaviour of dogs housed in a rescue shelter." *Animal Welfare*, Volume 11, Issue 4 (2002)

Wells, Deborah et al. "A note on the effect of auditory stimulation on the behaviour and welfare of zoo-housed gorillas." *Applied Animal Behaviour Science*, Volume 100, Issue 3-4 (2006)

Wingfield, John C. et al. "Ecological bases of hormone-behavior interactions: the 'emergency of life history stage.'" *American Zoologist*, Volume 38, Issue 1 (1998)

Wolchover, N. "Why Dogs Chase Laser Beams (And Why It Can Drive Them Nuts)." Retrieved from http://www.livescience.com (published July 26, 2012)

Woody, Erik Z. and Szechtman, Henry. "Adaptation to potential threat: the evolution, neurobiology, and psychopathology of the security motivation system." *Neuroscience and Biobehavioral Reviews*, Volume 35, Issue 4 (2011)

Woody, Erik Z. and Szechtman, Henry. "A biological security motivation system for potential threats: are there implications for policy-making?" *Frontiers in Human Neuroscience*, Volume 7 (2013)

Yin, S. "Dominance Versus Leadership in Dog Training." *Compendium on Continuing Education for the Practicing Veterinarian*, Volume 29, Issue 7 (2007)

Yin, S. "Dominance vs. Unruly Behavior." *Low Stress Handling, Restraint and Behavior Modification of Dogs and Cats*. Davis, CA: CattleDog Publishing (2009)

Resources

Interpreting and Understanding Science

This website has a more in-depth explanation as to what empirical evidence is: https://www.livescience.com/21456-empirical-evidence-a-definition.html

This one beautifully explains the scientific process: https://www.sciencebuddies.org/science-fair-projects/science-fair/steps-of-the-scientific-method

Wikipedia has a comprehensive list of logical fallacies, their definitions, and in many cases links to more comprehensive explanations here: https://en.wikipedia.org/wiki/List_of_fallacies

This article is a great place to start learning how to evaluate research: http://spring2017.iaabcjournal.org/evaluating-research-2/

Canine Nutrition and Safety

A list of books from Dogwise on canine nutrition: https://www.dogwise.com/health-anatomy-breeding-nutrition-books/

Fascetti, Andrea J. and Sean Delaney. *Applied Clinical Veterinary Nutrition*. Wiley-Blackwell, 2011.

The canine Body Condition Score chart is available here: https://www.aaha.org/public_documents/professional/guidelines/weightmgmt_bodyconditionscoring.pdf

You can download the nutrient requirements for dogs for free here: https://www.nap.edu/catalog/20184/nutrient-requirements-of-dogs

For lists of toxic foods and plants for your pets, visit http://www.aspca.org

Canine Ethology and Neurobiology

To learn more about canine olfaction, read Chapter 1 of *Domestic Dog Cognition and Behavior.*

In addition to the must-read article on dominance and aggression that can be found in the References section, we highly recommend reading these other related articles on dominance and aggression by Dr. Abrantes:

- https://rogerabrantes.wordpress.com/2011/12/11/dominance-making-sense-of-the-nonsense/

- https://ethology.eu/aggressive-behavior-the-making-of-a-definition/

To learn more about the factors that influence behavior and dogs' social needs, we highly recommend reading the following books:

- Steven Lindsay's three-volume series *The Handbook of Applied Dog Behavior and Training*

- *Decoding Your Dog* by several of the veterinary behaviorists at the American College of Veterinary Behaviorists

- *Dog Sense* by Dr. John Bradshaw

- *Inside of a Dog* by Dr. Alexandra Horowitz

- *Puppy Start Right* by Dr. Ken and Debbie Martin

Eileen Anderson wrote a fascinating article about the differences between dog and human hearing here: https://eileenanddogs.com/blog/2019/03/21/dogs-hearing-vs-human-hearing/

Science-Based Training and Behavior Modification

Applied Behavior Analysis

For more discussion on the Humane Hierarchy and how it is designed to be used, check out these articles by Dr. Susan Friedman:

- "What Went Wrong With the Humane Hierarchy Is Still Wrong With the Revisions": https://summer2018.iaabcjournal.org/2018/07/02/editorial-humane-hierarchy/

- "What's Wrong With This Picture?: Effectiveness is Not Enough": http://behaviorworks.org/files/articles/What's%20Wrong%20With%20this%20Picture-General.pdf

And also the IAABC's LIMA (least intrusive minimally aversive) position statement: https://m.iaabc.org/about/lima/

And this article by Eileen Anderson: https://eileenanddogs.com/2018/06/28/quadrant-cornerstone-operant-learning/

There are many, many excellent books related to science-based training, but in our opinion these are the best books to get a solid introduction to science-based training:

- *How Dogs Learn* by Burch & Bailey

- *How 2 Train A ___* by Dr. Patricia Barlow-Irick

- *Excel-erated Learning* by Dr. Pam Reid

- *Don't Shoot the Dog* by Karen Pryor

- If you decide you'd like to go more in-depth, Paul Chance's *Learning and Behavior* is an essential textbook—along with, as we've already mentioned, Steven Lindsay's three-volume *Handbook*.

Dr. Zazie Todd's compilation of research on training methodologies and their effects: https://www.companionanimalpsychology.com/p/resources.html?m=1)

General Training Recommendations
Retreat & Treat protocol

1. Toss a high-value treat in front of the dog.

2. When they eat it, toss a lower-value treat behind them so they get to go away from you.

3. Repeat this process until the dog willingly approaches you to take treats from your hand.

Variation of Retreat & Treat for dogs whose behavior is more severe, such that approaching new people is not yet appropriate:

1. As soon as the dog makes eye contact, toss a high-value treat past the dog so they can retreat to eat it.

2. When the dog turns around or tries to approach again, repeat the high-value treat toss.

3. Continue with this strategy until the dog's body language is relaxed upon approach, then switch to the standard Retreat and Treat protocol.

For more information about this protocol:

- This is an article from Dr. Ian Dunbar about his Retreat and Treat Protocol: https://www.dogstardaily.com/training/retreat-treat

- You can also find several videos on YouTube by searching for "treat retreat."

Other training tips/protocols
To learn more about Chirag Patel's Bucket Game: https://www.animal-trainingacademy.com/podcast/training-tidbits/chirag-patel/

To learn more about how to shape creativity by playing 101 Things to Do With a Box, go here: https://www.clickertraining.com/101-things-to-do-with-a-box

Several resources exist to help people learn more about training dogs for medical, grooming, and basic handling skills. These are a few of the big ones:

- https://lowstresshandling.com/

- https://fearfreepets.com/

- https://coopcare2018.wordpress.com/

Our favorite YouTube channels for how-to training tips, body language exercises, and other valuable science-based topics, include:

- Eileenanddogs: https://www.youtube.com/user/eileenanddogs

- Kikopup: https://www.youtube.com/user/kikopup

- Donna Hill: https://www.youtube.com/user/supernaturalbc2009

- Behavior Works: https://www.youtube.com/user/behaviorworks1

- Laura Monaco Torelli: https://www.youtube.com/user/
  lauramonacotorelli

Selecting a Trainer or Behavior Professional

While there are many good dog trainers out there who can teach you how to teach your dog basic manners, dog sports, and other relationship-building exercises, behavior disorders such as resource guarding should be seen by behavior professionals who have specialized education and training in the behavior sciences. You can find such professionals through the following organizations:

- Veterinary behaviorists can be found at https://www.dacvb.org

- Behaviorists (that is, professionals who have an advanced degree in one of the behavior sciences) can be found at: http://www.animalbehaviorsociety.org

- Certified behavior consultants can be found at: https://www.iaabc.org/

- The Certification Council for Professional Dog Trainers also offers a behavior consultant certification. You can look on their site for CBCCs: http://www.ccpdt.org/

This article has excellent advice on how to select a competent, ethical behavior professional: https://thebark.com/content/tips-picking-dog-trainer

See also the Joint Standards of Practice espoused by the International Association of Animal Behavior Consultants (IAABC), the Certification Council for Professional Dog Trainers (CCPDT), and the Association of Professional Dog Trainers (APDT): https://m.iaabc.org/joint-standards-of-practice/

Becoming a Trainer or Behavior Professional

If you are interested in learning how to become a science-based behavior professional, there are many wonderful resources available to you.

Regardless of your level of interest, Dr. Susan Friedman's course Living and Learning With Animals is an essential foundation upon which to build your education: http://www.behaviorworks.org/htm/lla_professional_overview.html

These courses will set you on the path to become a competent, knowledgeable, science-based dog trainer:

- Karen Pryor Academy: https://karenpryoracademy.com/

- The Academy for Dog Trainers: https://academyfordogtrainers.com/

- CATCH Canine Academy: https://catchdogtrainers.com/

- Victoria Stilwell Academy: https://www.vsdogtrainingacademy.com/

- Pat Miller Academy: https://peaceablepaws.com/peaceable-paws-intern-academies/

To become a behavior consultant (that is, someone who is qualified to address more severe behavior disorders), there are fewer options available. Although the authors have heard of a few exciting programs in development, to our knowledge at the time of printing these are the only programs designed specifically to train people to become behavior consultants in the United States:

- The International Association of Animal Behavior Consultants offers several courses, mentorships, and other continuing education resources: iaabc.org/

- The authors have recently launched their own apprenticeship program specifically designed to prepare people for a career in animal behavior consulting. Our website is: https://firsttrainhome.org.

Agency and Choice
Dog Park Safety signs: https://iaabc.org/resources/dog-park-public

Toy Preference Assessment: https://centerforshelterdogs.tufts.edu/wp-content/uploads/2016/03/ToyPreferenceAssessment.pdf

You can find Eileen Anderson's video on petting consent by searching YouTube for "Does Your Dog REALLY Want to Be Petted?" or going directly to this link https://youtu.be/-cGDYI-s-cQ

Enrichment Ideas and Support

Everywhere
This is the S.P.I.D.E.R. framework, which zoos, aviaries, and other conservation organizations utilize to assess the efficacy of their enrichment program: http://www.animalenrichment.org/spider

For more ideas and inspiration for foraging and other enrichment opportunities for your dog, we highly recommend joining the Facebook group Canine Enrichment: https://www.facebook.com/groups/canineenrichment/

Dr. Karen Overall's relaxation protocol can be found in her book *Clinical Behavioral Medicine for Small Animals*.

You can purchase Suzanne Clothier's Really Real Relaxation DVD from Dogwise at: https://www.dogwise.com/really-real-relaxation-creating-authentic-connected-relaxation-with-your-dog-dvd/

Eileen Anderson's pyramid pan article: https://eileenanddogs.com/blog/2017/01/11/making-500-non-crumbly-dog-treats-from-a-mold/

In shelters
Allie and Emily founded and run a philanthropic project called First Train Home to help shelters address behavior issues and logistical husbandry issues more ethically and effectively. Our website is: http://www.firsttrainhome.org

We also highly recommend Drs. Erica Feuerbacher and Lisa Gunter's shelter workshops. Their website is: https://www.instituteforshelterdogs.org/

We also highly recommend the Shelter Playgroup Alliance as a resource for learning how to run safe and ethical playgroups: https://www.shelterdogplay.org/

More information about Karen Pryor Academy's shelter enrichment course can be found here: https://karenpryoracademy.com/courses/shelter-training-and-enrichment/

About the Authors

Emily Strong, CDBC, CPBT-KA, SBA, is co-owner and behavior consultant at Pet Harmony, LLC, and co-founder and president of First Train Home. She has been involved in various animal welfare fields since 1990, working and volunteering in animal shelters, rescue groups, veterinary hospitals, stables, wildlife rehabs, an aviary, and finally as a behavior consultant. While a behavior consultant in Austin, Texas, she was on the board of Wings of Love Bird Haven, and co-founded and ran Austin Parrot Society. She then relocated to Kanab, Utah, to work as a behavior consultant in both the Parrot and Dog Departments at Best Friends Animal Society for almost three years before moving to Salt Lake City to go back into business for herself, publish her book, and launch First Train Home. She has been training animals of many species her whole life, including (but probably not limited to): dogs, cats, parrots, a wide variety of other species of birds, rabbits, ferrets, hamsters, rats, mice, horses, miniature donkeys, pigs, goats, tortoises, leopard geckos, snakes, pygmy octopuses, fish, and even praying mantids. In addition to running her businesses and writing books, she is also a national speaker, has written articles for multiple publications, and has an international client base.

Allie Bender, CDBC, CPDT-KA, SBA, is the founder and co-owner of Pet Harmony Animal Behavior & Training and co-founder of First Train Home. Allie is a national speaker, published author, and an animal welfare advocate. She has been working with rescue groups and shelters since 2006 in various capacities, including founding a student-run animal welfare organization. Allie started dog training professionally in 2012, and by 2015 became the lead dog behavior consultant at Best Friends Animal Society, the largest no-kill animal sanctuary in the nation. There she had the opportunity to work with dogs and cats with serious behavior challenges as well as speak at national conferences, write for the Best Friends magazine, and make TV and commercial appearances. Allie has a BS in animal science from Iowa State University and is certified through the International Association of Animal Behavior Consultants and the Council for Certification of Professional Dog Trainers.

INDEX

A

restricted activity, 177–180
Retreat & Treat protocol (Dunbar), 40–41
role model dogs, 117–118
routines, 62–63, 151, 159, 173

S
safety
 agency and, 45
 enrichment practices, 63–67
 exercise and, 55
 foraging and, 85–86
 importance of, 58–63
Salmon, Peter, 48
scent work
 calming enrichment, 136–137
 enrichment practices, 170–171
 instinctual behaviors, 70–73
 scent detection sports, 124
 in shelters, 184–185, 191
 stress detection, 157–159
Schenkel, Rudolph, 98–99
Schipper, Lidewij, 121
secure space, 61–62
security
 comfort building exercises, 147–148
 enrichment practices, 63–67
 identification of basic needs, 17
 importance of, 58–63
Seligman, Martin, 28, 30, 37
sensitivity periods, 106
separation anxiety, 33, 147–148
serotonin, 48
shaping, 118–119, 122–123, 164, 171–172
shelter facilities
 enrichment practices, 69–70, 121, 138–139, 168, 183–192
 learned helplessness, 29, 31, 33
 social interactions, 109, 113
 space utilization, 39–40
Shepherdson, David, 35, 39
Shyne, A., 121
sight enrichment, 74
Simonet, Patricia, 138
sleeping patterns, 76–77, 141

Made in the USA
Monee, IL
06 August 2024

63348777R00131